COMPENSATION STRUCTURES

FOR VENTURE-BACKED COMPANIES

By

Joseph Bartlett & Ross P. Barrett

Mat #40686942

BOOK & ARTICLE IDEA SUBMISSIONS

If you are a C-Level executive, senior lawyer, or venture capitalist interested in submitting a book or article idea to the Aspatore editorial board for review, please email AspatoreAuthors@thomson.com. Aspatore is especially looking for highly specific ideas that would have a direct financial impact on behalf of a reader. Completed publications can range from 2 to 2,000 pages. Include your book/article idea, biography, and any additional pertinent information.

ISBN 1-58762-180-0
Library of Congress Control Number: 2004101126

For corrections, updates, comments or any other inquiries please email AspatoreEditorial@thomson.com.

First Printing, 2004
10 9 8 7 6 5 4 3 2 1

About ASPATORE BOOKS –
Publishers of C-Level Business Intelligence

www.Aspatore.com
Aspatore Books is the largest and most exclusive publisher of C-Level executives (CEO, CFO, CTO, CMO, Partner) from the world's most respected companies. Aspatore annually publishes a select group of C-Level executives from the Global 1,000, top 250 professional services firms, law firms (Partners & Chairs), and other leading companies of all sizes. C-Level Business Intelligence ™, as conceptualized and developed by Aspatore Books, provides professionals of all levels with proven business intelligence from industry insiders – direct and unfiltered insight from those who know it best – as opposed to third-party accounts offered by unknown authors and analysts. Aspatore Books is committed to publishing a highly innovative line of business books, and redefining such resources as indispensable tools for all professionals.

Author Notes

I would like to thank and credit all the partners and associates at my prior firms who have helped me with materials I used for clients and in transactions while at the firm. The helpers are too numerous to cite so I cite the firms...Gaston & Snow, Mayer Brown & Platt, Morrison & forester and my current firm, Fish & Richardson. I would also like to thank my longtime assistant and right hand, Joan Taylor.

- Joseph W. Bartlett

I would like to thank the contributing editor board at VC Experts for their numerous contributions to the website and to this book, specific instances of contribution are acknowledged below. I would also like to thank my lovely wife Allison and my daughters Grace and Georgia.

- Ross Barrett Philippians 4:13

Compensation Structures
For Venture-Backed Companies
CONTENTS

1

Compensation Generally

Since both start-ups and buyouts depend in large part on extraordinary performance by managers, one principal aim of the planners of new ventures is to put stock or stock equivalents in the hands of senior managers without incurring tax liability to motivate such individuals. Indeed, managers may be required to accept stock instead of cash compensation in order to preserve cash flow for the operations of the enterprise or the benefit of the lenders.[1]

The trick is to use stock as currency without incurring immediate taxable (or to minimize the) consequences to the recipient. This is not a simple exercise since stock is being awarded for past or future services, which is a taxable event in classic terms. Under existing rules (which are changing as this is written) the equity is customarily allocated, if possible, in a way that has minimal effect on the business' reported earnings. A majority of the commentaries on this issue are written by tax practitioners; when a compensation scheme enables the company to take a tax deduction, they view that as an unalloyed "plus." However, a scheme that generates an expense on the profit and loss statement of the business enterprise is generally undesirable for several reasons, including the importance of earnings in negotiations to raise financing.

All other things being equal, of course, tax deductions are favorable. But, if the cost of casting a system in a given way is a "hit" to earnings as reported to shareholders, then again, under existing rules, there is (or was) occasion to revisit the question. Assuming the issuer so elects,[2] the grant of stock options as a form of employee compensation impacts the income statement as of the date of the grant, which is to say not at all, since the value of the option itself as of that date is indeterminate if the grantee's exercise price is equal to "fair value." As the option grows in value, culminating on the day it is exercised, the grantor's earnings are unscathed. However, FASB had introduced proposed rules that would require companies to expense their stock option grants. In fact, many companies, such as Coca-Cola, voluntarily expense their options (more recently Microsoft has moved in this direction). Mandatory expensing of stock option seems likely to come sooner rather than later. Many practitioners predict mandatory expensing in the United States, perhaps as early as 2004 and more probably by 2005. In any event, footnote disclosure is required by GAAP, the result of a late 1990's political compromise between FASB and the high tech lobby. By way of contrast, a phantom stock plan, which periodically awards to employees "units" ultimately redeemable in cash (the value of the units being tied to stock performance), can have an enormous negative impact on earnings.[3] (To be sure, any issuance of rights to purchase shares has a potential effect on the all-important earnings per share number.)[4]

A central planning imperative is to tie equity to the performance of the employee. Thus, if shares (or options or stock equivalents) are awarded, it is important that employee "fat cats" are not thereby created, (i.e., employees who can relax from and after the date of the award and watch their colleagues make them rich). Accordingly, awards, once made, usually "vest" over time, meaning that the price is fixed as of the date of the grant but the employee acquires unfettered ownership of the options or stock over a period of time commonly known as the vesting schedule. As a result, if the employee elects to quit before some or all of his stock or options have vested, then she either forfeits the unvested portion or the corporation can buy back the unvested portion for nominal consideration.

Regardless of how sophisticated the stock or stock option plan may be, it is likely that the employee will have to pay tax at some time on the value she has received. The trick is to match the employee's obligation to pay tax with his receipt of income with which to pay the tax.

---

[1] Anderson & Feit, *Restructurings in the 1990s*, in Corporate Restructurings 1990 7, 101 (PLI Course Handbook Series No. 685). Stock may be used as currency for the rank and file as well; for instance when the employees "pay" for stock donated to an ESOP by agreeing to a cut in hourly wages.

[2] [Under FASB Statement 123 and APB Opinion No. 25, unless the option has values based on trading in an organized market or the issuer elects, the issuer of an option records compensation expense as of the date the option is issued only if the exercise price is less than fair value.]

[3] FASB Interpretation No. 28, 11 3, 4 (Dec. 1978); *see also* Miller, Comprehensive GAAP Guide 39.01-39.20 (1987); APB Opinion No. 25, 1 32. The distinction lies in the fact that, under the typical stock option plan, the option price and the amount of option shares are fixed as of the date of the grant, APB Opinion No. 25, 1 10b, and therefore any "compensation" is fixed as of that time as well, while, under a phantom stock option plan and other stock bonus and purchase plans, the amount of stock or other compensation varies as circumstances dictate. The fact that the employee must remain in his job for a period to vest the options does not, as of now, mean that the plan has variable terms. If, however, options vest according to performance standards-i.e., Newco profits-the possibility of periodic expense allocations is real.

[4] Options and warrants are considered "common stock equivalents" and, for purposes of calculating earnings per share, are assumed to have been exercised if the market price has exceeded the exercise price for three consecutive months. The calculation includes issuance of the option stock and use by the issuer of the exercise price to purchase its own stock at market. APB Opinion No. 15, 36, 51.

Securing the Key Employees

It is essential that VC investors do all that is reasonably practicable to secure the services of key employees during the vital growth stages of a business. In addition to motivating key employees through share options in the company, VCs should ensure that each key employee enters into a service agreement or contract of employment. That might includes the following:

- Notice periods help to secure the services of the key employee during a specific period of time following the employee or the company giving notice. Clearly, a balance must be achieved between severance costs that are likely to be higher if the notice period is longer, and the ability to hold onto the employee that is enhanced if the notice period is longer.

- Garden leave clauses will give the company the option to suspend the key employee from his or her duties and keep them from joining a competing business during the notice period. Garden leave is when an employee is not required to attend work but continues in employment, receiving normal pay and benefits. The advantage of garden leave is that there is no contact between the employee and your important clients during this period.[1]

Confidentiality clauses prohibit an employee from disclosing or using any confidential information or trade secrets of the company. To be enforceable, this clause should clearly define what is meant by confidential information, which should include confidential business plans, product specifications, designs and customer lists.

- However, this clause should include carve outs for information which enters the public domain, is ordered to be disclosed by a court or, in some jurisdictions such as the U.K., is the subject of a protected act (such as whistle blowing).

---

[1] See, e.g. http://www.smallbusiness.co.uk/newsArticle.php?EntryID=2551&thesectionID=1

2

Restricted Stock to Employees

Stock Subject to Vesting (Substantial Risk of Forfeiture)

Section 83(a) of the Internal Revenue Code[1] states that if "property" is issued "in connection with the performance of services,"[2] the difference between the "fair value" of, and the amount paid by the recipient for, the property-usually stock-is taxable to the recipient (and deductible by the corporation) as additional compensation as of the earlier of (1) the first date forfeiture restraints (if any) lapse, or (2) the first date the property is transferable, value being calculated without regard to restrictions other than those which by their terms never lapse.[3] If an employee is buying stock at a bargain and there are no "substantial" forfeiture risks (other than those which will never lapse) attached, then the impact of § 83 is relatively simple-he pays tax on the bargain element upon receipt of the stock.

Section 83 becomes of cardinal importance in venture financings in which employees are acquiring "restricted" stock, meaning stock subject to contractual restraints on transferability and risks of "forfeiture." Despite the fact that "restricted" stock (in the sense of nonvested stock) can be issued at any time during a corporation's lifetime, the issue is discussed in this chapter since it routinely arises on corporate organization.[4]

The purpose of vesting restrictions is to tie footloose employees to the corporation with "golden handcuffs." Typically, an employee will be allowed to purchase at bargain prices shares of stock subject to the company's right to buy them back at the employee's nominal cost if the employee prematurely terminates his employment for reasons other than death or disability. Thus, a five-year vesting restriction will typically provide that one-fifth of the shares issued shall vest in each of the five years following the employee's receipt of stock; that is, they are no longer repurchasable by the corporation at cost. The vesting constraint goes hand-in-hand with an absolute, albeit limited in time, restraint on alienation; the employee cannot dispose of shares to anyone until they are vested. Without that constraint (unless it is clear the forfeiture restriction is binding on transferees, in which case no one would buy at any sensible price), the forfeiture restriction would have little economic bite.[5] If the employee were originally issued 1,000 shares and left of his own accord in the third year following the employee's receipt of stock, the employee would own 400 shares outright and 600 shares would be repurchasable at the employee's cost.

Under § 83(a), an employee "lucking" into the opportunity to buy restricted, nonvested stock at a bargain has a problem. He receives a piece of paper he cannot readily sell; and he incurs a contingent liability to pay at some later date tax on the difference between his nominal cost and the artificial "value" of that security as at a future time. For purposes of computing the tax, such value is calculated as if, contrary to fact, the employee could sell the shares into an auction market since "investment letter" restrictions do not count in computing value.[6] Arguably, therefore, the receipt of nonvested stock is no bargain because, when the tax becomes payable (i.e., the forfeiture risk lapses), the stock may be (indeed it is expected to be) highly "valuable" and the tax burdens accordingly aggravated. The potential "Catch-22" is apparent: A owes tax on a $ 10 stock which he cannot sell-perhaps at any price-and has no way of realizing the cash with which to pay the tax; he pays out of other assets and holds, expecting an IPO which never materializes, and his stock eventually becomes worthless.

The answer to the predicament lies in the provisions of § 83(b). As long as value can be measured when the shares are initially issued, the tax problem is not calamitous because the employee is receiving stock at a time when its value, however calculated, is low. Thus, if the early-round cash investors are coming in at $1 per share and the employee is paying 60 cents a share, at least the amount of the tax is calculable-40 cents times the number of shares sold, times the employee's effective rate of federal tax. (Indeed, if the cash investors buy preferred stock, then the employee may claim no tax is due.) And, the privilege afforded by § 83(b) is that the taxpayer may make an election; that is, he may file, within 30 days after the stock has been originally purchased, notice of his choice to pay tax on the difference between the value of the stock received at that time and the amount actually paid for the stock. Once that tax is paid, then vesting restrictions become irrelevant. The stock may go to $100 per share when the employee finally vests with respect to the last share, but no taxable event will occur.

The § 83(b) election also changes the nature of the income. If the election is made, then the subsequent tax event occurs upon the sale of stock, and any gain at that time is capital gain. In the absence of the election, the tax event occurs upon vesting and the character upon vesting will be ordinary income. Only the post-vesting appreciation will be capital gain.

It is important to keep in mind that the § 83(b) election is available and should be made, even though the employee purchases shares at full value at the time of issuance.[7] It is not, in other words, the fact that the employee is purchasing cheap stock but that he's purchasing stock *subject to a substantial risk of forfeiture*, which casts the taxable event out into the future; it's usually true that such stock is cheap stock-else why would anyone agree to the forfeiture restrictions-but such need not always be the case. The virtue of the § 83(b) election is that it pulls that event back to the present day, when the gap between the employee's payment and the value of the stock is presumably at its narrowest.

The § 83(b) election is not without its risks. If the property declines in value, then the loss would be capital loss. Under such circumstances and in the absence of the election, the compensatory element would be reduced or disappear. Thus if A receives stock worth $1,000 for free, the § 83(b) election results in $1,000 of taxable ordinary income. If the stock declines in value to $400 when A vests and immediately sells the stock, A would have a $600 capital loss. In the absence of the election, A would only have $400 of ordinary income upon vesting.[8]

Section 83 also obtains when an employee acquires restricted stock pursuant to a "nonqualified" stock option, an option which does not fit the rules in the Code governing "incentive stock options."[9] The tax on shares received under a nonqualified option is measurable at option *exercise;*[10] that is, before the stock is or can be sold to the public (unless it is registered for sale at the time of exercise). Accordingly, it may be an advantage to the optionee, if the option shares are still subject to a risk of forfeiture, to forgo the § 83(b) election; by so doing, he avoids a tax at a time when the stock may not be able to be sold advantageously. Any method of postponing tax (i.e., by suffering forfeiture restrictions) may be preferable, particularly since an IPO may occur in the interim and, thus, liquidity become obtainable if an S-8 is effective. On the other hand, a dramatic increase in value between option exercise and sale can render that strategy a mistake.

The idea that the § 83(b) election is no longer an attractive option for taxpayers receiving restricted stock has been advanced in a prestigious journal.[11] The analysis is bottomed on the assumption that (i) the differential in tax between income and gains is not substantial (more so now that the Bush tax cuts have gone into effect) and (ii) the employee will sell the stock at the same time as receipt of the stock is no longer subject to a substantial risk of forfeiture." On those assumptions, the conclusion necessarily follows: If one assumes that a sale occurs coincident with vesting, tax will be paid in the year of vesting on the entire gain remaining untaxed, meaning that § 83(b), under the scenario posed by the authors, is only a prescription for requiring an employee to pay some tax earlier than he otherwise would elect.

Note that an employee is often unable to sell shares (if they are liquid) as of the date of vesting if an S-8 is not on file and/or because the employee is in a "control" position; § 83(b) is very useful in such circumstances. The employee pays a small amount of tax initially and is protected against a potentially ruinous amount of tax at a time when the employee may be unable to effectively sell the stock at its fair market value. Indeed, absent § 83(b), a "Catch 22" situation may occur: The employee finds himself taxed on exercise under § 83(a) on a gain measured by fair market value and yet must, nonetheless, sell the stock at a discount in a private transaction to try to collect enough money to pay tax on a gain not actually achieved. The authors have made, in effect, a serious error. The § 83(b) election is (as it always was) most useful in allowing an employee to choose the date on which shares will be sold. If the employee must sell as of the year of vesting (because of the tax effect of § 83(a)), then an important incident of ownership has been lost.[12]

The "Catch 22" posed by § 83(a) is illustrated by the case of Grant v. United States[13] The employee enjoyed a nonqualified stock option at a strike price of $6.67 per share, which he exercised at a time when stock of the same class was selling on the New York Stock Exchange for $23.37 a share. The employee sold his unregistered stock in a private placement for $14 a share. He attempted to report his gain based on the difference between the option price and the price he realized. Under § 83(a), however, the fact that the employee couldn't sell the shares in the public market is a restriction that lapses over a period of time and, therefore, is not taken into account in valuing the shares for purposes of calculating the tax upon option exercise. The employee, in other words, had to pay tax on a gain of $16.70, the difference between $6.67 and $23.37 per share, even though he only in fact realized $7.33, the difference between $6.67 and $14 per share.

When drafting a complex employee stock restriction, one should study § 83 with care. The gloss on the statutory provisions is important.[14]

Thus, the concept of "transfer" entails "beneficial ownership" of the stock residing in the transferee; this is taken to imply that stock which is issued subject to a restriction requiring return of the stock upon an event that is "certain to occur" may be deemed never to have been "transferred," a potentially confusing proposition when one compares the concept of restrictions which never lapse.[15] Thus, assume stock worth $1 per share is sold to an employee for $100, subject to recapture at cost if he leaves his employment voluntarily within five years and in any event resalable only to the corporation at fair market value upon leaving the company's employ. When his employment terminates (an event bound to happen sometime), the transaction can be viewed in several lights. As stated, it can be argued that there never was any "transfer";[16] the stock only serves as security for the issuer's promise to pay fair value some day and, thus, the interim forfeiture restriction (during the first five years) has no tax-postponing effect. If there is deemed to have been a transfer, the permanent restriction is a nonlapse restriction; however, it can be argued that such restriction does not impact value for § 83 purposes because the price is set at fair market value.[17] Suppose the employer and employee elect to cause the permanent restriction to be mutually rescinded? What happens then? The Service may argue that the employee has received a taxable increase in value as of that time, based on his inability to establish, in the language of § 83(d)(2)(A), that the cancellation was "not compensatory." As with most Code sections, the thought experiments can go on forever.

There are other subsidiary issues which come up frequently and deserve special mention. For example, stock which is forfeitable because a noncompetition covenant is breached is presumed not to be subject to a substantial risk of forfeiture, nor are stock grants conditioned on the issuer achieving certain performance goals.[18] A source of practical problems arises by dint of the fact that the employer gets a deduction when the employee incurs tax under § 83[19] but only if the employer withholds[20] under the FICA, FUTA, and Wage Withholding at the Source provisions of the Code. Thus, the deduction can be lost if there are no payments from which to withhold; if, for example, the employee does not make the § 83(b) election and is no longer on the payroll when the forfeiture condition lapses. Further, it is an open question how § 83 interacts with a transfer of an interest in partnership or limited liability company profits. A so-called "carried" partnership interest in profits is often subject to vesting; if the partner or member withdraws prematurely, his interest is bought back at a penalty price. The norm is to make the § 83(b) election when receiving a carried interest in partnership profits on the theory that one has nothing to lose.

To illustrate the operation of Sections 83(a) and 83(b) consider the following examples.

Example 1: Suppose Employer transfers 10 shares of stock to Employee on January 1, 2000 (worth $1.00 at the time of the transfer), however, the stock vests ratably over 5 years of continued employment. If Employee remains employed for a year from the date of the grant, Employee must include 1/5 of the fair market value in income, which is determined by the fair market value of the stock on January 1, 2001. Suppose the company is a start-up company, which goes public in December 2000, and because of its desirable business-to-business software, its stock price rockets to $200.00 a share by January 1, 2001. Employee would have to include 1/5 of $200.00 ($40) in income for his 2001 taxable year. Should Employee remain employed with Employer through January 1, 2005, she would have to include in income for each portion of the stock vesting an amount equal to the difference between the fair market value on the vesting date and the price she paid for the stock. For instance if the stock rose to $210 a share on January 1, 2002, then Employee would have to include 1/5 of $210 ($42) for his 2002 taxable year. Employee would have to recognize a corresponding amount for each year she remained employed with Employer until his stock had completely vested (e.g., by January 1, 2005).

This does not appear fair to Employee, who essentially gets punished with higher taxes for helping to build an incredibly valuable company (according to the stock market). However, Employee can make an election, which would accelerate the timing of the taxation of his stock to the year of the transfer of the stock, which would be the grant date (year 2000 in Example 1), as opposed to when the stock vests over the course of the vesting schedule for the stock. Commonly referred to as the "§83(b) Election," this election can greatly reduce the tax impact of receiving stock if the stock has the potential to increase dramatically over the course of its vesting period. Although the requirements for an election under §83(b) are both simple and set forth explicitly in the Treasury Regulations, the most important point of which to beware is that the election must be made, which means it must be mailed to the IRS, within 30 days after the transfer of stock.

For instance, in Example 1, had Employee made a §83(b) Election on or before January 1, 2000, she would only have included in income 1/5 of $10.00 ($2.00) in year 2000. In contrast, without making the election, Employee would have included $40 and $42 in income for the years 2001 and 2002 respectively, as well as additional amounts for each year through 2005, until his stock had totally vested.

In spite of the huge benefits of the §83(b) election, there is some risk where the employee is paying less than fair market value for the stock. If the employment relationship ends before the stock vests, the employee is not entitled to a deduction to offset the tax she paid as a result of making the election in the year of the stock grant.

For instance, in Example 1, if Employee makes the §83(b) election, she pays $10 in tax for the 2000 taxable year. If Employee is fired or leaves the company before any stock has vested (e.g., before January 2001), then Employee forfeits all of his stock. The Employee's taxable loss is measured by the difference between the amount Employer paid for his stock upon forfeiture ($0) and the amount she paid for the stock at the grant date ($0) -

- e.g., Employee has no taxable loss upon forfeiture according to the facts of Example 1.

Finally, when the employee subsequently sells the stock, she recognizes gain equal to the difference between the price received for the stock and his basis in the stock -- the amount she paid for the stock, plus the amount of ordinary income she recognized for receiving the stock (e.g., determined either when the stock vested or when she made the §83(b) election). The holding period for determining whether the stock qualifies for long-term capital gain also begins immediately after the stock vests or when the employee makes the §83(b) Election.

It is important to note that before §83 is invoked, and therefore before an employee can actually make an election under §83(b), there actually must be a "transfer" of stock. Although this seems like a no-brainer, the transfer of an option to purchase stock is generally not considered to constitute a transfer for the purposes of §83 with respect to the stock underlying the option. Additionally, the option itself does not constitute a transfer unless (i) the option is a nonqualified stock option (e.g., does not constitute an incentive stock option), and (ii) the company has options that trade on a public market. See generally §1.83-3(a), 1.83-7. There are some exceptions to this rule as noted in the section below.

There is one very practical situation in which the transfer of stock can be treated as an option, which would therefore preclude an election under §83(b) and have disastrous consequences if an employee desired to make the election. A company is often inclined to require its employees receiving a grant of restricted stock to purchase the stock for fair market value at the date of the grant–the arrangement could be advantageous for general accounting purposes, the company might want to avoid tax withholding problems or the company might want to offer restricted stock on terms similar to the terms of an incentive stock option (incentive stock options have a strike price at the fair market value of the stock as of the date of the grant). However, the employee might not either desire or possess the money to purchase the restricted stock upon the date of the grant, because she does not obtain unfettered ownership in the stock until the occurrence of some event in the future. As a result, the company may be willing to loan the money to the employee.

If the loan is structured as a non-recourse loan that is not secured by property at least equal to the fair market value of the underlying stock on the grant date, then the Internal Revenue Service will characterize the arrangement as an option to purchase stock. According to this approach, §83 would not apply until the employee pays off the balance of the loan, at which point the employee would include in income the difference between the fair market value of the stock (determined as of the date of the loan payoff) and the amount paid for the stock (the loan payoff amount).

Example 2: Building on Example 1, suppose Employer grants Employee 10 shares of stock with a fair market value of $1.00 on January 1, 2000, and requires the employee to purchase the stock for $1.00 a share. To facilitate the purchase Employer loans Employee $10.00. Employee files a §83(b) Election with the IRS on January 2, 2000. The stock climbs to $200.00 on January 1, 2001, at which time 1/5 vests. Feeling confident that the stock will not decline in value below $1.00 a share, Employee pays off the loan balance. If the loan was non-recourse, without sufficient loan security (e.g., other property with a fair market value equal to the loan balance), then the IRS will require Employee to recognize the difference between the loan balance $10 (e.g., assuming no interest on such a nominal loan) and $2,000 in income for the year 2001. The §83(b) Election was invalid, because a "transfer" didn't occur on grant date of the restricted stock (e.g., January 1, 2000).

One might be inclined to question whether stock would fall under the ambit of §83 if transferred to an employee who pays the company an amount equal to the fair market value of the stock? §83 can apply to a purchase at fair market value if the transfer is compensatory. Although this is a complicated issue, which should be explored at length according to the facts of any given situation, generally a transfer for fair market value will be treated as compensatory in nature, unless the employee receiving the stock can prove that other parties would able to purchase stock from the company on the same or similar terms.

---

[1] At first blush, § 83(a)(1) appears to say that tax is postponed in an instance where a restraint on alienation not accompanied by a risk of forfeiture lapses. However, the import of the section (see § 83(c)(2)) is that both nontransferability and risk of forfeiture must combine if the tax is to be postponed. If there is no restraint on transferability, as a practical matter the risk of forfeiture is nugatory; it can be defeated simply by selling the stock. And if there is no risk of forfeiture, there is no reason to postpone the tax.

[2] A case of great interest to practitioners held that a shareholder/employee purchasing stock subject to a substantial risk of forfeiture at its fair value was, nonetheless, a transferee of property "in connection with" the performance of services. Alves v. Commissioner, 79 T.C. 864 (1982), aff'd, 734 F.2d 478 (9th Cir. 1984). In Alves, the employee paid fair market value for the stock, which was nontransferable and subject to a substantial risk of forfeiture. When the stock vested, the fair market value had increased, which according to the court resulted in a taxable event to Mr. Alves, equal to the excess of the fair market value at that time over the amount paid by Mr. Alves. The "cure" is a § 83(b) election.

[3] As the statutory source for imposing tax on the employees, § 83(a) overlaps with § 61 (definition of gross income). See Banoff, *Conversions of Services into Property Interests: Choice of Form of Business*, 61 Taxes 844, 850 (Dec. 1983).

[4] Nonvested stock is most common in the early stages of a firm's existence because nontaxable bar gain purchases of cheap stock are most easily defended before widespread trading ends the issuer's and employee's discretion to set prices for tax purposes. If an employee is paying full value for his or her shares or paying tax out of pocket on the bargain element (which amounts to almost the same thing), naturally it is difficult for the issuer to negotiate a vesting restriction, except perhaps a restriction to resell to that company at fair market value which, under Treas. Reg. § 1.83-3(c)(1), is not a "substantial" forfeiture restriction for purposes of § 83.

[5] Careful practitioners consider making § 83(b) elections where there is a tax-free reorganization in which founder stock that is substantially or fully vested is exchanged for stock in another corporation, and the acquiring corporation requires that forfeiture restrictions be imposed on the stock received by the founders. Such forfeiture restrictions would require the founders to forfeit their stock if they terminate their employment before a certain time. In this situation, it is possible that the IRS would take the position that a new transfer occurred in connection with the performance of services because the founders received newly issued stock subject to additional restrictions relating to their employment. Even tough the exchange is otherwise tax-free, in the absence of a § 83(b)

election, when the additional restrictions lapse, the founders could have additional compensation income in an amount equal to the difference between the value of the stock exchanged and the value of the stock received at the time of the restrictions lapse.

[6] "Investment letter restrictions are not restrictions which "by [their] terms never lapse" and, therefore, are ignored in computing § 83(a) "value." I.R.C. § 83(a)(1). Restrictions which by their terms never lapse include a permanent right of refusal and an agreement that the stock be sold to the company whenever employment (as it someday must) terminates, in each case at some value other than fair market value.

[7] See Alves v. Commissioner, 79 T.C. 864 (1982), aff d, 734 F.2d 478 (9th Cir. 1984). As the Text suggests, to pay "fair value" for § 83 purposes, one must actually pay more than current value because, contrary to common sense, "section 83 fair market value" does not admit of the dampening effects of lapse restrictions. See Martin, Raising Capital for a Closely Held Company, 43 N.Y.U. Inst. Fed. Tax'n § 8.06[2] (1985).

[8] Also, if the stock is forfeited, a loss is only allowed for the amount paid, and not for the compensatory element reported in income. Treas. Reg. § 1.83-2(a).

[9] Incentive stock options escape the ambit of § 83. I.R.C. § 83(e)(1).

[10] Section 83 deals with "transfers" of property and the option stock is not transferred until the option is exercised. Treas. Reg. § 1.83-3(a)(2). The grant of the option itself is not taxable under § 83 if, as is usually the case, it lacks a "readily ascertainable fair market value." I.R.C. § 83(e)(3).

[11] Lassila & Wiggins, The Demise of the Section 83(b) Election, 66 Taxes 512 (July 1988). The authors also based their conclusion in part on the fact that capital gains and ordinary income were taxed at the same rate-a fact no longer true.

[12] Of course, if the employee pays fair market value, the § 83(b) election is a foregone conclusion and avoids the Alves problem.

[13] 15 Ct. Cl. 38 (1988).

[14] The section does not apply to "unfunded and unsecured" promises to pay money in the future since the same are not "property," meaning that the most frequently encountered category of deferred compensation is unaffected. Treas. Reg. § 1.83-3(e). Payments pursuant to such promises are taxable only on receipt. Rev. Rul. 60-31, 1960-1 C.B. 174, modified by Rev. Rul. 70-435, 1970-2 C.B. 100, and Rev. Rul. 64-279, 1964-2 C.B. 121.

[15] Treas. Reg. § 1.83-3(a)(3). The concept of "transfer" is most important for purposes of the § 83(b) election. The election can only be made if in fact there is a "transfer." If not, then the benefits of the election described above are not available.

[16] A transfer probably will be found even if the forfeiture event is certain if the employee stands to lose either his 100 per share or the bargain element in the stock when it was issued (900). It can be argued that there was a transfer, and therefore (given the proper election), a tax is payable on the

difference between (1) 100 and, (2) $ 1.00 (diminished perhaps, by the effect, if any, of the nonlapse restriction).

[17] As previously stated the obligation to return the stock at fair market value is not a "substantial" forfeiture condition at all since fair market value negates the idea of a forfeiture. Treas. Reg. § 1.83-3(c)(1). It is not clear that any nonlapse restriction other than one involving a "formula" price clause (see § 83(d)(1)) will impact value.

[18] Treas. Reg. § 1.83-3(c)(2).

[19] Treas. Reg. § 1.83-6(a)(1).

[20] Treas. Reg. § 1.83-6(a)(2).

Section 83 and LLC Units

Revenue Proc. 93-27; Profits interests as "property;" Section 83(b) election.

How carefully does one have to review the buyout provisions in a limited partnership or LLC for SRF (substantial risk of forfeiture) purposes of an unvested profits interest to see if the buyout price is at "fair market value"? There are some options: How about payment with an interest-bearing note at a rate that could be viewed as non-competitive? How about payment of the capital account, without posing unrealized gains (or losses)? Should this be viewed as a forfeiture for 83(a) and (b) purposes?

Several law firms take the position that Section 83(a) of the Code should not apply to interests in profits allocated to members of the LLC which is the general partner of a private equity fund. Hence, a Section 83(b) election is unnecessary. However, experienced counsel often advise a precautionary rule – *simply make the election because it does not hurt.*

Nota bene: The issue may soon be settled: An attorney in the executive compensation division of the IRS spoke on a panel addressing advanced taxation issues at the NASPP (National Association of Stock Plan Professionals) annual meeting. He mentioned that the IRS expects to release a ruling that the principles of Rev. Proc. 93-27 shall apply to grants of a forfeitable profits interest in a partnership. Recipients of such profits interest shall not be subject to tax at the time of grant and, provided the interest is held for the requisite period of time, shall be entitled to capital gain treatment when the interest is sold. Further, the recipient need not make a Section 83(b) election to get this tax treatment, even if the recipient has a capital account at the time the interest vests.

Form of Section 83(b) Election

This statement is being made under Section 83(b) of the Internal Revenue Code of 1986, as amended, pursuant to Treas. Reg. Section 1.83-2.

(1) The person making this election, and various information relating to such person, are as follows:

Name: _____

Address: _____

_____

Taxpayer Ident. No.: _____

(2) The property that may be subject to Section 83, with respect to which the election is being made, is such person's stock in Newco, Inc., a Delaware corporation.

(3) The stock was acquired on _____, 2004, and the taxable year for which the election is being made is calendar year 2004

(4) The stock is subject to a repurchase right lapsing over an approximately ten (10) year period pursuant to which the partnership or its assigns, under certain circumstances, has the right to acquire a portion of such person's stock at a price specified by formula.

(5) The fair market value of such stock at the time of transfer (determined without regard to any restriction other than a restriction which by its terms will never lapse) was $_____ .

(6) The amount paid for such stock was $_____ .

(7) A copy of this statement has been furnished to Newco, Inc.

Date:_____

_____
Spouse, if applicable

Note that the IRS requires that the election be made no later than 30 days after the date of transfer which is date of acquisition of stock.

3

Use of Preferred Stock to Shelter the Disproportionately Low Price to the Sweat Equity

Again to state a fundamental proposition, there is no available cash in an early stage financing with which to pay federal and/or state income taxes. Consequently, anything that smacks of a taxable event is verboten. The norm, however, is that the founders will obtain their interests in the new entity in consideration of past services and/or the capitalized value of the founders' talents and services to be rendered; the promoters, if different from the founders, are obtaining stock for their organizational efforts. The omnipresent danger is that the IRS will successfully assert the position that all or a portion of the stock issued to the founders has been, for tax purposes, issued for services and a current tax is payable. Since that position reflects the economic reality, it is dangerous.[1]

There are, however, three principal weapons on the side of the taxpayer.[2] First, § 351 of the Code provides for nonrecognition of gain or loss upon the exchange of property for shares if the shareholders contributing cash or property are in "control" (meaning ownership of 80 percent of the stock) of the corporation after the transaction. The trick, within the bounds of reasonableness and good faith, is to argue that the founder's contribution is not "services" but intangible property-that is, a secret process or other proprietary information-because secret processes can be "property" under the Code. The second, the "passage of time" approach, is described in the next section " 'Lapse of Time' Approach."

Thirdly, if the consideration paid by the founder cannot in good conscience be labeled "property," and the investors all come in together, then the inquiry turns to the value of the stock being issued. Assume the founder pays, as he always can, some small amount of cash. Is that cash sufficient to equal the "value" of the stock received so that no gain is recognizable? At first blush, if the founder pays $100 per share and the investors contemporaneously pay $10 per share, it looks as if the founder has made a bargain purchase and an element of taxable compensation has changed hands. However, the compensatory element may disappear if the investors receive preferred stock. The Internal Revenue Service has never challenged successfully the view that the issuance of shares with a liquidation prefer-preference-ordinarily labeled preferred stock-can "eat up" value in an amount equal to the preference, thereby reducing the common stock (the "cheap stock") to marginal value.[3] Put another way, if the liquidation preference of the preferred is equal to the cash contributions of the parties contributing cash capital, then a balance sheet test immediately after organization suggests that the common is "worth" only the nominal consideration the founders have paid, thereby excluding any element that can be attributed to past or future services. See the table below for a hypothetical balance sheet.

Assets		Liabilities	
Cash	$ 10,100	. . . .	-0-
		Shareholders' Equity Preferred Stock (1000 shares) outstanding, $10 par, convertible into 1,000 shares of common stock)	$10,000
		Common Stock 1,000 shares outstanding, 10¢ par)	$100
$10,100			$10,100

An uncritical examination of the balance sheet might suggest that 10¢ a share paid by the common would compare equitably-that is, no bargain purchases with the $10 paid by the preferred, since the preferred appears superior to the common on the balance sheet in the full amount of the cash paid. Certainly, if the issuer were liquidated immediately after it was formed-that is, on the date the taxable event, if any, occurred-the common shareholders would get back just what they put in: 10¢ per share. Of course, since no one intends to liquidate the corporation either right away or, for that matter, ever (and, indeed, if it is liquidated, it is unlikely that either the common or the preferred will get anything), the liquidation value test is dependent on a contrary-to-fact convention, but nonetheless a convention that has stood the test of time in view of what appears to be the silent acquiescence of the Internal Revenue Service.

The power of the preferred to "eat up" value for tax purposes is enhanced to the extent the preferred shareholder owns additional superior rights, that is, senior as to dividends (of which there are usually none), special voting rights, registration rights, and the like. These rights are often significant to the cash investors in the early going and are helpful on the tax issue; from the founder's point of view, the fact that (other than the dividends) they fade away upon the exit date-the IPO for example-means he can be relatively indifferent. It could, of course, be argued that one must weight the common's value upwards because half of the "upside" belongs to the common; however, making the preferred convertible, albeit at a price of $10 per share, means that the preferred shares in the "upside" as well. In short, ordinarily the cash investors take convertible preferred shares (a choice which, parenthetically, excludes an election of S Corporation status) and the founder common.

The principal caveat has to do with excess. In the example quoted, the cash investor's payment per share is 100 times the amount of the founder's payment. Some practitioners are uncomfortable with a spread that great. Others tend to take a more aggressive view.[4] The belt and suspenders technique is to combine the "eat 'em all up" preferred approach with the "passage of time," or "Bruce Berckmans" approach.[5]

As indicated, it can be important to contributing shareholders other than the founder that the "eat 'em all up" approach works. To be sure, the biggest risk is to the taxpayer held to have received stock for services. However, any shareholder contributing appreciated property may be required to pay tax if the taxpayer deemed to have contributed services gets more than 20 percent of the resultant stock since, as stated, § 351 only works if the contributors of cash and property, not services, get 80 percent or more of the stock.

---

[1] The entire question of tax minimization for persons arguably providing services corporations and partnerships in the process of organization is discussed in a helpful article, Banoff, *Conversions of Services into Property Interests: Choice of Form of Business*, 61 Taxes 844 (Dec. 1983).

[2] The Treasury has, in turn, formidable weapons: § 61 (gross income includes income "from whatever source derived"); § 83 (the "assignment of income" doctrine); § 482 (IRS has power to reapportion income to reflect clearly the facts).

[3] In the estate tax arena, the Service has issued its position regarding the relative values of preferred and common stock. *See* Rev. Rul. 83-120, 1983-2 C.B. 170. This ruling suggests the "soak-up" preferred stock approach is not correct. However, Rev. Rul. 83-120 was issued in response to an estate tax planning technique-the estate freeze-and the Service's attack on the technique ultimately had to be memorialized by statute before being legitimatized. *See* I.R.C. § 2701.

[4] One experienced venture capital lawyer has suggested a 1: 10 ratio is acceptable, although "higher risk start-ups may justify greater discounts." Auftnuth, *Selected Tax and Accounting Issues in Early and Mezzanine Financings, and Venture Capital Partnerships,* in Venture Capital After The Tax Reform Act of 1986, at 55, 84 (PLI Course Handbook Series No. 422, 1987); *compare* Treas. Reg. § 1.83-5(c), Ex. 4 (where the IRS takes the view that book value, which is "ordinarily determinate," does not control if the parties expressly agree the common stock is issued for services).

[5] This issue should be viewed alongside the so-called Sol *Diamond Campbell* question-when a partnership issues a "carried" interest in profits to a service partner.

4

'Lapse of Time' Approach: Incorporate and Issue Stock Early, Prior to Cash Investors

The complementary device for allocating the founder his cheap stock tax free involves organizing the start-up entity as soon as the founder starts to consider a maiden voyage. To the extent the founder receives his shares well prior to the first round financing, the founder/taxpayer can argue that the passage of time and events account for the increase in value-$10 for the investors stock versus 10 cents for his shares. The risk is that the IRS will successfully argue "step transaction." However, that argument is vitiated if the financing was only a contingency when the founder's stock was issued. The moral of the story being that it usually does not cost anything to organize the start-up as early as possible and may provide substantial tax comfort.

This approach is sometimes labeled the "Bruce Berckmans" approach, after Berckmans v. Commissioner, 20 T.C.M. (CCH) 458 (1961). One commentator makes the point that the failure to pay "reasonable" salaries to founder/employees weakens their case that stock was not awarded for services. See Martin, *Raising Capital for a Closely Held Company*, 43 N.Y.U. Inst. Red. Tax'n § 8.06 21(b) (1985).

The lesson, in sum, signaled by the discussion in this and the previous section is that the early bird catches the worm. Once the first-round of financing has occurred, the dimension of the "cheap stock" issue changes. It is considerably dicier to contend that the preferred "eats up" value when common shares have traded in the interim or otherwise been priced in arms-length transactions. The planning process must shift to the arena of executive compensation, that is, stock equivalents, stock options, restricted stock bought with borrowed company funds, and so forth. (The importance of the question whether the employee shares are issued at less than fair market value is not confined to the tax arena. Bargain stock will create compensation expense on the company's books, impacting earnings.)

5

Stock Options

A *stock option* is a right issued to an individual to buy shares of stock in a given issuer at a fixed or formula price (subject to adjustments).[1]. It is a "derivative" security in that the option itself derives its value from the value of the underlying stock. An option and a warrant are conceptually the same; however, an option is a warrant exercisable, usually by an employee (rather than a corporation) and usually over a longer period. An option is usually issued by the company itself, to be satisfied by newly issued stock, but such is not necessarily the case. Any owner of stock can sell an option-a "call" in trading parlance-on his stock on whatever terms are mutually agreeable but this type of option will not be an "incentive stock option."[2]

To the company planning on issuing the options, there are several events in the process (each of which could be the occasion for a tax of some kind).[3] If the option is an ISO, and, thus receives favorable tax treatment (and even if it is not), the first step is for the directors to adopt, and the stockholders to ratify,[4] a stock option plan. Adoption of a plan does not, of and by itself, involve the grant of options to any individuals. The plan, first and most importantly, identifies the maximum number of shares which can be issued to all the recipients in the aggregate; this is usually about 10 percent to 20 percent of the total stock outstanding, depending on the caliber of the employees and the willingness of the investors to dilute their equity in the company. The plan tells the stockholders the maximum amount of dilution they will suffer if all options are granted and exercised. It also sets out the basic provisions in each option contract, most of which are required under the Internal Revenue Code of 1986, as amended (the "Code"), if the options are to be "incentive stock options" under § 422 of the Code.

Options are granted to individuals pursuant to individual contracts. The scope of the plan contemplates the issuance of incentive stock options (ISOs) and/or nonqualified stock options ("NSOs") and, perhaps, cash buyouts of the options in lieu of exercise, in the discretion of the issuer or the employee (Stock Appreciation Rights, or "SARs").

---

[1] The exercise price is routinely adjusted in the case of stock dividends, splits or other forms of nonacquisitive reorganizations. If the issuer is to disappear in a merger, the customary method is to vest all options immediately and allow the employee to exercise them for a short specified period of time prior to closing; tax and securities law consequences may dictate alternative strategies-i.e., cash out all options and/or replace them with equity incentives in the acquiring corporation.

[2] If the major or sole shareholder grants options to key employees on stock she owns, under the Code the transaction is generally treated as if the issuer granted the options. Treas. Reg. § 1.83-6(d)(1). See Kimpel, Compensation Planning for "High Tech" Executives, in Tax Planning for High Tech and New Ventures 67 (70th Forum Fed. Tax Inst. New Eng. 1984) [hereinafter Kimpel]. An incentive stock option is an option issued by the "employer corporation" or a parent or subsidiary, I.R.C. § 422(b) of the Code, however, options granted by a shareholder are nonqualified options.

[3] ARB No. 43, Ch. 13, 1 6, reprinted as Appendix B to APB Opinion No. 25, identifies six events in the life of an option: the four mentioned, plus the date the right to exercise the option vests and the date the option is first exercisable, two dates that are often simultaneous.

[4] Shareholder approval within 12 months before or after the adoption of the plan is required if the options are to be ISOs under § 422(b)(1) of the Code. Except as may be required by applicable stock exchange rules, if the options are not designed to qualify under § 422 of the Code, shareholder approval is not required. Stockholder approval is also required for § 16b purposes under the Securities Exchange Act of 1934, as amended.

Incentive Stock Options

Incentive stock options (usually abbreviated as ISOs) are rights to purchase stock structured to comply with the requirements of § 422 of the Code. If the requirements are satisfied, then §83(a) of the Code does not apply. As a result, the holder, who must be an employee of the issuer (or its parent or subsidiaries), will not be subject to federal income tax either at the time of the grant of the option, or at the time of its exercise; and gain realized on a sale of the underlying stock will be capital gain. Note, however, that upon exercise, the employee may be subject to the alternative minimum tax because the difference between the fair market value and the strike price is a preference item for alternative minimum tax purposes.

To qualify as an incentive stock option under §422 of the Code, all of the following requirements must be met:

1. The grantee must be an employee.[1]
2. The exercise price must be equal to the fair market value of the stock as of the day on which the option is granted. However, if the grantee has more than 10% of the voting power of the stock (a 'ten-percent stockholder), then the exercise price must be 110% of fair market value of the stock. Fair market value is easily determined if the stock is publicly traded. However, if the stock is not publicly traded, the employer corporation must make a good faith effort to determine the fair market value of the stock, which will depend on the facts and circumstances of the situation. As opposed to the rule under § 83 of the Code, value may be discounted for purposes of § 422 of the Code if the stock is restricted. Gresham v. Commissioner, 79 T.C. 20 (1982).
3. Upon exercise, the employee must receive stock of his employer corporation (or a parent or subsidiary corporation to his employer).

4. The ISO must be issued pursuant to a qualified stock option plan established by the employer corporation, which meets the following requirements:

5. The plan must be in writing and set forth the total number of ISOs that may be issued pursuant to the plan; and

6. The plan is approved by the shareholders of the employer within 12 months (either before or after) the date the plan is adopted.

7. The ISO grant must specifically state that it cannot be transferred by the employee or exercised by anyone other than the grantee.[2]

8. The option must be granted within 10 years from the earlier of the date that the plan was adopted, or approved, by the shareholders.

9. The option granted pursuant to a valid ISO plan must be exercised within 10 years from the date that it is granted (5 years in the case of an ISO grant to a ten-percent stockholder). It should be noted that an employee can exercise an ISO up to three months after termination of his employment, and such period is extended up to one year in the event of the employee's death (i.e., the employee's estate would exercise the ISO in such an instance or disability).

10. The holding period requirement (see *infra.*) is satisfied.

Finally, a portion of stock exercised pursuant to an ISO will be treated as though issued pursuant to a NSO grant, if the fair market value of the stock capable of being exercised in any given year exceeds $100,000. The fair market value of the stock may be determined on the date of the option grant. *See* § 422(d) of the Code. The employer could issue separate stock certificates that clearly indicate which stock is ISO stock and which is not ISO stock; however, the default rule would treat a proportionate amount of each share of stock according to the rules for ISOs and NSOs.

Example: Assume Employee receives an option to purchase 15,000 shares of Employers stock when the fair market value of the stock is $10. The option is issued pursuant to a valid incentive stock option plan and the option grant complies with all of the ISO structural requirements (i.e., the requirements listed in number 1-8 listed above) have been satisfied. The option is fully exercisable -- e.g., assume there are no vesting restrictions. Since Employee received an option to purchase up to $150,000 in one given year, the grant exceeds the $100,000 limitation as described above and, therefore, the option will be bifurcated at the time that the employee exercises the option. Upon exercise, two-thirds of each share will receive ISO treatment and the remaining one-third will be treated according to the rules for NSOs. Alternatively, the employer could issue stock certificates identifying 10,000 shares as ISO stock and 5,000 shares as NSO stock.

An incentive stock option may provide that the employee may exercise his option by paying with stock of the issuer and she may have a "right" to receive "property" in lieu of stock at option exercise.[3] Usually, the plan also establishes a committee of the board (for public companies the committee should be comprised of two or more individuals who qualify as both "outside" and "non-employee" directors)[4] to "administer" the plan-that is, to grant the options-and establish a system for tying options to performance.

Scattering grants of options over a period of time can work to tie rewards to performance but such a procedure means, in a rising share value scenario, that the grantee's exercise price will escalate. Hence, the better drafted plans overgrant the number of options in the early stages and then provide for "vesting"; that is, the power of the issuer to recapture granted options lapses in decreasing amounts as the employee's longevity increases. Once an employee terminates or is terminated, she must exercise his options (only those vested, of course) within a short period: usually a month (and not more than three months if the grantee wants to preserve ISO status)[5] after termination, meaning she loses the ability to postpone his investment decision. The short fuse on post-termination exercise periods increases the possibility that a terminated employee's vested options will lapse (and go back into the pool for someone else) since the exercise price will be (again given a rising stock price scenario) closer to actual value when she quits rather than at the tail end of the option period.

The benefits of receiving ISO treatment can be substantial. The employee does not recognize income when the ISO is granted and does not recognize income when she exercises the option. The tax consequences to an employee depend on when the employee sells the ISO stock. Generally, when an employee sells stock that she received pursuant to a valid ISO grant (i.e., the option meets the above requirements and the holding periods described below), all gain will be treated as capital gain -- and therefore be subject to a maximum federal rate for capital gains as opposed to the maximum ordinary income rate.

1. Two years from the date that the ISO was granted; and
2. One year from the date on which the employee exercised the ISO.

Except as discussed below, the employer is not entitled to a deduction should the employee satisfy the Holding Period requirements.

Generally, if the employee transfers the ISO stock before the expiration of the Holding Period, then she must recognize compensation income for the year of the disposition in an amount equal to the difference between the fair market value of the ISO stock as of the exercise date and the strike price. Certain transfers will not violate the Holding Period such as a transfer upon death or certain non-recognition transactions.

If an employee recognizes compensation income from selling ISO stock before expiration of the Holding Period (i.e. a disqualifying disposition), the employer is entitled to a corresponding deduction if the employer satisfies the applicable Form w-2 or Form 1099 reporting requirements under §§ 6041 or 6041A of the Code. See also Prop. Treas. Reg. §1.6039-2(a) (lists informational requirements that must be provided to employees). However, should the employer fail to timely report such income, then the employer is entitled to a corresponding deduction only if it can prove that the employee actually included the amount in income. See Treas. Reg. §1.83-6(a). A special rule applies to amounts includible in an employee's income by reason of a disqualifying disposition. In the case of such a disposition, a Form W-2 or Form W-2a as appropriate, will be considered timely if it is furnished to the employee and filed with the IRS as or before the date on which the employer files its tax return claiming the deduction relating to the disqualifying disposition.

There is currently a lot of debate in whether the IRS should impose a withholding obligation with respect to the income received from a disqualifying disposition. Pursuant to IRS notice 2002-47, the IRS will not access FICA or FUTA taxes or impose federal income tax withholding on the exercise of an ISO or the disposition of stock acquired by exercising an ISO. As of January 1, 2003, the IRS has stated that this rule will remain in place until it completes its review of comments on recent proposed regulations and issues future guidance which would apply on a prospective basis. Individual taxpayers are not relieved from their obligation to include compensation income upon a disposition of stock acquired pursuant to the exercise of an ISO and does not relieve employers of their reporting obligations.

If an employer grants an option that meets all of the requirements of an ISO, but the employer does not intend for the option to receive ISO treatment, then the option grant should specifically state that the option does not constitute an ISO.

While one might think ISOs are advantageous from a tax perspective, the alternative minimum tax ("AMT") rules cast a cloud over ISOs. Specifically, the difference between the fair market value and exercise price is included as an adjustment for determining alternative minimum taxable income. As a result, any significant ISO grants will be subject to the AMT, which would trigger a tax upon exercise of the ISO. Thus, an employee with a significant grant of ISOs would prefer to exercise his ISOs before the underlying ISO stock significantly appreciates (i.e., measured from the time of the ISO grant date).

In 2000 and 2001, the impact of the AMT on ISOs has received a considerable amount of attention. Several key employees, who received large ISO grants, margined their stock to cover their AMT payments, which was done partially to obtain the benefit of holding the ISOs for the requisite one-year period after exercise. However, the stock market crashed, subjecting this employees to margin calls by their brokers, and in some cases the employees did not have enough assets to pay their tax bills.

The attractiveness of Incentive Stock Options generally is subject to question in today's volatile markets. The one-year holding period after exercise means that the holder, lured by the possibility of capital gains treatment, is at risk that the stock price will decline below the exercise price and he or she will wind up losing money on the trade.

---

[1] The grantee must have been employed by the issuing corporation, or its parent or subsidiary, at all times between the date of the option's grant and a period ending not later than three months before the date of exercise (except in the case of death or disability of the employee, whereupon exercise of the option is permitted up to one year following the date of termination of employment for such reasons, § 422(c)(7)) of the Code. The Regulations define *employees* for this purpose as persons involved in the "legal and bona fide relationship of employer and employee." Treas. Reg. § 1.421 - 7(h)(1), (2) and § 31.3401(c)-l. The definition incorporates the concepts in 3401(c) of the Code, which defines an employee for purposes of tax withholding. One of the games often played by planners is attempting to qualify valued directors and consultants as "employees."

[2] § 422(b) of the Code.

[3] *Id.* §§ 422(c)(4)(A), (B) of the Code.

[4] With respect to public companies that grant options, the requirement that the members of the committee be "outside" or "non-employee" directors is found in Section 162(m) of the Code and Section 16(b) of the Securities and Exchange Act of 1934, as amended.

[5] I.R.C. § 422(a)(2).

Nonqualified Stock Options

Nonqualified stock options ("NSOs") are "nonqualified" in the sense that they do not meet the requirements of § 422 of the Internal Revenue Code of 1986, as amended (the "Code"). NSOs may be taxable upon transfer (i.e., when granted to an employee) if the option itself (and not just the underlying stock) trades on a public market. See Treas. Reg. §1.83-7. Nonpublicly traded options may trigger taxation upon grant if all of the following are met:

1. The option is transferable by the employee;
2. The option is immediately exercisable in full;
3. The option is not subject to a restriction that would diminish its fair market value; and
4. The "option privilege" (i.e., the opportunity to benefit during the exercise period from any increase in the fair market value of the option) is readily ascertainable.

This exception is rarely ever satisfied in the context of the grant of NSOs to an employee, because the NSOs are rarely transferable by the employee. Employers prefer to limit who may become shareholders. Also, the ability to either exercise may not be exercisable in full, or the option may be restricted (i.e., so as to secure performance or provide motivation to the employee). Finally, the "option privilege" is rarely ascertainable with respect to a startup company. If, however, this exception is met, then the option would be taxable upon transfer and would receive the same treatment as if it were restricted stock.

Assuming the NSOs do not meet the exception above, then the NSOs do not trigger any tax consequences until the employee exercises the NSOs. Unlike restricted stock, NSOs do not trigger tax consequences as they vest. The exercise of NSOs triggers the application of §83 of the Code, at which point the following occur: (1) the employee includes in income the difference between the fair market value of the option and the strike or exercise price (i.e., the amount paid for the stock upon exercise), and (2) the employer is entitled to a corresponding deduction. *See* Treas. Reg. §1.83-7(a).

Example. Suppose (i) employer transfers 10 NSOs to employee on January 1, 2000; (ii) the strike price is $1.00 a share; and (iii) the NSOs vest ratably over 5 years. After 5 years have passed, on January 2, 2005, and employee is fully vested, she decides to exercise the NSOs when the stock has a fair market value of $50 a share. There are no tax consequences to employee until she exercises the NSOs, at which point she must include $490 in income as compensation -- the fair market value of the stock ($50 x 10 shares), minus the strike price ($1 x 10 shares).

By the time an employee exercises his NSOs, the fair market value of the stock could increase dramatically, which would in turn dramatically increase his taxes attributable to the exercise of the NSOs. Moreover, the amount included in income is treated as compensation and therefore is subject to ordinary income tax rates.

Additionally, it should be noted that the holder's (i.e., the Employee's or it could be an independent contractor's) compensation is not a tax preference item for purposes of the alternative minimum tax.

The impact on the company's earnings depends on the exercise price of the option on the grant date. The employer will have a charge against its earnings if, as of the date of grant, the fair market value of a share of stock subject to the option exceeds the exercise price, (i.e., the spread). The change will be equal to the number of options granted multiplied by the spread.

Since few specific legal requirements are applicable to the issuance of NSOs, great flexibility is permitted in the terms of such options. The following features are typically found in nonqualified options due to applicable state and federal tax and securities laws:

1. The exercise price may be at or below market price at the time of the grant.[1]
2. Only a minimal holding period is required to meet general state law requirements of adequate consideration.
3. The employee's ability to exercise the option need not be limited to the period of employment.
4. The option is (usually) not transferable except by will or the laws of descent and distribution.

---

[1] It is arguable that, if the purchase price is too low in comparison with existing value, the instrument is not an option but a sale of the option stock, triggering a tax under § 83(a) of the Code.

6

Deep Discount NSOs

The use of "deep discount" stock options has become popular in recent years. A *deep discount option* is a nonqualified stock option issued at an exercise price substantially less than the current fair market value of the option stock. Assuming on the grant date that the NSOs are not publicly traded, nor have a readily ascertainable fair market value on the date as defined by the Treasury Regulations (see "Nonqualified Stock Options"),[1] the employee is not taxed as of the date of the grant -- i.e., §83(a) does not apply to the NSO so as to trigger taxable consequences on the date of the grant. The beauty of deep discount options is that the executive is immediately vested with value (i.e., the spread) without, however, the necessity of paying tax until exercise.[2] There is some apprehension in the tax bar that, if the discount is too steep, the IRS may argue that exercise is certain, and, therefore, the employee has actually purchased the option stock at a bargain, or that the option stock has been constructively received.[3]

---

[1] The flagship case is *Commissioner v. LoBue*, 351 U.S. 243 (1956). Under Treas. Reg. 1.83-7(b)(2), the option must be transferable, immediately exercisable, unconditioned, and entail readily ascertainable value if it is to be taxable upon grant-conditions which are rarely extant. *See generally*

O'Neill & Schende, *Using Discount Stock Options as Executive Compensation,* J. Tax'n 348, 349 (June 1990).

[2] The discount, under APB Opinion No. 25, is an immediate charge to the employer's earnings.

[3] Rev. Rul. 82-150: Priv. Lin Rul. 88-29-070. The appropriate taxation of options issued at a discount is currently under IRS study. Levin & Ginsburg, Mergers, Acquisitions, and Buyouts 1311.012 n.141 (CCH Tax Transactions Library) or Levin & Ginsburg, Structuring Venture Capital, Private Equity, and Entrepreneurial Transactions: 2002 Edition.

ISOs Versus NOSs

The principal advantage[1] of an ISO is that it postpones tax on the holder's gain (exercise price versus sales price) until the option stock is sold; the tax on an NSO holder occurs upon exercise, measured by the difference between exercise price and fair value as of that time.[2] This is a major distinction.[3] The NSO holder has to come up with her tax money earlier in the process, provoking a potentially unacceptable investment risk unless she can sell immediately after exercise. However, as per SEC Rule 144, she cannot sell publicly; that is, she must either hold for one year or sell at a stiff discount, unless she is able to register her stock for sale.[4]

Indeed, the interaction of the Code and Rule 144 can produce a script Yossarian could appreciate. On exercise, the NSO holder owes tax on the difference between exercise price and "fair market value" calculated without regard to the restriction which will lapse,[5] that is, the inability to sell publicly for two years. Let us say the trading price of the stock is $10 and the exercise price is $6. Tax is owed on $4 of gain. Mr. Yossarian can sell right away in a private transaction but at a gain of only $2. He has to pay tax on $2 of gain he cannot then realize, forcing him to choose an immediate sale at an economic loss so as to develop a countervailing loss for tax purposes. Alternatively, he can pay his tax and hold the stock one year and sell without a discount, but, Catch-22, the stock may have gone down in price in the interim. He has paid tax on a gain he has not seen and, one year later, he may have an economic loss in the stock because the price falls. Moreover, the deduction for interest on the money he has borrowed has been severely limited.[6] He gets a tax loss after one year of agony, but, by that time, he may be broke. Further, assuming the NSO is subject to vesting in the form of a right to repurchase at the option price if the executive's service terminates prior to a specified time, the dilemma is increased when the individual must decide whether to make an I.R.C. § 83(b) election (unless the option price equals the fair market value at the time of the election), since, if he makes the election, he will be taxed on the value of appreciation he will not receive if his service terminates before the shares are vested. Note, however, certain avenues of opportunity-when the issuer goes public, it often will maintain an evergreen registration statement on Form S-8, registering shares issued upon the exercise of employee options.

There is more, however, to the comparison between ISOs and NSOs. The second major advantage of the ISO over the NSO-that the gain on sale is capital gain if the stock is held for a year after exercise (and the sale succeeds the grant by two years)-was rendered relatively immaterial by the 1986 Tax Reform Act (since the differences in tax rates became relatively small to the point of triviality). However, with the 1993 Deficit Reduction Act,[7] the distinction has been significantly restored and ISOs are back in fashion. Moreover, if the option stock is "qualified small business stock," it may be that the spread will be even more dramatic.[8] On the other hand, exercise of an ISO[9] produces tax preference[10] in an amount equal to the difference between the "fair market value" of the stock on exercise and the amount paid unless the option stock is sold in the year of exercise-an event which voids preferential treatment under § 422.[11] This feature led some commentators to forecast the death of ISOs.[12] The alternative minimum tax (AMT) result is not an unmitigated disaster since, in most instances, the excess tax paid is recovered when and if the option stock is subsequently sold at a gain.[13] Finally, under the 1993 Deficit Reduction Act, the spread on NSOs will enter into the calculation of executive compensation for purposes of measuring whether the $1 million threshold has been achieved and, thus, deductibility disallowed. The short of the matter is that, in an era in which the tax law changes annually, there is considerable luster to what might be called the "wait and see" approach. According to that strategy, the issuer constructs a plan involving ISOs. Then, as some critical date nears-an IPO looms, for example-the employee enjoys alternatives. She can exercise the option and hold the shares if alternative minimum tax is not a problem as a practical matter, thereby postponing tax while the Rule 144 period runs, or she can do something to disqualify the option as an ISO-sell before the one-year holding period lapses, for example.[14]

In this connection, the situation must be addressed from the issuer's point of view as well. A corporation is not allowed a deduction at any time in connection with ISOs granted to its employees (unless there is a disqualifying disposition of the ISO).[15] A company can deduct the amount of ordinary income an employee is deemed to have received in connection with an NSO at the same time ordinary income is includable in the employee's taxable income. The value of the deduction allowed to a profitable corporation in connection with an NSO may well exceed the value to the executive of an ISO over an NSO. Perhaps the issuer will want a tax deduction and would be willing to pay the employee a bonus, accordingly, to make a disqualifying disposition. Moreover, in the event of a disqualifying disposition, the gain is the lesser of the putative gain on exercise or the actual gain on sale.[16] [Also, as indicated, the accounting treatment of NSOs and ISOs is the same; a "hit" to earnings only if the option is granted at less than fair value,[17]] or unless the issuer elects

The point is that there is no one "right" answer to the ISO/NSO decision, particularly in view of the uncertainty posed by the FASB proposals and the irresistible impulse of politicians to tinker with the Internal Revenue Code; it is impossible to set out any general rules. The ISO versus NSO question should be examined carefully in light of the facts of each case and the tax, securities, and accounting rules in effect at that time.

[1] Newco's alternatives are not "either/or." A qualified ISO plan can be combined with an NSO plan.

[2] The tax is owed under I.R.C. § 83(a), on the receipt of "property" (*i.e.*, the option stock) in connection with services.

[3] The ability to time one's disposition of the underlying shares has "cash value," even though that value is difficult to quantify in advance.

[4] Rule 144 omits options from the situations in which the "tacking" of holding periods is permissible. Compare Rule 144(d)(1) and (3).

[5] The restriction on the ability to transfer by itself does not, despite the language of I.R.C. § 83, impose a restraint which allows the holder to postpone tax under I.R.C. § 83(b). Compare Robinson v. Commissioner, 805 F.2d 38 (1 st Cir. 1986).

[6] I.R.C. § 163(d). Under the statute prior to the Tax Reform Act of 1986, the individual's annual maximum deduction for interest on debt to "purchase or carry property held for investment," I.R.C. §§ 163(d)(1)(A), (B), was net investment income plus $10,000; after the phase out, it is solely net investment income. I.R.C. § 163(d)(1).

[7] The spread depends on the adjusted gross income of the taxpayer but it may be subject to AMT effects. I.R.C. § 56(b)(3).

[8] See discussion of new I.R.C. § 1202, which excludes one-half the gain on the sale of such stock if held for 5 years. See Note on Qualified Small Business ("QSB") Stock and Rollovers Sections 1202 and 1045.

[9] The alternative minimum tax puzzle has been well summarized by the author's then-partner (now an officer of Fidelity Corp.) John Kimpel, in these words:

The employee's exposure to the alternative minimum tax on the exercise of an ISO can create serious problems. Consider the following nightmare: Company X grants an ISO to a key employee to purchase 100,000 shares of its stock at $.60 a share, its then fair market value (total exercise price $60,000). Four years later ... the company goes public at $10 a share. The employee exercises his option and acquires 100,000 shares of stock for $60,000. The amount of the tax preference item potentially subject to alternative minimum tax is $940,000 ($1 million -$60,000). Since the alternative minimum tax is the excess, if any of (a) 20% [now 24% for individuals] of the amount by which taxpayer's adjusted gross income plus items of tax preference less certain itemized deductions exceeds an exemption amount of $30,000 ($40,000, subject post '86 to certain reductions, if a joint return if filed), over (b) the regular income tax paid, the employee in the example above may face a staggering tax bill without having sufficient funds to pay the tax.

Kimpel at 53.

[10] Alternative minimum tax calculations involve comparing the tax calculated at standard rates without regard to AMTI-$100,000 say, on $400,000 of income-with the tax which would be assessed

were all income, including tax preference items, to form the base amount times the AMT rate-i.e., 24% for individuals.

[11] If the optionee "disposes" of the stock received pursuant to the exercise of an ISO in the year in which she exercised the ISO, she will not be required to add the spread to his AMTL Treas. Reg. § 1.57-1(f)(5). Generally, an optionee will be considered to have disposed of the stock if she recognizes gain upon such disposition. See I.R.C. § 425(c).

[12] The Tax Reform Act: What to Do About Stock Options" XI Corporate Counsel I (Sept.-Oct. 1986).

[13] If the exercise of an ISO results in an AMT liability, the optionee will, to the extent not limited by I.R.C. § 53(c), be entitled to claim a credit (the "AMT credit") against his regular tax liability in the succeeding taxable year or years equal to the AMT paid. I.R.C. § 53(a). I.R.C. § 56(c) limits the AMT credit, in any given year, to the excess of a taxpayer's regular tax liability over his AMT liability for that year.

[14] A disqualifying disposition may, however, itself raise tax issues, if, for example, the stock received upon a disqualifying disposition is subject to a substantial risk of forfeiture. Kimpel at 56-57.

[15] In order for the employer to take the deduction for compensation expense allowed upon a disqualifying disposition, the employer must withhold tax from the income received by the ISO upon the disqualifying disposition. In fact, the employer **must** deduct and withhold an appropriate amount of income tax from any wages recognized by the employee upon exercise of the NSO. The employer must also deduct and withhold the employee's 7.65% portion of FICA taxes from such wages (although no withholding is necessary for the Social Security portion of such FICA taxes to the extent that the employee's wages have exceeded the relevant Social Security Act contribution and benefit base limit for the current year). The employer is responsible for reporting the withheld amounts on an IRS Form 941, as well as reporting the spread as wages in Boxes 1, 3 and 5 of the IRS Form W-2. Note that if the employer timely prepares and delivers an IRS Form W-2, the employee will be deemed to have included the amount of the spread in his or her gross income such that the employer is entitled to a corresponding business expense deduction.

[16] I.R.C. § 422(c)(2). Exercise and sale within six months may pose problems for directors, officers, and 10% stockholders under § 16(b) of the '34 Act. In order to mitigate that result, the plan (ISO or NSO) should be drafted pursuant to the provisions of Rule 16b-3.

[17] Aufmuth, Selected Tax Accounting Issues in Early and Mezzanine Financings and Venture Capital Partnerships, in Venture Capital After the Tax Reform Act of 1986, at 55, 76 (PLI Course Handbook Series No.422, 1987) [hereinafter Aufmuth].

Equity Compensation Structures for Venture-Backed Companies Post-Enron, Post-Market Bust[ii]

Equity compensation structures at venture-backed start-ups and other private companies have followed a standard pattern for many years-restricted common stock or time-vested common stock options. Historically, there have been three principal structuring considerations for employee equity compensation: business incentives, accounting impact and tax minimization. Although there have been significant accounting changes over the last couple of years that affect equity compensation, as well as changes in market perception relating to non-cash compensation, there has been little change in equity compensation structures. In addition, recent experience has created an increasing awareness on the part of sophisticated entrepreneurs and managers of the potential adverse impact on their equity from down round pricing and deal structures such as multiple liquidation preferences.

Companies and their employees are beginning to explore alternative structures that afford some protection from these events. Among these structures are: performance-based option vesting tied to achievement of individual or company-wide goals; options where the number of shares varies depending on the return outside investors receive on their investment in a liquidity event; "make-whole" guarantees entitling the employee to a cash payment on a liquidity event hypothetically linked to a deemed conversion of preferred equity, with or without a minimum percentage equity guarantee; options on preferred stock; and acquisition/IPO cash bonus pools.

Start-ups typically issue "restricted stock" to founders and to early-stage employees until the stock becomes too expensive for an employee to purchase because of valuations established by venture financings. Restricted stock is preferable to options from the employee's viewpoint since the employee will receive long-term capital gain treatment on a liquidity event if holding period requirements are met. In order to align the employee's incentives to the needs of the business, restricted stock typically has "golden handcuff" vesting provisions-unvested stock is forfeited back to the company at cost upon termination, with vesting occurring in increments over three or four years. For accounting purposes, because the stock is purchased at "fair market value," there is no charge to earnings if vesting is solely time-based and the number of shares is fixed.

After the company receives its first round of convertible preferred stock financing, the common stock typically is valued at a steep discount to the preferred stock price. Even so, the purchase price for restricted stock may be too high. The employee might be permitted to purchase the stock with a promissory note, but there are undesirable consequences to that structure, including the repayment risk in a "down round" (or worse) scenario. Because of these complications, post-financing incentive equity often takes the form of stock options that qualify for so called "fixed accounting."

Stock options can be structured for favorable accounting treatment (i.e., no compensation expense) if they are for a fixed number of shares with a fixed exercise price equal to fair market value of the underlying common stock at grant, and are solely time-vested (as opposed to performance-vested). One structure called a TARSAP mixes performance and time-vesting, but is rarely used due to accounting uncertainties. For tax purposes, if the options are at fair market value and meet certain other requirements of the tax code, they can also be granted as incentive stock options (ISOs). With an ISO, there is no tax or withholding on exercise and if a sufficient holding period is met after exercise, the spread is converted into long-term capital gain.

So what's wrong with this picture?

This question can be put a different way-if accounting and tax considerations were completely irrelevant, how would equity compensation be structured? We suggest that the structures would look a lot different. Further, although tax and accounting considerations are still relevant, we suggest that they may be increasingly less relevant in the post-Enron environment, thus permitting a fresh look at equity structures.

We suggest that the fixed number of shares, time-vested structure for restricted stock and stock options is not optimal from a business point of view. Certainly, it is not optimal in all cases. The business purpose of equity grants is to align the interests of the employee with those of other shareholders. The current accounting rules favor companies that grant options that vest with tenure over companies that grant options that vest based on performance. The employee should be incentivized to be as productive as possible as quickly as possible, not just productive enough to not be fired. Also treated adversely are structures which vary the amount of equity or the price of the grant based on performance or on external equity indexes. Structures with a fixed exercise price below market at date of grant and with time vesting are accounted for with a fixed charge to earnings over the vesting period. Structures where the price varies, or the number of shares varies other than by time vesting, result in a variable charge to earnings measured by changes in the value of the employer's equity over the vesting period. This treatment is particularly troublesome given that there is an open-ended charge to earnings.

As for tax, if the employee is granted an option that is not an ISO (i.e., a "nonqualified option"), the employee recognizes taxable income on the spread at exercise, which in the case of a private company, is not mitigated by the ability to do a simultaneous exercise and sale into the public markets. In reality, even employees who hold ISOs rarely time their exercises and sales to achieve long-term capital gain treatment. In addition, ISOs may create alternative minimum tax problems.

ISOs do have one significant advantage - there is no tax due on exercise, which is particularly useful to a departing employee, who typically must exercise vested options within a short time window after termination. The limited exercise period is not a requirement for an option to be an ISO at grant; however, if the option permits exercise beyond the specified tax-mandated post-termination exercise period, the option is automatically converted into a non-qualified option after that period.

Our thesis as to the new relevance of unconventional structures is simple: ISOs rarely result in long-term capital gain; non-cash accounting charges are irrelevant to a private company; changes in accounting principles have significantly reduced the impact of non-cash compensation charges in an acquisition; and, lastly, even for public companies, non-cash compensation charges increasingly are becoming irrelevant.

Therefore, why not structure employee equity to maximize business incentives? For private companies, accounting measures of performance are not what drives valuations. Cash flow and the promise of future financial performance are the real performance measures. Why then are equity grants structured around accounting considerations and not business incentives in private companies? The reason is the anticipated relevance of GAAP performance in an IPO or an acquisition - that is, even if non-cash earnings charges are unimportant for a private company, the impact that the historical financial statements will have on valuations in an acquisition or an IPO is relevant.

For the vast majority of start-ups, the exit strategy is a sale to a strategic buyer rather than an IPO. This trend is being reinforced in our public capital markets where the economics, market mechanisms and the diminished interests of bankers, analysts and institutional investors render all but a handful of small public companies almost invisible. It is in the rarefied atmosphere of public equity where the highest sensitivity to the accounting for option grants exists - where the word "dilution" refers to a reduction in earnings per share rather than a shift in economic value of equity rights. Even there, the sensitivity is diminishing.

This has always been the case. What has changed?

On the accounting side, there was one dramatic change several years ago - the demise of pooling-of-interests accounting. Perhaps more importantly, the financial community is increasingly beginning to ignore or discount non-cash equity compensation expense in measuring a company's performance.

In poolings, the financial statements of the acquired company were combined with those of the acquiror going backward and forward. Compensation expense from "non-qualifying" options would decrease the acquiror's historical and future earnings. Under currently mandated purchase accounting, the acquired company's historical financial statements are not combined with the acquiror's financials other than in possible pro forma disclosures in footnotes. This suggests that one important cornerstone of the existing compensation structures no longer applies - to optimize the accounting treatment of the private company's equity compensation in order to minimize any adverse effects on the acquiror's "pooled" historical financial statements.

Adverse accounting treatment of compensation at a private company may have an adverse impact on the acquiror's financial statements post-acquisition in the case of **unvested** options. Under purchase accounting, the cost of assuming **vested** options is treated as part of the purchase price with no negative effects on earnings.

Similarly, variable expense related to performance-based options does not affect the acquiror's income statement to the extent the performance milestones have been achieved or, as often happens at least for management, the vesting of the options accelerates on the acquisition under the terms of the original option grant. An expense issue remains, however, with respect to unvested, non-accelerated options. The "intrinsic value" of these options at the date of acquisition would be amortized into the acquiror's financial statements as compensation expense over the remaining vesting period. We suggest that the impact of this one circumstance is likely to be minimal because, in addition to the acceleration of many options at acquisition, the successful private company on acquisition most likely would have achieved the performance measures specified in any performance-based option grants. Also, the intrinsic value for "qualifying options" may not be significantly less than for more creative structures.

There is also an increasing change in the perception of the relevance of non-cash compensation expense for "non-qualifying" options. Post-Enron, incentive-based equity, or at least the favorable accounting for it, has taken on something of a public taint. A number of prominent public companies are electing to treat options under an alternative accounting treatment where the fair value of the option at the date of grant is amortized to earnings over the vesting or performance period. The advantage of this model for venture-backed companies is that such values exclude a volatility factor and so result in a lower valuation of the options than would be the case for a public company. This treatment also minimizes the compensation cost volatility associated with variable option grants under the existing prevalent accounting model which arises from changes in the value of the issuer's equity prior to the vesting of such variable options. These considerations make the granting of performance-based options an attractive alternative for companies electing this accounting treatment.

The new accounting regime and new perceptions of the decreasing relevance of non-cash compensation expense, as well as the real-world impracticalities of ISOs, have created an opportunity, particularly for private companies, to revisit the desirability of equity structures that maximize business objectives, but are less sensitive to accounting and tax considerations.

There is another unrelated factor at work here in the current financing "depression" in the private venture-backed technology company market. Dilutive or "down round" financings have become prevalent. In addition, new deal structures, such as preferred stock with multiple liquidation preferences, have significantly dimmed the prospect of common equity holders ever realizing a significant gain. In other words, as a result of greatly reduced enterprise valuations, the required payouts to preferred stock investors resulting from large prior investments and/or multiple liquidation preferences renders unlikely that the common equity will ever acquire significant value. Astute entrepreneurs and professional managers are increasingly seeking different forms of protection from these down scenarios from the company and its venture investors. For these economic reasons, accounting and tax considerations increasingly are taking a back seat in structuring equity compensation, at least for senior managers.

Among the structures that are beginning to emerge are the following:

Performance-based common stock options. Companies are granting common stock options where the options are vest-based on the achievement of individual or broader-based performance goals. If the goal is reached by a certain date, a portion of the option vests; if the goal is not reached by a specified date, a portion of the option is forfeited. For example, a portion of the option vests when a software developer successfully completes development of a particular module by a certain date, with or without additional vesting for early achievement. Another example is the non-qualified option where the number of shares varies depending on the return outside investors receive on their investment in a liquidity event. In this case, the option might have time-based vesting milestones, but once vested, the option could be exercised post termination and only on a liquidity event. In an IPO, the option might vest six months after the offering, imposing a built-in lock-up agreement. Thirdly, vesting schedules or the number of shares subject to an option can be made dependent on achievement of company-wide milestones, or a combination of individual and company milestones, which may be dependent on timeframes as well.

Equity-based incentives with dilution protection devices. In the case of negotiated equity grants, the employee could be given a deeply discounted option that vests on performance milestones, so that the employee potentially is rewarded for individual performance even though the equity has not increased in value due to market conditions or other factors not related to individual performance. Employees can be given contractual "make-whole" guarantees, such that on an acquisition, the employee would be entitled to a cash (or stock) payment equal to the difference between the amount actually realized by the employee and the amount that would have been received on the hypothetical basis that all convertible senior securities had been converted into common stock. Alternatively or in addition, an option might specify that the number of shares subject to the option could not go below a specified percentage of the fully diluted equity compensation. A variation on this theme, frequently used by universities that license technology to early stage companies, is to specify that the option represents the right to buy a specified percentage of the fully diluted equity after the company has raised a specified amount of outside capital. Another technique being used is to grant options to buy preferred stock, but that doesn't afford much protection against subsequent down rounds, or subsequent rounds with onerous terms.

Cash incentive payments. Structures that do not utilize restricted stock or stock options are even more flexible and avoid the risk of the dilution of equity-based compensation. A bonus pool could be established payable in cash on an acquisition equal to a specified percentage of the amounts payable to investors in an acquisition, or after the investors have received their original investment together with a specified return. An IPO could be treated as a deemed acquisition of the company at its pre-money valuation, with the employee being paid in stock valued at the IPO price; such a payout would be a taxable event and some liquidity for the equity would be necessary. A similar structure would be for the employee to be contractually entitled to a cash payment equivalent to a "carried interest" on the investors' returns. (There is, of course, a certain irony in that structure.) To the extent such models are contingent upon a specific contingent event outside of the employee's control, they may not have any current accounting implications until such time as the contingency is resolved; this charge would be "washed" in the purchase accounting for the acquisition.

Each of these alternatives has its own advantages and disadvantages. We expect, however, that given the trend away from rigid adherence to historical structures with favorable accounting consequences or perceived tax benefits, a number of these structures will become increasingly commonplace.

[ii] Contributed to VC Experts by Edwin L. Miller, Jr. Partner, Morse, Barnes-Brown & Pendleton, P.C., Waltham, Mass. Christopher J. Lindop, Partner, Ernst + Young LLP, Boston, Mass. *All Rights Reserved by the Authors*

7

An Analysis of Compensation For Senior Public Managers– And a Proposed Alternative to Stock Options[1]

'Enronitis' has stimulated the suspicion that Corporate America is irremediably corrupt, in turn spreading the malaise which drags the market averages down just as the economy recovers nicely. Good news cannot fix the Dow and NASDAQ, the troubles of which in turn may reverse the good news.

The Administration appears hapless, in part because its options are so limited. On the one hand, massive government regulation is a cure worse than the disease; on the other hand, simply jawboning and increasing the penalties for crimes already on the books is perceived (correctly) as doing nothing.

The following paper suggests a new approach, which recognizes certain realities in today's ugly climate (including the above-named) and attempts to (i) understand and accommodate them; and (ii) leapfrog the current quagmire.

First, some realities as I see them, namely:

- Stock options, *per se*, are not the problem. Most of the attacks on options are lamentably uninformed.

- However, the 1997 FASB failure to require expensing options as of the date of grant has acquired iconic importance–a "reform" which now must happen to combat corporate "greed." The fact that the "reform" is (a) unnecessary and (b) unlikely to have much impact is beside the point.[2]

- The ability to pay the help with options has been critical to the success of the venture capital-driven, hi-tech miracle in this country (the envy of every competitive economy) for three reasons:

> (i) It ties reward to performance. *Nota bena*: Performance driven pay, ironically, was the battle cry of the "reformers" in the `80s; management was then accused of neglecting the stock price, wedded to their fixed salaries and cushy, non-stressful jobs. Today's "reformers" are, by and large, the same people, but they have done a 180° turn.
> (ii) The corporation does not use cash–which, in the case of venture-backed start-ups, none of them have.
> (iii) Tax is postponed until the employee realizes cash– and can, therefore, pay the tax.

- If stock options are the required sacrificial lamb, the equivalent of the human sacrifice which cures the primitive tribe of its angst, then some regime has to be installed in their place, hopefully a regime which can be better calibrated to where we as a society want to go– *i.e.*, pay rationally tied to long-term performance with little or no built-in incentives to cheat.

- The root cause of the problem cannot easily be fixed but only recognized and dealt with because it is not based on the CEO's greed or independent bias towards criminal behavior; the problem's foundation lies in the climate in which a typical CEO operates–i.e., today's market insistence on quarter-by-quarter performance, the company meeting estimates to the exact penny so that the stock can be precisely and comfortably positioned in the portfolio of the major asset managers. Note again the ultimate (and unreachable) locale of this problem–not (directly at least) in how CEOs get paid, and how much, but in the first instance in how (and how much) the asset managers, the people who buy the CEO's stock, get paid. In financial services, the only real money these days is in asset management, not commercial or investment banking or brokerage; asset managers are graded quarter-by-quarter, which filters down to the people who control the firms in which they invest.

- Given the natural propensity of CEOs to please the people who own their companies (the institutional asset managers), there is a large incentive to hit the number, even if you have to cook the books a bit to do it. For genuine efforts at reform to succeed, the trick, obviously, is to create counter-incentives, to lift the typical CEO's horizon towards the long term, despite pressure from the analysts and institutional managers.

- One virtue of lengthening the reward horizon is that creative accounting usually has a short shelf life; sooner or later, someone rings an alarm bell–maybe even the SEC.

- The two "solutions" currently advertised most prominently do not work. Thus, requiring the CEO, et al., to hold the option stock for a year post-exercise, at least in today's volatile market, is an invitation to personal ruin. In the first place, where does the CEO get the money to exercise? Under the Sarbanes-Oxley Act, the CEO can no longer borrow from the company. Let's say she borrows on margin. The problem is, if you put a CEO in that position (having paid the exercise price, with the option out of the money a year later) just watch her really push the envelope in order to goose the stock price. Moreover, the idea to issue stock versus options, advanced recently by some commentators who feel options distort incentives, does not work for these reasons. If the stock is a gift, the company must "gross up" in order to pay tax (plus tax on the gross up) on the trade–an inefficient use of capital. And, the traditional fix for this problem, a company loan, is now a crime under Sarbanes-Oxley.

Against this background, please consider the following proposal: a fix which I submit: (i) does not require much government action (except a bit of comfort from the IRS); (ii) preserves fundamental benefits of option plans; (iii) is cash flow positive for the Treasury; (iv) opens up the opportunity of a totemic sacrifice, meaning companies can substitute the new regime for the option plan so as to purge themselves of the evil spirits everywhere lurking; (v) lengthens time horizons; and (vi) fixes some secondary problems in the bargain.

Discussion

The critics are, as am I, flabbergasted at the inflation in CEO compensation over the past decade-$10 million a year is small potatoes for some executives. Think, in fact, $100 million a year, a fair amount in actual cash but principally driven by option awards. The seeming overpayments, particularly against the backdrop of company failure, has called into question the entire system of option compensation. If the CEOs made out like bandits and the little people lost their jobs and their savings, the system must be wrong. All aspects of option plans are now under fire–how they are accounted for, taxed, sized, awarded, etc.

How We Got There

First, why has so much been paid to CEOs, CFOs, *et al,* during the past decade? Lush stock options, huge bonuses, limitless loans went well beyond historical norms. The principal answer stems from relentless commitment, I think, to the pay-for-performance mantra, which was all the rage in the 80s, repeatedly chanted by critics (whom the liberal press applauded as tribunes of the people) of what was then perceived to be entrenched, sedentary and risk averse managers. Much of that criticism was self-serving, propaganda by wolves in sheep's clothing–*i.e.,* the corporate raiders pretending to defend the moral high ground in aid of their pet greenmail and hostile takeover initiatives. But the notion stuck–tie the managers' pay to the shareholders' outcomes. If the company remains stodgy, its stock performance less than outstanding, fire the senior management, replace the same with entrepreneurs (or predators, if you like, to borrow Jim Stewart's label). The SEC, indeed, put its official imprimatur on the movement; ironically the very option schemes which are now reviled were heralded as the solution, the way to a solid future for Corporate America in the `80's, the delight of the very 'reformers' who are in the vanguard of today's necktie parties. As a consequence, I suggest, the board's view of the ideal CEO has changed, often morphing a board's perception of the CEO to the equivalent of an asset manager, and in particular the manager of a private equity fund. I suggest the critics (the managers of LBO funds engaged in hostile takeovers) and the criticized [CEOs] began in terms of image and internal dynamics, to merge-to look, act and be regarded alike, a common phenomenon in social relations case studies; just as cops and robbers (husbands and wives, people and their dogs) tend to take on common characteristics because of their continually being in each other's company. Hence, the raiders (*i.e.*, the general partners of LBO funds who were doing all the talking during the heyday of private equity investing) and their victims (*i.e.*, the managers of the target companies) began to resemble identical twins. Please recall Abe Lincoln's story about the two gents who wrestled with each other so long, they wound up in the other's overcoat. If Harold Simmons, Boone Pickens, Carl Ichan *et al.*, preached that Corporate America needed to be shook up, the CEOs to look and act like Simmons, Pickens and Ichan, the logical extension of that thesis is as follows:–since Ichan, *et al.*, normally took a 20% carried interest in the profits earned on their investors' capital, why shouldn't an outstanding CEO be paid in like vein?

The logic had, in fact, enormous surface appeal, as per the following scenario:

- Ichan, on behalf of KKR, criticizes management and seeks to take over Company X; the current team is too timid, too paranoid, too concerned about a regular paycheck vs. shareholder value;
- Ichan takes control of Company X in order to unlock shareholder value, buying 50% of the stock, and installs Superhero as CEO;
- Superhero cuts costs, boosts profits and Company X's market cap goes from $1 billion to $3 billion in a year's time. Ichan makes $300 million (20% of $2 billion x 50%). What should Superhero and his team make? Well, how

about $150 million, a modest share of the new wealth
created; the larger the company, the larger the award.

I further suggest this theme proved to be catching. As the market boomed in
the `90s, management boomed along with it. If the stock prices tripled on
Superhero's watch, why shouldn't she get what amounts to a percentage
deal–a carried interest in the appreciation in market cap? The directors were
influenced by the fact that (a) good managers were and are scarce (and they
are); and (b) everyone was making out–particularly (on paper) the very
shareholders Boone Pickens said he cared so much about.

The huge awards, part stock (including options) and part cash, were not
noteworthy as long as the music kept playing. The asset managers became
super rich but only because they "deserved" to–their pay was tied to profits.[3]
And so with the CEOs, whether installed by Ichan or just mimicking his
nominees, pay tied to profits, perfectly aligned with investors, whether the
public shareholder or the limited partners of the LBO fund.

The problem, of course, is obvious. The music stopped. Superhero became
an ordinary mortal as her company share price stumbled, either because the
company had special problems in continuing double digit growth (as almost
all do) and/or was caught in the general downdraft. In some cases, Superhero
was fired but with a generous severance award, negotiated where the music
was at its loudest. In others, the annual awards were cut back, but were still
pretty rich in view of the lofty heights from which the cut backs were
calculated–a 90% cut in pay is not so punitive if the beginning point is
$50,000,000.

And so now, at last, we get to the real problem. The CEOs, during the boom
years, were analogized to the managers of private equity, and paid
accordingly, but the analogy was not extended to its logical conclusion. The
CEOs were and are paid like hedge fund managers, not the general partners
of venture and buyout funds–a critical error. The hedge fund partners

manage, by and large, public equities. They enjoy a big interest in profits, which they take annually and do not give back but their investors are relatively liquid because the fund itself is usually liquid (to a point). If the fund does not perform, the investors depart. Ken Lipper is the most recent example of a hedge fund manager with not much left to hedge.

The CEO, on the other hand, is best analogized, if at all, to the managers of a private equity fund whose investors are stuck over a long term–i.e., venture or buyout. By and large, the LPs in such funds are mired in place. To be sure, the individual shareholders of the public company Superhero is managing can sell; but the shareholders as a group, particularly the large institutions with unwieldy blocks, are stuck, like the LPs of a venture fund.

And, thereby hangs the tale–or, to put the same in context, thereby appears the solution. If CEO, our Superhero, is to be paid like a venture or buyout general partner (i.e., her pay a carried interest in the "profit," measured by increases in market cap), then he should be burdened with the customary protective provision–the so-called 'clawback.'

In venture and buyout funds, the clawback operates to true up allocations and distributions of profits over the ten to twelve year life of the fund. If the general partner pockets big money because of extraordinary profits early on, and those early achievements are not sustainable, she owes hard cash back to his investors at the end of the day, when the fund liquidates. If it turns out the fund wound up making no money at all, then she has to give it all back.

Why not, in short, apply the clawback to Superhero, the CEO of Company X? The logic is that the CEO is, first, hired to obtain long-term results, likened, say, to Henry Kravis.[4] She gets modest base pay annually, and a carry–again like Kravis. Finally, her carried interest in profits (net of what she needs to pay taxes) is escrowed until the end of the day (and why not ten years?)[5], when the hits, runs and errors during her stewardship are calculated and her pay trued up, again like Kravis'. After true up, her escrow account may be a big number, or it may be zero.

The point is that, since the boards have bought into only half the 'fund manager' analogy, today's CEOs have it "heads I win, tails you lose." In good years, they take home big numbers; in bad years (like hedge fund managers), they do not give anything back. Who wouldn't be tempted to try an accounting trick or two, or plunge into a glamorous but unwise merger under those circumstances?

In short, if we were to measure long-term performance (and, if the analogy is extended as it should have been, for once we would really mean it), the CEO obtains no advantage (or almost none) by loading up in a particular quarter. She can exercise her options and sell into a temporary rally; but the 'true up' means she will have to give it all back when and if the market takes its revenge.

The Fix

Replace Stock Option Plans? With What?

Some wag once said (Mencken, I believe) that all difficult problems have solutions which are both simple and wrong. The test of the foregoing analysis, assuming it survives as a plausible hypothesis, comes when the board of a public (or, indeed, a private) company attempts to implement the same. Can the present system in fact be improved on in the above-mentioned critical detail, and perhaps a number of others as well? The proof of the pudding, they say, is in the eating.

The seemingly simplest way to achieve "reform" is, as many of the loudest voices would have it, to junk stock option compensation entirely and shift to a bonus plan or, if you want to dress up a bonus plan and make it look equity-flavored, a phantom stock plan. However, there are obvious problems with a straight bonus plan (and I will leave aside the accounting issues for the moment). If the management team is entitled to, say, a share of the upside (as measured by increases in market capitalization) which approach stock option levels (say, 15%, plus or minus, of total outstanding shares), then the cash drain on the company could be out of sight. Let's say the compensation committee eliminates the entire stock option plan and substitutes a phantom stock plan. In our hypothetical case, the company stock price surges from $1 billion to $3 billion, based on the promise of a couple of break through oncology therapeutics; but the company still does not have much in the way of cash flow. How do you pay out $300 million in cash to the executive team (15% of $2 billion) without breaking the bank?

Currently, the only way to achieve that result (by and large) is with options. The cash representing the executive's profit share comes not from the company (which doesn't have it) but the stock market. (Note that the solution outlined herein does <u>not</u> mean a retreat to fainthearted CEO compensation; the working assumption is that the essence of the `80s analogy should be preserved–but radically improved. While the cascading criticism of options is so intense and pervasive, albeit often unfair and typically uninformed,[6] that a search for a replacement solution is in order, nonetheless, we do not want to throw the baby out with the bath water, I submit; we need to offer extraordinary compensation to extraordinary CEOs and, not revert to the European model. In the right circumstances, the opportunity for 'venture capital' type rewards is what generates an aptitude for constructive risk on management's part and, in the process, helps create great companies.

The second, and equally necessary, element of option grants is that the tax paid by the recipient is postponed until realization–until there is cash with which to pay the tax. With rare exceptions, options are not taxed as of the date of grant; the tax is not due until exercise (in the case of non-quals, exercise being usually accompanied by sale) or sale of the option stock in the case of ISOs. Stock grants lack that quality.

The keys, in short, to the underlying, and constructive, economics of option plans have little or nothing to do with accounting legerdemain or tax avoidance; they are (i) the ability to pay percentage of "profits" compensation; (ii) the necessary cash requisitioned from the market, not the company; and (iii) tax paid only when and if the cash is available with which to pay it.

Having concluded that stock options are a continual source of contention, I repeat the question: Can the entire concept be replaced with a new, improved version which preserves the economics mentioned above? Can companies bent on compensating desirable executives with equity simply junk the stock option plan, thereby eliminating the difficulties which are inherent in dealing with accounting for derivative securities, which are by their nature complex and entail hard-to-quantify impacts on a company's financial statements?

Let's say we eliminate the structure entirely. That done, we still need to face up to the cash flow problem. We need to continue to tie executive compensation to performance, and to reward the 'best in breed' executives competitively. Cash from the company's resources is not the answer, not at the levels we are talking about. Restricted stock awards and other equity flavored solutions lack one or more of the three key advantages discussed earlier, usually the tax postponement feature.

The New Concept

Rather than escrowing, in effect, say, 20% of the company's outstanding stock into a stock option pool, the "fix" I am suggesting contemplates issuing outright 20% of the outstanding stock into a private equity fund, organized as a limited liability company (the "LLC"). The question of accounting for dilution is, as of the date of issuance of the shares, settled. The shares are currently outstanding; they have been issued to a limited liability company (taxed as a partnership) of which the company is initially the sole member, with an opening capital account equivalent to the then fair market value of the shares so deposited. The managers of the LLC are the compensation committee of the company's board. The members (other than the company) are the executives who otherwise would have participated in the stock option pool. They each are issued profits interests which can be adjusted annually or periodically by the managers without the imposition of tax (as long as capital accounts are not shifted). New executives join the pool, others withdraw and the assets are "booked up" annually so as to start all newcomers on a level playing field, so to speak, with the existing employee members. Each executive will be required to contribute sufficient cash to the pool to qualify as a true "partner" for tax purposes, a reasonable burden usually pegged at 1% of the 'value' of the fair market value of the shares. (This is one of the tricky parts; if this solution has traction, I assume a relevant Revenue Ruling can issue to bless the arrangements we are describing, so as to take any tax suspense out of the equation.)

Each member has a special profits interest, representing an interest in a fixed number of shares, and if she dies, becomes disabled or her employment terminates, the LLC sells the shares into the stock market and distributes the profit, meaning price minus tax basis as marked to market, and minus any contractual give backs–if the CEO quits and joins a competitor, for example. The shares may be distributed (tax free) earlier, in whole or in part on petition of the executive and agreement of the managers (death, disability, discharge other than for cause, pressing need), and presumptively will be distributed upon a change of control (subject to negotiated vesting restrictions), provided that, in the CEO's case, shares of the acquirer may be held in her capital account until the merger works as the CEO advertised it. The company's profits interest is, in effect, the reservoir; as awards are made and/or lapse each year, the company's interest is enlarged or diminished. The compensation committee may elect to sell shares in lieu of distributions in kind and distribute proceeds, depending on market conditions and legal considerations. The shares in the account may be subject to a buy/sell arrangement if the parties so agree and, in any event, a right of first refusal in the company is presumed. Distributions to the departing executives are subject to an escrow of, say, 50% of the profits to satisfy the clawback requirement. That means that the executive takes (depending on the provisions of her employment contract) half the realized profits, pays tax at capital gains rates and puts the remainder in her pocket, subject to a clawback calculation which cuts in at the end of ten years. (Note the clawback is a general claim on all the executive's assets, not limited to the escrow.) Until the expiration of the ten-year period, the executive leaves in her capital account escrowed profits in the form of stock, or cash which the managers can use to buy more stock, the capital account standing as collateral for the clawback at the end of the ten-year period, when the true up occurs and the departing executive either pays up or not, depending on the fortunes of the company over the period.

Advantages

The advantages of this system include: (i) the fact that it carries the analogy all the way through to its conclusion; the executive is paid like an asset manager–with not only the benefits but also the burdens, including the clawback; (ii) taxes are paid at capital gains rates (assuming the Treasury and the Internal Revenue Service go along and treat the members as true partners for tax purposes) when, as and if cash is realized; in fact, the gains tax can be further reduced under I.R.C. §§ 1045 and 1202 if the executive joined the plan while the company was still a Qualified Small Business; (iii) there is no advantage to an executive attempting to play the quarter by quarter game; the clawback *cum* true up means that the profits are not finally vested in their entirety in the executive until the tenth anniversary of her initial participation; (iv) the company spends no money for this element of executive compensation; the cash reward at the end of the day comes from the stock market itself; (v) there is no question about hidden dilution; dilution occurs outright, as the shares are deposited in the plan and are, outstanding for all purposes—including the all important earnings-per-share calculation; (vi) since the company gets no deduction on the sale of the shares and the executive pays a capital gains tax, from the Treasury's point of view this produces more tax revenue than a system which entails a 100% deduction to the company and a 100% tax payment by the executive, personal and corporate ordinary income rates being close to equal; (vii) the management of the entire plan is in the hands of the independent board members *qua* compensation committee and, since the tax code provisions governing partnerships are more flexible, the committee's power to adjust its decisions to current circumstances is enhanced; (viii) no chance of "inside information" temptation to the executive; (ix) no §16(b) problems and no reason for the company to loan cash to the executive—the 1% can and should come out of her pocket; (x) there is no need to re-price options; if the stock tanks, the executive has a loss (up to her cash contribution) in her account, which will be included in the true up calculation on the tenth anniversary; she balances that loss against gains in the account by reason of awards in past or future years.

To illustrate the new system, consider the following:

A Case Study

Early in Newco Inc.'s existence, when the CEO is hired, Newco deposits 20% of its outstanding shares (8,000,000 shares) into an LLC. The FMV is $1.00/share (last round price). Newco owns 80% of the LLC's profits interest and 100% of the capital accounts. CEO pays $1,000, being 1% of $100,000 (100,000 shares x $1.00) to LLC and receives a special profits interest in a separate account representing 100,000 shares.

On January 1 of the next 3 years, the fair market value of Newco stock is $2, $3 and $4/share respectively. CEO is awarded another 100,000 shares on each such occasion; she contributes $2,000, $3,000 and $4,000 to Newco's capital *seriatim*. In year 4, Newco goes public at $10 share. The stock shoots up to $30 per share shortly thereafter.

In year 8, CEO resigns and asks to cash out her interest. The stock has settled down to $10. The LLC distributes 400,000 shares which she sells for $4,000,000, representing a capital gain of $3,990,000. The company, at that price, elects not to exercise its first refusal right.

By year 10, Newco is in trouble (or the market itself has tanked). The stock is selling for $2.00 per share. The true up is exercised, as follows:

The CEO's after tax profit: $2,793,000 ($3,990,000 minus 30% assumed tax of $1,197,000).
For true up purposes, the CEO's notional net profit over the 10 year period is $100,000 (the shares in account #1, and only those shares, have appreciated.. $1 to $2.)

True Up calculation: Credit given for her $10,000 cash contribution and $100,000 net notional 10 year profit, for a total of $110,000. After tax profit of $2,793,000 minus $110,000 equals a give back by the CEO of $2,683,000.

Conclusion

Why is the above change in compensation methodology, a change which
smacks of a technically-driven tweak, superior to those current proposals in
Congress and trumpeted in the newspapers? We are facing a crisis, why does
not the crisis call for dramatic remedies, i.e., "throw them all in jail." Let me
recite the reasons I think the suggestion outlined above trumps the far more
theatrical so-called "solutions" currently on the table.

Thus, the current emphasis on increased penalties ('lock em up and throw
away the key') ignores elementary psychology. A significant number of the
individuals involved are unlikely to be deterred by increasing the
punishments facing wrongdoers because they don't believe (and it may turn
out that they are right, when all is said and done) that they did anything
wrong. To be sure, some number of the offending CEOs/CFOs are aware
they are over the edge but nonetheless think they can get away with it–or
thought so, anyway. For that cohort, simply increasing the penalties doesn't
do much good either. For those who are genuinely convinced they can get
away with it, the penalties are irrelevant. For those who acknowledge the
risk, the difference between a ten-year and a five-year sentence is trivial; in
either event, the individual has been ruined. The idea of playing super cop in
a situation like this may be appealing to one's sense of machismo, but, in
reality, the likelihood of that approach inducing a significant change in
behavior is remote.

So also with the change from the Financial Accounting Standards Board to
an entity composed of government appointees. The expertise of the
nominees is unlikely to improve because the FASB representatives are
eminently well qualified senior members from within the profession. It is true
that, on the issue of expensing stock options, FASB was compelled to cave to
political pressure and the Board rescinded mandatory expensing; I happen to
think the result was right but the fact that the politicians won the day
through pressure tactics is lamentable. The question before the house,

however, is whether a board composed of government appointees will be *less* sensitive to political pressure than an independent, self-regulatory organization. If you believe that, as they say, I have a bridge over the East River I would like to sell you.

Further to idea of imposing sanctions, I challenge the common sense of the rule compelling separation of the audit and consulting functions, as in the public interest. The idea is that accountants hired by a public company as consultants will admire the revenues from that assignment so enthusiastically that they will roll over and play dead with their audit hats on, in order to hold on to the combined business. There may be something in this; but the solution has no apparent logic. Once the consulting function is stripped out of the major (and indeed minor) accounting firms, then it becomes harder for the members of those firms to make the same compensation they have become accustomed to. In order to hold on to existing customers, and to attract new ones, why wouldn't the temptation (with the wolf at the door, so to speak) to bend the rules be even stronger, rather than milder, amongst the individuals whose judgments are the only judgments that count in this equation?

Similarly, the requirement that each public company board be dominated, at least numerically, by independent directions is a "reform" without much in the way of new teeth. The independent directors are well represented on the boards of most companies today, and in fact already control the key committees–nomination, audit and compensation. The fact is that companies are run by their managements. If the company is in fact being *managed* by a board of directors, it is usually a train wreck on the way to happening. There is only so much a board of directors can do in preventing a management chicanery; it is not at all clear simply how in adding more directors the equation will have much impact on the ultimate results.

The ultimate cop out is the idea that the financial statements will be sanitized if we insist that individuals in effect warrant them–the risk of a breach of warranty (viewed in hindsight, of course) being a jail sentence. This smacks, of course, of *per se* liability, the presumption of guilt in effect and is unlikely to survive judicial and fundamental scrutiny, given our constitutional notion that criminal penalties are applied only in the presence of so-called *mens rea* intent or recklessness that borders on intent. Moreover, the requirement can be defanged by careful attention to procedural details.

Counselors are already in the arena (i) challenging the constitutionality of what is ultimately the essence of the politicians' cop out; and (ii) constructing systems whereby the risk of error is disseminated widely enough so that no one individual is guilty. If a CEO is asked in effect to warrant financial disclosure, then that individual (assuming he or she is well advised) will lay down a paper trail which rebuts entirely the idea of an intent crime. First the individual reads the financial statement from start to finish; the fact that the statements may not mean anything to that individual is irrelevant–she has read them. Secondly, the inferior personnel in the company will be asked, individually and collectively, to provide written comfort that each and every item is appropriately accounted for. If there is any doubt in anybody's mind on a particular issue, then an outside consultant will be brought in and paid to express an opinion. That opinion is likely to be a so-called 'reasoned' opinion, which means that it contains a sufficient number of assumptions and qualifications that the maker of the opinion cannot be prosecuted–or, indeed, successfully sued. As I tell clients from time to time, I can sit in my office on a Tuesday and give a reasoned opinion (assuming I am in control of the qualifications) that the day of the week is actually Thursday. Once there have been enough people looking over the other guy's shoulder, sufficient memoranda, comfort letters, reviews, *et al.*, then the chance of a CEO/CFO, even one bent on cheating, stubbing her toe becomes infinitesimal.

The short of the matter is that reform in this space should focus on the 'carrot' rather than the 'stick'. What is it that drives management today, and how do we adjust the process so that the key managers behave themselves? In the 80s, the notion was that the ultimate reward was lifetime employment at a steady salary–job security, in other words. The reformers felt that the parochial, turf-conscious, self protective instincts of management in the 70s and 80s were holding back the growth of Corporate America–and, I think they were right. Risk aversion can become epidemic in a large organization and ultimately stifle it. While Dick Foster and Sarah Kaplan used one very wrong example in their book, *Creative Destruction* (Enron), their fundamental thesis was right: The S&P over a twenty-year span loses about 90% of its membership. For companies to survive in today's global economy, the fundamental imperative is: "innovate or die." This necessarily requires a management which is, in very important respects, the opposite of risk averse, which entertains a healthy appetite for taking calculated risks in order to keep the growth curve in line with society's expectations. You cannot ask an individual to take risks if she is paid according to a formula which is essentially static; the two notions are mutually exclusive. Accordingly, pay tied to performance, and generous pay for generous performance, are axioms which we accept as self proven in our economy, a necessary cornerstone of the United States' modern prosperity.

If all the above are more or less right, then the discussion comes down to a simple point. How do you preserve the risk/reward calculus which the reforms of the 80s introduced into our economy, without creating incentives to game the system. If you are able to do that successfully, I submit, you don't have to do much else. Adequate penalties, I argue. are already in place. There are plenty of sections of Title 18, U.S. Code on the books which enable prosecutors to go after criminal behavior; and, if the behavior is not criminal, then it is not fair to convict simply because somebody has to be the villain, this is not the American way. Moreover, scapegoating would not do much good even if it were legal; it never has.

One is necessarily led therefore to the 'carrot' and, such is what this paper and the system it advances are all about.

---

[1] Long form version of paper published in *Innovation Review, Intelligence from the Berkley Center for Entrepreneurial Studies*, Bartlett, "To Expense or not to Expense? Looking for a third option in the great stock option debate," Fall 2002.

[2] To show how irrelevant the "reform" is, AOL is considering the current expense alternative which FASB 123 allows. AOL will incur significantly increased charges to earnings, of course, but AOL seeks to trade on the basis of cash flow; as the old saying goes: "GAAP is an opinion; cash flow a fact." If AOL is willing to throw in the towel on this issue, what is the fuss all about? Even more alarming (see the principle of unintended consequences), Barry Diller has announced that USA Interactive will (i) expense option grants and (ii) in the future give up the plan entirely in favor of restricted stock grants, because options are "far too democratic."

[3] Pete Peterson likes to denigrate the *amour propre* of the managers of the '80s LBO funds, boasting of the double digit IRRs they delivered to their LPs, by pointing out that, if the Man From Mars could have leveraged the S&P index by 80% (vs. 50%) during that period, he would have delivered a compounded 35% IRR.

[4] Although all coincidences are viewed with suspicion in today's cynical environment, in fact my conclusions were arrived at independently and not borrowed from a strikingly similar analysis (antedating mine) which appear in a paper authored by Harvard Business School Professor Brian J. Hall, *Incentive Strategy: Executive Compensation and Ownership Structure* (Part II) 4 (May, 2002) (herein cited as "Hall").

[5] A Booz Allen study, coincidentally, puts the average term of a U.S. CEO at 9.5 years, a number which appears to be shortening as CEOs come under increasingly intense pressure.

[6] For example, the charge that stock options involve sham accounting is simplistic. The dilutive effect of stock options are, in fact, accounted for in the all-important earnings per share number; in-the-money options are treated as outstanding for purposes of that calculation. On the tax issue, since today's executives either obtain non-qualified options initially or turn their incentive stock options into non-qualified options, the tax effect is neutral; the company gets a deduction because, and only because, the executive pays tax on the spread. If the company didn't get a deduction, then simple rules of tax equity require that the executive will be relieved of her tax burden. In either case, as far as the Treasury is concerned, it's a wash.

8

Stock Appreciation Rights (SARs)

A SAR is a "stock appreciation right," meaning that the issuer purchases for cash (or shares) the right to cancel the holder's options at a price equivalent to the spread-the difference between fair market value of the option stock and the exercise price.

Payment in shares is taxable to the employees; cashless exercise is not available. The payment should be deductible to the issuer (and income to the employee),[1] assuming the payment is not "unreasonable compensation" under § 162(m) nor offends the "Golden Parachute" rules in § 280G.[2] If an option plan entails a built-in SAR-i.e., the employee has a right to elect an SAR-the issuer incurs expense[3] as its stock appreciates. Often "put" rights of this sort are built into plans adopted by nonpublic companies, which don't care much about reported earnings.[4] If the SAR with a put feature lapses when the issuer becomes public, there is a one time charge to earnings, measured by the strike price versus the IPO price.

Assuming the Series A Round is not viewed as the purchase of a "security" but the equivalent of a bonus measured by security price, historically, the reasons for granting SARs was to avoid the problems that option holders who are also insiders for '34 Act § 16 and Rule 16b purposes encountered when and if they sold the option stock within six months after the date of acquisition (*i.e.*, exercise). Rule 16b-3 has made it relatively easy for that problem to be solved and hence, even insiders (assuming no misuse of material nonpublic information) can exercise and sell simultaneously, the compulsion to substitute SARs being pro tanto alleviated.

SARs Issued By LLCs

The significant advantage of issuing SARs to LLC employees is that the employees never acquire an interest in the LLC, thereby avoiding the potentially adverse tax consequences attendant on partnership status while accomplishing the objective of tying employee compensation to the value of the LLC. The valuation and cash outlay obligations continue as the primary disadvantages when comparing options to SARs.

Accounting for SARs

SARs must be accounted for as variable plans. This is because the amounts of equity which an employee may acquire upon exercise of an SAR is not known until the employee exercises the SAR. Variable plan accounting means that the final measurement of the compensation cost which must be expensed for an SAR is equal to the cash and/or fair market value of equity which the employee receives when she exercises the SAR.

APB Opinion No. 25 and FASB Interpretation No. 28 require interim calculations of the amount of compensation inherent in SARs. A new measurement must be made at the end of each reporting period based on the current market price of the stock. Normalization or estimation of the annual compensation costs to compute the quarterly impact is not allowed.

Under FASB Interpretation No. 28, which must be applied to variable plans, there will be a very significant difference in the interim measurement of compensation expense for SARs depending on whether the SARs cliff vest at the end of a designated period or vest ratably over the designated period.

Assume a company grants SARs to an employee on January 1 of Year one on 100,000 "shares" when the value of the shares is $10 per share. The SARs vest at the end of three years and have a term of ten years. When the SARs are exercised, the employee receives equity or cash with a value equal to 100 percent of the appreciation of the equity subject to the SARs since the date of grant. Assume further that all of the SARs are exercised at the end of the fifth year.

Since the SARs will cliff vest at the end of three years, FASB Interpretation No. 28 requires that 33.33 percent of the compensation cost computed as of the end of Year One be expensed in Year One; 66.66 percent of the compensation cost computed as of the end of Year Two (less the compensation cost previously expensed in Year One) be expensed in Year Two; 100 percent of the compensation cost computed as of the end of Year Three (less the compensation cost previously expensed in Years One and Two) be expensed in Year Three; and 100 percent of any additional compensation expense (resulting from future increases in value of the equity) or income (resulting from future declines in the value of the equity) be recognized in Years Four and Five.

Example 1 illustrates how compensation expense would be determined for each year based on the assumed facts. (In actual practice, interim computations would need to be made at the end of each quarter.)

EXAMPLE 1
VARIABLE ACCOUNTING -- CLIFF VESTING
MEASUREMENT OF PERIODIC COMPENSATION EXPENSE

	Year				
	1	2	3	4	5
Option price - same for all years	$10.00	$10.00	$10.00	$10.00	$10.00
	12.00	12.00	17.00	16.00	24.00
Value at end of period					
Spread per share	2.00	2.00	7.00	6.00	14.00
	100,000	100,000	100,000	100,000	100,000
Total shares					
Aggregate compensation	200,000	200,000	700,000	600,000	1,400,000
	33.3%	66.7%	100.0%	100.0%	100.0%
Cumulative percent accrued					
Cumulative compensation	66,667	133,333	700,000	600,000	1,400,000
	---	66,667	133,333	700,000	600,000
Compensation previously recognized					
Compensation expense (income) for the year	$66,667	$66,667	$566,667	($100,000)	$800,000

NOTE: Negative compensation expense occurs in Year 4. Negative compensation is limited to the amount of compensation expense previously recognized (i.e., in no event can cumulative compensation expense be negative).

If the employee in Example 1 above had exercised his SARs upon vesting at the end of Year Three, the company would have issued shares with a market value of $700,000. Since the measurement date occurs at exercise, no further compensation cost measurement would be required for Years Four and Five.

The assumptions are identical to the SARs previously illustrated in Example 1 above, except that the SARs vest ratably at 33.33 percent per year over a three year period, instead of 100 percent cliff vesting at the end of the third year.

In this situation FASB Interpretation No. 28 requires compensation expense to be determined separately for each one-third portion of the SAR, as if three separate SARs were granted. The compensation cost for the one-third portion of the SAR which vests at the end of Year One will be expensed 100 percent in Year One; the compensation cost for the one-third portion of the SAR which vests at the end of Year Two will be expensed 50 percent in Year One and 50 percent in Year Two; and the compensation cost for the one-third portion of the SAR which vests at the end of Year Three will be expensed 33.33 percent in each of Years One, Two and Three. Example 2 illustrates how the aggregate cumulative percentage of compensation accrued by the end of each year of the vesting period is determined based on the facts assumed above.

EXAMPLE 2
VARIABLE ACCOUNTS - RATABLE VESTING

	Aggregate Cumulative Percentage of Compensation Accrued by the End of Each Year of Vesting Period		
	YEAR		
For Rights Vested in:	1	2	3
Year 1	33.33%	33.33%	33.33%
Year 2	16.67%	33.33%	33.33%
Year 3	11.11%	22.22%	33.33%
Aggregate percentage accrued at end of each year	61.11%	88.89%	100.00%
Rounded	61%	89%	100%

Accordingly, ratable vesting over a designated period results in a substantial acceleration of expense recognition when compared to cliff vesting at the end of the designated period. Example 3 illustrates how compensation expense would be determined for each year based on the facts assumed above where the SARs vest ratably at 33.33 percent per year over a three-year period.

EXAMPLE 3
VARIABLE ACCOUNTING - RATABLE VESTING
MEASUREMENT OF PERIODIC COMPENSATION EXPENSE

	YEAR				
	1	2	3	4	5
Option price - same for all years	$10.00	$10.00	$10.00	$10.00	$10.00
	12.00	12.00	17.00	16.00	24.00
Value at end of period					
Spread per share	2.00	2.00	7.00	6.00	14.00
	100,000	100,000	100,000	100,000	100,000
Total shares					
Aggregate compensation	200,000	200,000	700,000	600,000	1,400,000
	61.0%	89.0%	100.0%	100.0%	100.0%
Cumulative percent accrued					
Cumulative compensation	122,000	178,000	700,000	600,000	1,400,000
	?	122,000	178,000	700,000	600,000
Compensation previously recognized					
Compensation expense (income) for the year	122,000	56,000	522,000	(100,000)	800,000

Tax Treatment of SAR to Employee

In general, the holder of a SAR will recognize ordinary income on the date when the SAR is exercised.[5] The amount of income an employee realizes on exercise of the SAR is equal to the cash [6] and/or FMV of equity received (unless the equity is restricted).[7] No tax is imposed on the grant of a SAR to an employee. A SAR is not "property" under section 83, which taxes property transferred in connection with performance of services.[8] An employee does not have constructive receipt of income during the period when she has the right to exercise the SAR.

Revenue Ruling 80-300, 1980-2 C.B. 165, addresses the income tax consequences of the vesting of a stand-alone SAR (i.e., a SAR not granted in tandem with a stock option). It cites Treasury Regulations section 1.451-2(a) (1979), which provides that income is not constructively received if the taxpayer's control of its receipt is subject to "substantial limitations or restrictions." It continues:

The courts and the Internal Revenue Service have recognized that a requirement of surrender or forfeiture of a valuable right is a sufficient restriction to make inapplicable the doctrine of constructive receipt. See Hales v. Commissioner, 40 B.T.A. 1245 (1939), acq, 1940-1 C.B. 2. See also Rev. Rul. 58-230, 1958-1 C.B. 204, which holds that a requirement of a six-month suspension from participation in an employees' profit sharing plan upon an employee's withdrawal of the employer's contributions and earnings thereon, and the employee's consequent loss of the benefit of the employer's contributions that would have been made for the six-month period, is a substantial limitation that precludes constructive receipt of the withdrawable amounts.[9]

Based on this rationale, Revenue Ruling 80-300 holds that an employee who has a SAR is not in constructive receipt of income by virtue of appreciation of the employer's stock, but is subject to tax when she exercises the SAR. It states:

> The forfeiture of a valuable right is a substantial limitation that precludes constructive receipt of income. The employee's right to benefit from further appreciation of stock, in this case, without risking any capital is a valuable right. However, once the employee exercises the stock appreciation rights, the employee loses all change of further appreciation with respect to that stock and the amount payable becomes fixed and available without limitation. Accordingly, an employee will be in receipt of income on the date the SARs are exercised.[10]

Revenue Ruling 82-121, 1982-1 C.B. 79, addresses the income tax consequences of a SAR granted in tandem with a stock option. In this ruling the SAR was capped (payment under the SAR could not exceed the exercise price of the option) and reached its maximum value, but the stock option was not limited. The IRS ruled that an employee who possesses such a tandem stock option/SAR is not in constructive receive of income by virtue of appreciation of the employee's stock, but is subject to tax when she exercises the stock option or SAR. It stated:

> In order to exercise the SARs, [employee] must surrender the related options and thereby forfeit the right to benefit from any appreciation of the optioned stock in excess of the price at which the related option could have been exercised. In this case, the loss of the stock option purchase rights is the loss of a valuable right and, therefore, is a substantial limitation that precludes the constructive receipt of the appreciation in the SAR when it first reached its maximum value.[11]

---

[11] Treas. Reg. § 1.83-7(a). Timing of the deduction is tricky if the Host is buying out the Target employees' options; the Host may want the deduction to fall in a particular tax period and the rules are confusing. *See* Levin & Ginsburg, *Corporate Mergers, Acquisitions and Leveraged Buyouts, in* Tax

Strategies for Leveraged Buyouts and Other Corporate Acquisitions, Restructurings and Financings 581 (PLI Course Handbook Series No. 293, 1989).

[2] If the option is vested and the payment is made in connection with the acquisition, the payment may be subject to the "Golden Parachute" rules.

[3] APB Opinion No. 25, amending ARB 43.

[4] Once the issuer is public, and assuming the publicly held stock is eligible for margin loans, a structuring variation enables the issuer and employee to obviate the necessity of using SARs and yet achieve roughly the same result. The ways the wrinkle, called cashless exercise, works is that the employee who enjoys an option obtains from a broker a margin loan to purchase the option stock. This is particularly useful for directors and 10% shareholders subject to § 16(b) of the '34 Act, the so-called "recapture of short-swing profits" section. The loan enables the employee to pay the exercise price, but she does not have to sell immediately to develop the necessary funds; the stock is held by the broker in a margin account. Indeed, the need for an employer to grant SAR rights is eliminated and, therefore, earnings are preserved. To protect the employee who must hold the shares because of § 16(b) or because the waiting period under Rule 144 has not yet lapsed, the employer may issue what is called an SDR (a Stock Depreciation Right) to compensate for depreciation until sale. The broker, having financed the transaction, resells the shares for the employee as soon as they are salable-actually for the account of the issuer, since the issuer has assumed the downside risk during the period prior to sale. 2 Corp. Executive 7 (Jan.-Feb. 1988). If the issuer, as is often the case, maintains an effective registration statement on Form S-8, the shares can be sold in effect, simultaneously. The possibility of this device was opened by a liberalization of Regulation 7 by the Federal Reserve Board. See the discussion of the January 25, 1988, amendment in Barron, *Control and Restricted Securities*, 16 Sec. Reg. L.J. 289, 292, (Fall 1988).

[5] I.R.C. § 451(a).

[6] Id. § 61.

[7] Id. § 83(a).

[8] Treas. Reg. § 1.83-3(e) (as amended 1985).

[9] Rev. Rul. 80-300, 1980-2 C.B. at 166.

[10] Id.

[11] Rev. Rul. 82-121, 1982-1 C.B. at 80.

9

Options on LLC Units: Difficulties in Drafting and Implementation*

Some of the significant disadvantages of an LLC are associated with the issuance of membership interests to employees of a LLC upon exercise of employee options. Generally, the grant of an option to purchase LLC equity to an employee does not have an immediate taxable consequence for the LLC or the employee. However, upon the exercise of such an option by an employee who then becomes a holder of LLC equity, several significant tax consequences appear likely. Although the issue is not free from doubt, once an employee acquires LLC equity, he or she is likely to be treated as a partner for tax purposes.

When the employee is considered as a partner, some of the significant tax consequences the employee and the LLC will confront are the following:

---

* **Contributing Editors:** John L. Cleary II of Sills Cummis, John M. Cunningham of Ransmeier & Spellman, P.C.

- Receipt of a Schedule K I (instead of a W2) reflecting the employee's allocable portion of the LLCs income and deduction items and any guaranteed payments for capital or services provided.

- Obligation to make quarterly estimated tax payments rather than income tax withholding on wages.

- Liability for the full amount of employment taxes as a self-employed LLC member rather than the LLC bearing one-half of the employment taxes.

- Taxation (rather than exclusion) of certain fringe benefits such as group term life insurance and, more important, employer-provided health care insurance (although for 1998, self-employed individuals may deduct 45 percent of the cost of health care insurance and for later years, the deductible portion will increase under a schedule in the Internal Revenue Code to 100 percent in 2007). I.R.C. §162(l).

- If the LLC equity includes a capital interest and there is unrealized appreciation in the LLCs assets, the transfer of the LLC equity may trigger taxation to the employee.

One fairly straightforward solution is to forestall option exercise until after the date the LLC converts to a C corporation in anticipation of an IPO or an acquisition or merger, Options would "vest" under a schedule to be determined, but would not be exercisable until the "first exercise date." For option holders who leave employment prior to this first exercise date, the post-termination exercise period would continue until the conversion of the LLC. By extending the post-termination exercise period, no departing employee will feel compelled to exercise the option that would otherwise expire due to termination of employment. Preventing option exercises also will save the LLC the costs associated with accounting and reporting obligations to a holder of a relatively small interest in the LLC. It also simplifies the management of the LLC when membership votes are required.

[1] FASB, *Invitation to Comment*, Accounting for Compensation Plans Involving Certain Rights Granted to Employees (May 31, 1984).

[2] See the letter of Senator Riegle to FASB, *quoted in* 19 Corp. Fin. Wk. 4 (Mar. 1993); Steinberg & Wexher, *Stock Compensation: The Latest Accounting Controversy*, 7 Insights 26 (Nov. 1993).

[3] Norris, *Accounting Board Yields on Stock Options*, N.Y. Times, Dec. 15, 1994, at D 1.

10

Convertible Debt Plans

Under the typical plan, an executive is offered a subordinated debenture which, after a fixed number of years of employment (or death or disability), becomes convertible at the executive's option into common stock. The issuer loans[1] the executive the amount necessary to purchase the debenture. Provided the conversion price is at least equal to or greater than the fair market value of the conversion shares at time of purchase and the interest rate on the loan to the executive is competitive,[2] the thinking is that the executive will not realize compensation income. Postponed vesting (if any) of the conversion privilege is not considered a substantial risk of forfeiture, and, consequently, no § 83(b) election is required unless the debentures themselves are subject to a substantial risk of forfeiture. The executive recognizes no gain or loss upon the conversion of the debentures into common stock,[3] and the employer is not entitled to a deduction for compensation expense.[4]

The convertible debenture plan, assuming the same is not successfully challenged, combines the best of nonqualified stock options and restricted stock, while maintaining advantages over incentive stock options. The executive may wait and see the company's success before purchasing stock.

She neither realizes taxable income upon the subsequent acquisition of stock, nor recognizes any item of tax preference subject to the alternative minimum tax. The tax holding period of the stock begins upon the purchase of the debenture, while the special holding period and other restrictive rules of incentive stock options are not applicable.[5] In the view of some experienced practitioners, convertible debt plans are too good to be true; the IRS may argue that the entire transaction is a nonqualified stock option. In fact, in PLR 1999 3104 (May 6, 1999) the Service took the view, agreeing with the taxpayer, that: "The grant of a Convertible Bond and a corresponding Employee Loan constitutes the grant of a nonstatutory option having no readily ascertainable fair market value at grant for purposes of section 83."

---

[1] Certain state statutes, e.g., Del. Code Ann. tit. 8, § 143, specifically authorize the corporation to make loans to executives-unsecured and without interest-if the directors judge the loan to be one which is "reasonably expected ... to benefit the corporation." See generally Barnard, *Executive Loans from Corporate Funds*, 17 Sec. Reg. L.J. 257 (1989). Some states require shareholder approval. Id. at 260. A few courts have voided "sweetheart" arrangements in an action by shareholders.

[2] Under I.R.C. § 7872, a below market rate loan is restated as compensation paid by the company to the executive in the amount of the foregone interest. Under I.R.C. § 163(h)(2)(B), investment interest is deductible by an individual only to the extent of investment income.

[3] Rev. Rul. 72-265, 1972-1 C.B. 222.

[4] For a description of one such plan, see the prospectus disclosure in the Mass Comp initial public offering:

"In 1984, the Company issued to August P. Klein, the President and Chief Executive Officer and a director of the Company, an 8 3/4% convertible debenture in the amount of $1,350,000, payable on December 31, 1994, in consideration for Mr. Klein's payment to the Company of $4,500 in cash and his delivery to the Company of a 9% promissory note in the principal amount of $1,345,500 which was originally payable in installments commencing March 31, 1987, the final installment to be due March 31, 1989. In January 1987, the Company extended the date of payment of the first two installments so that the entire amount is currently payable on March 31, 1989. The debenture is convertible into 450,000 shares of common stock of the Company at a price of $3.00 per share (subject to adjustment in the event of splits and similar capital changes). Except in certain events, including Mr. Klein's death or disability, no conversion rights were exercisable until December 15, 1984, at which time such rights, subject to continued employment, became exercisable as to one-fourth of the debenture, and thereafter such rights become exercisable as to the remaining portion of the debenture in equal increments on a monthly basis so that the full amount of the debenture is convertible on June 15, 1989. The debenture is also fully convertible at the option of the Company after April 15, 1989, and, in certain circumstances, earlier."

[5] If the conversion stock is "margin stock," then a loan above Federal Reserve Board limits may run into Regulation G. The trick then is to put together an "eligible plan," meaning one approved by the stockholders, in which case "good faith loan value" is the limit.

'Grossing Up'

An employee may be issued stock at bargain prices (or for free), plus a cash bonus in an amount sufficient to allow the employee to pay tax on the bargain purchase element, plus the tax on the bonus. This is a relatively simple transaction called "grossing up." The result is that the employee gets the stock, after all taxes are paid, at the bargain price she agreed to pay and the employer takes the deduction. The problem is that "grossing up" costs the company money at a time when cash may be scarce and it debits earnings when every drop of reported income may be precious in valuing the company's stock.

Phantom Plans

There are any number of variations on the foregoing themes, including the issuance of junior common stock (no longer favored), so-called "haircut" programs,[1] "book value" stock plans,[2] ESOPs, stock bonus plans and the like, several of which raise tax, accounting, and ERISA issues.[3] Perhaps the most frequently used are phantom equity programs, attempting to replicate the advantages of equity incentives without using real equity. Phantom plans can be divided into three general categories:

- plans in which the value of the payout is tied directly to the price of the issuing company's equity. SARs are an example of this type of plan;

- plans in which the value of the payout is tied to the price of the company's equity, but the public market for the equity is illiquid or nonexistent; and
- plans in which the value of the payout is tied to a measure that is different from the company's equity price, but which attempts to provide a surrogate for the value of the organization. Such plans typically are used by privately held firms or to provide equity-like incentives within business units of publicly traded firms.

In terms of plan design, phantom plans can take on the characteristics of any equity program. Most often, however, phantom plans mirror fair market option plans. They are appreciation-only plans which entitle the executive to the increase in value over a specified term or performance measurement period.

The typical phantom equity plan is structured around units. Each unit represents a percentage of the increase in the value of the organization over a specified time period as determined either by changes in the firm's actual equity price or by a surrogate for such changes. Like stock options, units typically vest over time and are subject to forfeiture upon early termination.

Surrogate performance measures for phantom plans attempt, to the extent possible, to measure value as if the organization were publicly traded. Typically, valuation is based on one of the following measures:

- the book value of the organization, adjusted to disregard extraordinary dividends;
- returns in excess of the organization's cost of capital (economic value or EVA);
- discounted cash flow of the organization as a function of invested capital (CFROI); or
- earnings or book value multiplied by a market multiple based on the multiple of comparable publicly traded firms.

Valuation also is sometimes based on a third-party appraisal of the organization at predetermined intervals.

The choice of the appropriate valuation technique should largely be a function of the sophistication of the company's planning process, cash flow considerations, and the overall validity of the technique for the particular situation. Book value growth represents the simplest alternative, but often is a poor measure of true value creation. In contrast, more sophisticated measures such as EVA and CFROI, while providing a more accurate picture of true value, are often difficult to communicate and understand.

Compared to plans that use real equity, phantom plans offer greater flexibility in design, particularly in the area of linking performance measurement to an entity other than the entire firm. Additionally, phantom equity plans often are not subject to securities regulations and therefore would not require the approval of shareholders.

The major disadvantage of phantom plans is the need to accrue the full value of the award as a charge against income. Unlike plans using real equity, this requirement typically leads firms using phantom equity to place a limit or "cap" on the maximum award available under the plan.

Since most phantom plans are based on a surrogate measure of value (with the exception of SARs, phantom plans tied to actual equity price are rare), they also have the inherent disadvantage of the need to develop an acceptable valuation mechanism.

With the expected demise of SARs, the primary application of phantom equity plans is within privately held firms and business units of publicly traded companies. Of course for an LLC, phantom equity programs satisfy the competitive and strategic need to offer executives a wealth accumulation and incentive opportunity comparable to the stock plans more readily available within C corporations.

Phantom equity plans are similar to SARs and are accounted for in the same manner. Any dividend equivalents which are credited as part of the phantom equity arrangement will be recognized as compensation expense when dividends are declared. If dividend equivalents are not paid currently and do not bear interest, the compensation cost may be based on the present value of the future cash payments.

In general, employees are taxed on phantom equity awards when the awards are settled in cash, equity, or a combination of both.[4] The award is taxable as ordinary income, whether payable in cash or equity (unless the equity is restricted).[5]

The foregoing tax treatment is clear for phantom equity plans which provide for payment upon a fixed event or date (such as retirement, termination of employment, or some other fixed date). It is less clear for phantom equity plans which allow participants to exercise phantom equity units at any time after the units vest and thereby determine their own settlement dates.

---

[1] A "haircut" or fixed differential plan entails selling stock to an employee at a discount from fair market value, say, $ 10, subject to the right in the company to repurchase, in the case of a proposed transfer, the stock at the same discount ($ 10) from then-existing market value. The "accounting and tax considerations are subject to some uncertainty." Aufmuth, *Selected Tax Accounting Issues in Early and Mezzanine Financings and Venture Capital Partnerships*, in Venture Capital After the Tax Reform Act of 1986, at 79.

[2] A "book value" stock plan entails the issuance of a special class of stock whose value is based on book value or some objective formula. To the extent the "book value" stock is convertible upward into common stock, the arrangement smacks of junior common stock. *See* Buoymaster & Frank, *Employee Benefit Plans, in* Harroch, Start-Up Companies: Planning, Financing and Operating the Successful Small Business § 14.2[6] (1990).

[3] A useful summary of the array, including qualified retirement plans, deferred compensation plans, and incidental benefits, is contained in the article by Messrs. Buoymaster & Frank, *id.*

[4] I.R.C. § 451.

[5] I.R.C. §§ 61, 83.

11

Life Insurance (Split-Dollar)[ix]

The Tax Reform Act of 1986 impacted a corporate benefit some emerging
development-stage companies had found attractive and, indeed, mature
companies as well–corporate-owned life insurance ("Split-Dollar").[1] Under
a Split-Dollar plan, a corporation arranges life insurance on a key employee
and pays the premiums, contingent on recovery from the death benefit. The
net (post) death benefit is received, tax free, by the estate of the employee;
and the internal buildup of cash values is tax deferred. From the
corporation's standpoint, the kicker was Internal Revenue Code § 264,
which allowed a tax deduction for interest paid on a policy loan, opening up
tax arbitrage opportunities when the taxpaying company borrowed up to the
maximum allowable against the cash value of the policy.[2] The 1986 Tax
Reform Act added § 264(a)(4), which limits the deduction for interest paid
to an aggregate maximum loan of $50,000 per employee.[3]

Split dollar is particularly useful if the company can convince its accountants
that the benefit program for the executives should not be reflected on the
corporate books because the cost recovery through the insurance
arrangement makes the expense immaterial.[4] There is still life in split-
dollar, however the IRS has announced it will "provide comprehensive
guidance regarding the tax treatment of split-dollar arrangements." The

situation, pending the new regulations, has been outlined in a useful commentary, as follows:

Taxpayers may rely either on Notice 2002-8 (including a reasonable application of the proposed regulations) or on Notice 2001-10 for split-dollar programs entered into before final regulations are published. One important assurance - and clarification - made by Notice 2002-8 is that the IRS will not tax increases in the equity portion of the policies in existing split-dollar arrangements. As for existing arrangements terminating before 2004, the policy will not be taxed on a "roll-out" when the employer no longer has an interest in the policy. Nor will employees be taxed on the termination of an equity split-dollar arrangement if the employee recognizes the value of current life insurance protection as income.[5]

[1] See I.R.C. § 764(a)(4).

[2] See Weiner & Kotner, *Use of Corporate Purchased Life Insurance in the Post-Tax Reform Environment,* 16 Tax Mgmt. Compensation Plan. J. 144 (June 3, 1988).

[3] See I.R.C. § 5264(a)(4).

[4] See Weiner & Kotner, *Use of Corporate Purchased Life Insurance in the Post-Tax Reform Environment,* 16 Tax Mgmt. Compensation Plan. J. at 145, n.4 (June 3, 1988).

[5] See CCH Standard Federal Tax Report, Issue 3, Report 3, Vol. 89 (January 10, 2002).

[ix] Contributed to VC Experts by *Jeffrey R. Shearman*

Is Split Dollar Dead: What to Do With Existing Plans and Do New Split Dollar Plans Make Sense?

Over the past 30 years, split dollar plans have been a very popular fringe benefit that closely held and publicly traded businesses have made available to owners and executives in closely held and publicly traded businesses. Split dollar subsidized the purchase of permanent life insurance that was used to deal with a variety of planning issues owners and executives commonly encountered.

In its most basic form, split dollar was used to replace the owner/executive's income for the surviving spouse and children. In slightly more complicated arrangements, split dollar was used to fund survivorship life insurance policies designed to pay federal estate taxes, and was also used to pay the premiums on life insurance used to fund "buy-sell/business succession" agreements.

The term "split dollar" is somewhat confusing and doesn't accurately describe how the arrangement really works. Split dollar isn't a type of insurance policy, but rather is an agreement between the policy owner and the premium payor that describes the rights and obligations of each party to the arrangement. Many things are typically "split" in a split dollar agreement, but the most common, and important, are which party pays the premiums, and how the policy's death benefit and cash values are split.

Going back to 1964, the tax treatment of split dollar plans was fairly well settled in the eyes of the IRS. Under Revenue Ruling 64-328, the executive didn't have to take the corporation's premium payments into income, but rather paid income tax each year on the "economic benefit" provided under the plan. Because the economic benefit for a permanent policy was calculated using what essentially were term rates, the cost to the executive was very low in many if not most cases.

In the 1980's, compensation planners focused not only on the policy's death benefits, but also the significant cash values that could be accumulated in a permanent life insurance policy. At about this time, so-called "equity" split dollar plans came into vogue because the executive's "split interest" in the policy included not only a significant portion of the death benefit but also a significant share of the policy's cash values. Split dollar plans were attractive to corporations because they could be used to attract and retain key people. And because the split dollar agreement ensured that the corporation always received its premium payments out of the death benefit in the event the executive died, or out of the cash value if the executive lived and the agreement was terminated, it was quite easy to see why split dollar became such a popular fringe corporate benefit.

Starting in 1996, the IRS began to take a closer look at the tax treatment of split dollar plans. After issuing two Notices, one in 2001 and another in 2002, the IRS issued a comprehensive set of proposed split dollar regulations on July 3, 2002. The proposed regulations and Notices make it clear that there are now three sets of rules that apply to split dollar plans, and each depends upon when the plan was established.

Split dollar plans established prior to 1.28.2002 ("old" split dollar plans) enjoy one set of rules. Arrangements established after 1.28.2002 but before the proposed regulations become final ("transitional split dollar plans") must follow another set of rules, and arrangements established after the regulations become final ("new" split dollar plans) must follow another set or rules. While at first glance these rules may seem very complex, the Service has provided some clear "safe harbors" that need to be carefully considered.

Since there are thousands of "old" split dollar plans already in place (i.e., those plans established prior to 1.28.2002), let's review the rules that apply to those plans. For arrangements entered into before 1.28.2002, the IRS has said that participants have the option of using the insurer's term rates, the so-called Table 2001 rates. Additionally, government's PS58 rates to measure the economic benefit may be used in a compensatory arrangement.

If the "old" plan is an "equity" split dollar arrangement and was entered into before 1.28.2002, the IRS has essentially provided split dollar participants with what some planners are calling a "tax relief" program. If these arrangements are terminated before 1.1.2004 or are re-drawn as a loan transaction, the IRS has indicated that it will not assert a taxable transfer under IRC Section 83. Some commentators believe that it is possible that the IRS may assert a transfer under IRC Section 101 or a transfer tax provision of the Internal Revenue Code.

Some planners have developed what are being termed split dollar "rescue" programs that are designed to help answer the question: "what should I do with my existing plan?" In some cases, the policy arrangement is "rolled up" back to the corporation, and a "1035 exchange" occurs. In other "rescue" programs, the policy is sold to a defective life insurance trust by means of a balloon note and a "1035 exchange" occurs.

Many who never had a split dollar plan may be wondering if the good times are essentially over and it's too late to get in on the game. For "new" plans (i.e., those established after the regulations become final), the IRS is making the tax treatment dependent upon who owns the policy. If the executive is designated policy owner, the IRS will treat the employer's premium payments as a series of loans that are taxed under the below market interest rules of Section 7872. For "transitional" plans (i.e., those established after 1.28.2002 but before the proposed regulations become final), another set of rules applies.

12

Simplified Employee Pension Plans

Generally, small start-ups are not in a position to establish qualified pension or profit-sharing plans; indeed, the subject of tax-advantaged benefit plans is well beyond the scope of this Text. However, in 1978 Congress authorized the creation of an arrangement worth noting in this context-simplified employee pension plans (SEPs) available for businesses with 25 or fewer employees.[1] The Tax Reform Act of 1986 made such plans more attractive by establishing a salary reduction feature so that plan participants may make voluntary tax-deferred contributions.[2] Simplified employee pensions work on many of the same principles as individual retirement accounts, the difference being that SEP contributions are usually made by employers, not employees. Additionally, the amounts contributed by the employer may be larger than the amount allowable under an IRA-up to a maximum of $30,000. The employer may determine in each year how much to deposit in an SEP. Moreover, there are generally no filing requirements with federal agencies.

---

[1] See I.R.C. § 408(k). Employers can make contributions that are generally deductible from employee income to the extent they do not exceed $30,000 and 15% of the compensation, Id. §§ 408(j), 402(h).

[2] See id § 408(k)(6).

Employee Stock Purchase Plans

A tax qualified employee stock purchase plan ("ESPP") is designed to allow employees to purchase stock through payroll deductions at a discounted price. Under the Code, an ESPP permits employees to purchase up to $25,000 (in value) of employer stock per year, at a discount of up to 15 percent from fair market value. There is no tax to the employee at the time the stock is purchased. As with incentive stock options, if the stock is held for two years from the date of option grant and one year from the purchase date, gain is taxed at capital gains rates, other than the discount element which is taxed at ordinary income. As in most employee benefit plans (other than stock options), the plan cannot discriminate and employees owning over 5 percent of the company are not eligible to participate–not that they ordinarily would in any event. The employees generally participate through payroll deductions; employees are then granted an option to purchase a given number of shares and the price is 85 percent of the fair market value as of the first day of the option period or as of the last day, whichever is lower.

Shareholder approval must be obtained either 12 months or before or after the ESPP is adopted by the board. Certain employees, new hires and part timers can be excluded and payroll deductions cannot exceed 10 percent of the employee's compensation. By and large, given the unpopularity of investments in company stock these days and the requirement of a one-year holding period to obtain capital gains treatment, it is questionable whether ESPPs are currently much of a factor in stock-flavored employee compensation.

13

Deferred Compensation: Rabbi Trusts

Deferred compensation is currently popular, to quote one of the best known practitioners, due to "[t]he opportunity for (a) accumulation of investment returns on deferred amounts on a pre-tax basis and (b) future payouts (at the end of the deferral period) at a lower marginal income tax rate."[1] The use of funded trusts to bolster unsecured promises to pay deferred compensation in the future has become popular, mainly in more mature corporations but also in start-ups where deferred compensation plans, are, on the surface, difficult because it is not certain that the company will be around to honor the deferred compensation obligation. A device called a "Rabbi Trust," has been used frequently, so called because the first time the device was considered by the Internal Revenue Service, it was for the benefit of a rabbi.[2] The corporation responsible for the deferred compensation obligation deposits assets in the Rabbi Trust for the benefit of the employee,[3] but the deposit does not trigger immediate taxation, the notion being that the obligation is unfunded as long as the assets are available to the general creditors of the corporation.[4] That being the case, there is a risk that an executive will never realize the benefits of the funds placed in the Rabbi Trust. There is also pending legislation that, if enacted, would severally limit the deferral of taxes with respect to amounts deposited in certain "unfunded" arrangements.[5]

[1] Bachelder, "Deferred Compensation: Reasons for Its Growning Use," N.Y. L.J. (Aug. 31, 2001).

[2] See Priv. Ltr. Rul. 81-13-107 (Dec. 31, 1980), reprinted in 4 Stand. Fed. Tax. Rep. (CCH) 1 6973 (1981).

[3] Id. The IRS also requires that the trustee be independent and the rights to the trust be nonassignable.

[4] Id.

[5] See Walter, An Overview of Compensation Techniques Following TRA 1986, 14 J. Corp. Tax'n 139 (Summer 1987).

14

The 'Golden Parachute' Rules

In 1984, Congress was concerned that executive termination payments (that is, payments due to an executive upon termination of employment, usually after the employer was acquired) had grown too large, and were inhibiting useful acquisitions as well as impoverishing shareholders. It decided to use the tax law as a means of reducing the amount of such payments. The result is now set forth in sections 280G and 4999 of the Internal Revenue Code-- the "golden parachute" rules.

The Treasury Department promulgated proposed regulations under sections 280G and 4999 in 1989. These were quite comprehensive, and, by default, remained the primary source of guidance for practitioners until a new set of proposed regulations was issued in 2002.[1] Now, the 2002 proposed regulations form the principal guidance for taxpayers. The 2002 proposed regulations are proposed to apply to any payments that are contingent on a change in ownership or control occurring on or after January 1, 2004. Taxpayers may rely on these proposed regulations until the effective date of the final regulations. Alternatively, taxpayers may rely on the 1989 proposed regulations for any payment contingent on a change in ownership or control that occurs prior to January 1, 2004.[2] The drafters of the 2002 proposed regulations had the benefit of comments based on the past seventeen years during which the statute was in effect, and as a result the new proposed regulations answer almost all of the common questions arising under the statute.

The golden parachute rules impose a heavy tax on both the employer (in the form of the denial of a deduction that otherwise would be available) and the executive (as a nondeductible excise tax) if, in connection with an acquisition of the employer, the executive becomes entitled to an excessively large payment. The primary questions in determining whether this tax will apply are as follows:

1. Under what circumstances does the tax apply. That is, what is a "change in ownership or control?"
2. To what class of employees or other persons does the tax apply?
3. How large a payment can a company make without running afoul of the golden parachute rules?

Section 280G[3] denies a deduction to a corporation[4] for any excess parachute payment. Section 4999 imposes a 20% excise tax on the recipient of any excess parachute payment. The two provisions are not interdependent. For example, an individual may be subject to the 20% excise tax under section 4999 even though the payor is a foreign corporation not subject to United States income tax.

The 2002 proposed regulations apply to any payment that is contingent on a change in ownership or control that occurs on or after January 1, 2004. Meanwhile, taxpayers can rely on these rules for the treatment of any parachute payment made after February 20, 2002, or they can use the old proposed regulations. As the new proposed regulations are generally more taxpayer-favorable than the old proposed regulations, it is unlikely that a taxpayer would prefer to rely on the old proposed regulations.

Definitions

These rules are best introduced through a series of definitions. The definitions of primary importance are as follows:

Parachute Payment

A parachute payment is any payment, if: (a) the payment is in the nature of compensation for services; (b) the payment is to, or for the benefit of, a disqualified individual; (c) the payment is contingent on a change in the ownership of a corporation, the effective control of a corporation, or the ownership of a substantial portion of the assets of a corporation (a "change in ownership or control"); and (d) the payment has (together with other payments described in (a), (b), and (c) of this paragraph with respect to the same individual) an aggregate present value of at least 3 times the individual's base amount.[5]

There is a presumption that a payment is contingent on a change in ownership or control if the payment is made pursuant to:

1. an agreement entered into within one year before the date of a change in ownership or control; or
2. an amendment that modifies a previous agreement in any significant respect, if the amendment is made within one year before the date of a change in ownership or control. In the case of an amendment, only the portion of any payment that exceeds the amount of such payment that would have been made in the absence of the amendment is presumed, by reason of the amendment, to be contingent on the change in ownership or control.[6]

The presumption can be rebutted by clear and convincing evidence.[7] In the case of an agreement entered into within one year of the change in ownership or control, clear and convincing evidence that the agreement is one of the three following types generally will rebut the presumption:

1. A nondiscriminatory employee plan or program as defined in Q/A-26. These include: a group term life insurance plan that meets the requirements of section 79(d); a self insured medical reimbursement plan that meets the requirements of section 105(h); a cafeteria plan (within the meaning of section 125); an educational assistance program (within the meaning of section 127); a dependent care assistance program (within the meaning of section 129); or a no-additional-cost service (within the meaning of section 132(b)); qualified employee discounts (within the meaning of section 132(c)); qualified retirement planning services under section 132(m); and an adoption assistance program (within the meaning of section 137);

2. a contract between a corporation and an individual that replaces a prior contract entered into by the same parties more than one year before the change in ownership or control, if the new contract does not provide for increased payments (apart from normal increases attributable to increased responsibilities or cost of living adjustments), accelerate the payment of amounts due at a future time, or modify (to the individual's benefit) the terms or conditions under which payments will be made; or

3. a contract between a corporation and an individual who did not perform services for the corporation prior to the one year period before the change in ownership or control occurs, if the contract does not provide for payments that are significantly different in amount, timing, terms, or conditions from those provided under contracts entered into by the corporation (other than contracts that themselves were entered into within one year before the change in ownership or control and in contemplation of the change) with individuals performing comparable services.

In addition, Q/A-8 exempts payments from qualified retirement plans.

Payment in the Nature of Compensation

A payment may be a parachute payment (and therefore potentially an excess parachute payment) only if it is a payment in the nature of compensation for personal services. The payment can be in any form: cash, property, options, etc.[8] A bona fide payment to a disqualified individual to acquire stock of the acquired corporation would not be in the nature of compensation for services.

The party acquiring an interest in the corporation undergoing the change in control may make a parachute payment.[9] The actual employer of the disqualified individual need not make it.

Base Amount

The term "base amount" means the average annual compensation for services performed for the corporation with respect to which the change in ownership or control occurs (or for a predecessor entity or a related entity) which was includible in the gross income of the disqualified individual for taxable years in the base period, or which would have been includible in such gross income if such person had been a United States citizen or resident.[10] Deferred compensation payable in a future period and nontaxable fringe benefits are not part of the base amount.[11]

Base Period

In general, the base period is the five-year period ending on the last day of the taxable year prior to the year of the change in control.[12] If the base period of a disqualified individual includes a short taxable year, compensation for the short year must be annualized. In annualizing compensation, the expected frequency of payments to be made over an annual period must be taken into account. Thus, any amount of compensation for such a short or incomplete taxable year that represents a payment that will not be made more often than once per year (for example, an annual bonus) is not annualized.

Change in Ownership or Control

A change in the ownership or control of a corporation occurs on the date that any one person, or more than one person acting as a group,[113] acquires ownership of stock of the corporation that, together with stock held by such person or group, owns more than 50% of the total fair market value or total voting power of the stock of such corporation.[114] However, if any one person, or more than one person acting as a group, is considered to own more than 50% of the total fair market value or total voting power of the stock of a corporation, the acquisition of additional stock by the same person or persons is not considered to cause a change in the ownership of the corporation or to cause a change in the effective control of the corporation (within the meaning of Q/A-28). An increase in the percentage of stock owned by any one person, or persons acting as a group, as a result of a transaction in which the corporation acquires its stock in exchange for property, will be treated as an acquisition of stock for purposes of these rules.

The 2002 proposed regulations provide that, for purposes of determining whether two or more persons acting as a group are considered to own more than 50% of the total fair market value or total voting power of the stock of a corporation on the date of a merger, acquisition, or similar transaction involving that corporation, a person who owns stock in both corporations involved in the transaction is treated as acting as a group with respect to the other shareholders in a corporation only to the extent of such person's ownership of stock in that corporation prior to the transaction, and not with respect to his or her ownership in the other corporation.

Example: Assume individual A owns stock in both corporations X and Y when corporation X acquires stock in Y in exchange for X stock. In determining whether corporation Y has undergone a change in ownership or control, individual A is considered to be acting as a group with other shareholders in corporation Y only to the extent of A's holdings in corporation Y prior to the transaction, and not with respect to A's ownership in X. In determining whether Corporation X has undergone a change in ownership or control, individual A is considered to be acting as a group with other shareholders in Corporation X only to the extent of individual A's holdings in Corporation X prior to the transaction, and not with respect to individual A's ownership interest in Corporation Y.

Change in Effective Control

A change in control can also include a change in effective control.[15] A change in the effective control of a corporation is presumed to occur on the date that either:

1. any one person, or more than one person acting as a group, acquires (or has acquired during the 12-month period ending on the date of the most recent acquisition by such person or persons) ownership of stock of the corporation possessing 20% or more of the total voting power of the stock of such corporation; or

2. a majority of members of the corporation's board of directors is replaced during any 12-month period by directors whose appointment or election is not endorsed by a majority of the members of the corporation's board of directors prior to the date of the appointment or election.

This presumption is rebuttable by establishing that the stock acquisition or replacement of the majority of the members of the corporation's board of directors does not transfer the power to control (directly or indirectly) the management and policies of the corporation from any one person (or more than one person acting as a group) to another person (or group). If neither of the events set forth above has occurred, there is a presumption of no change in effective control.

Change in Control of Assets

The rules concerning changes in the control of corporate assets are as follows.[116] A change in the ownership of a substantial portion of a corporation's assets occurs on the date that any one person, or more than one person acting as a group, acquires (or has acquired during the 12-month period ending on the date of the most recent acquisition by such person or persons) assets from the corporation that have a total gross fair market value equal to or more than one third of the total gross fair market value of all of the assets of the corporation immediately prior to such acquisition or acquisitions. Such a provision places a great deal of pressure on valuation, because the one-third-of-value test does not establish a mere presumption; it is a substantive rule. Thus, at least theoretically, if the employer's valuation of the assets retained by the corporation (the fair market value assigned by the parties to the assets sold in an arm's length transaction would very likely be respected[117]) was challenged by the IRS and found to be too high, the parties could inadvertently have created a change in control and subjected themselves to the golden parachute rules. A well-considered and defensible appraisal is a very good idea in such cases.

Note that under Q/A-29, the change in control of assets test requires that one person, or group of persons acting together, acquire at least one third of the corporate assets. This implies that if a corporation sells, say 25% of its assets to one buyer, and another 25% to a different buyer, there is no change in ownership subject to section 280G unless the two buyers are acting in concert as a group.

Exempt Transfers

Certain transfers to related parties are exempt from these rules. These are (1) a transfer to a shareholder of the corporation (immediately before the asset transfer) in exchange for or with respect to its stock; (2) a transfer to an entity, 50% or more of the total value or voting power of which is owned, directly or indirectly, by the corporation; (3) a transfer to a person, or more than one person acting as a group, that owns, directly or indirectly, 50% or more of the total value or voting power of all the outstanding stock of the corporation; or (4) a transfer to an entity, at least 50% of the total value or voting power of which is owned, directly or indirectly, by persons who own at least 50% of the transferor. Thus, a typical spin-off would be exempt.

Excess Parachute Payment

The term "excess parachute payment" means an amount equal to the excess of any parachute payment over the portion of the disqualified individual's base amount that is allocated to such payment.[18] For this purpose, the portion of the base amount allocated to a parachute payment is the amount that bears the same ratio to the base amount as the present value of the parachute payment bears to the aggregate present value of all such payments to the same disqualified individual. The golden parachute taxes are direct functions of the amount of an excess parachute payment.

Example: E receives a single parachute payment of $1,000,000. His base amount is $330,000. Therefore, the parachute payment exceeds three times the base amount, and the golden parachute rules apply. The nondeductible excess parachute payment is $670,000 and the nondeductible excise tax is $134,000.

Disqualified Individual

Only a disqualified individual is subject to sections 280G and 4999. The term "disqualified individual" includes any individual (and therefore does not include an entity, other than a personal service corporation[19]) who is:

1. an employee or independent contractor who performs personal services for a corporation,
2. an officer, shareholder, or highly compensated individual,[20] or
3. a director, if at any time during the disqualified person determination period, the director is an employee or independent contractor and is either a shareholder or highly compensated individual with respect to the corporation.

Officer

An officer is someone who acts in the capacity of an officer, whether or not he or she holds an officer's title.[21] In a large corporation with many officers (such as a bank) the number of persons considered officers is limited to the 50 highest paid or 10% of the number of employees, if less; however, the minimum number of potential officers is three.

Shareholder

Under Q/A-17, an individual is a shareholder only if, during the disqualified individual determination period, the individual owns stock of a corporation with a fair market value that exceeds one percent of the total fair market value of the outstanding shares of all classes of the corporation's stock.[22] The disqualified person determination period is the twelve months ending on the date of the change in ownership or control of the corporation. The disqualified individual determination period is not affected by the date of the change in ownership or control.[23]

The constructive ownership rules of section 318(a) apply for purposes of determining the amount of stock owned by the individual. Thus, for example, stock subject to vested stock options is considered owned by the optionee. Also, a disqualified individual is deemed to own stock owned by his or her spouse, children, grandchildren, parents, and to varying degrees by entities in which he or she has an interest.

Highly-Compensated Individual

A highly-compensated individual is one who is, or would be if the individual were an employee, a member of the group consisting of the lesser of the highest paid one percent of the corporation's employees, or the highest paid 250 employees, of the corporation, when ranked on the basis of compensation (as determined under Q/A 21) paid during the disqualified individual determination period (as defined in Q/A 20, above).

To be considered highly compensated, an individual must have annualized compensation equal to at least the amount published periodically by the government.[24] This amount for 2002 is $90,000; it will be adjusted periodically for cost-of-living increases.

Events Triggering the Application of the Golden Parachute Rules

A payment is a parachute payment if it is contingent on a change in ownership or control. The 2002 proposed regulations use a "but for" test; that is, a payment is contingent on a change in control only if it would not have been made without the change in control.[25] The burden of proof is on the taxpayer, and proving the lack of a causal connection may be difficult. A payment generally is treated as one which would not in fact have been made in the absence of a change in ownership or control unless it is substantially certain, at the time of the change, that the payment would have been made whether or not the change in ownership or control occurred.

A payment may be contingent on a change in ownership or control, even if the payment is also contingent on a second event, such as termination of employment within a period following the change in ownership or control. In addition, a payment generally is treated as contingent on a change in ownership or control if (a) the payment is contingent on an event that is closely associated with such a change, (b) a change in ownership or control actually occurs, and (c) the event is materially related to the change in ownership or control.

Closely Associated with a Change. The following events are considered closely associated with a change in the ownership or control of a corporation:

1. the onset of a tender offer with respect to the corporation;
2. a substantial increase in the market price of the corporation's stock that occurs within a short period (but only if such increase occurs prior to a change in ownership or control);
3. the cessation of the listing of the corporation's stock on an established securities market; the acquisition of more than 5% of the corporation's stock by a person (or more than one person acting as a group) not in control of the corporation;
4. the voluntary or involuntary termination of the disqualified individual's employment or a significant reduction in the disqualified individual's job responsibilities; and
5. a change in ownership or control as defined in the disqualified individual's employment agreement (or elsewhere) that does not meet the definition of a change in ownership or control described in Q/A-27, 28, or 29.

Whether other events are treated as closely associated with a change in ownership or control is based on all the facts and circumstances of the particular case.

Example: A corporation and a disqualified individual enter into an employment contract within one year of a change in ownership of the corporation. Under the contract, in the event of a change in ownership or control and subsequent termination of employment, certain payments will be made to the individual. A change in ownership occurs, but the individual is not terminated until 2 years after the change. If clear and convincing evidence does not rebut the presumption that the payment is contingent on the change in control, because the payment is made pursuant to an agreement entered into within one year of the date of the change in ownership, the payment is presumed contingent on the change under Q/A-25. This is true even though A's termination of employment is presumed not to be materially related to the change in ownership or control under Q/A-22 because it took place more than one year after the change in control.

In the foregoing example, the payment is, by contract, contingent on the change in control, and also on the termination of employment of the disqualified individual. The parties need clear and convincing evidence to rebut the presumption.

Example: Executive E, a disqualified individual, is entitled to a bonus payment if the price of Corporation U's stock reaches $25 per share. It does so, and within 12 months after it does so there is an acquisition of U. This gives rise to a presumption that E's bonus is a parachute payment. E could rebut the presumption by showing that the run-up in the share price was due to an announcement that a patent infringement suit against U had just been decided in its favor, and that the change in control of U was due to a tender offer that did not commence until after the share price reached $25 (even though it was the settlement of the lawsuit that caused U to become an attractive acquisition target).

In this example, the event giving rise to the payment is one that is listed as "closely associated" with a change in control, and the change in control does in fact occur within one year of the event. However, in contrast to the preceding example, the payment is not explicitly contingent on a change in control, and the parties should be able to show that it was substantially certain that the payment would have been made absent the change in control.

Materially Related to a Change. The 2002 proposed regulations establish a rebuttable presumption that an event is materially related to a change in ownership or control if such event occurs within the period beginning one year before and ending one year after the date of change in ownership or control. If such event occurs outside of the period beginning one year before and ending one year after the date of change in ownership or control, the presumption runs the other way.[26] Thus, the burden of proving lack of a relationship between an event and a payment occurring within the same twelve months is on the taxpayer. The fact that a payment that is contingent on an event closely associated with a change in ownership or control is also conditioned on the occurrence of a second event does not affect the determination that the payment is contingent on a change in ownership or control as the result of the occurrence of the first event.[27]

Valuation of Parachute Payments

Most of the time the parachute payment is in cash and the amount is readily ascertainable. There are areas, however, in which valuation can be difficult. Primary among these is stock options. The 1989 proposed regulations provided that the transfer of a nonqualified stock option could be a payment in the nature of compensation, but did not address transfers of qualified (incentive) stock options. The 2002 proposed regulations provide that nonqualified and qualified stock options are payments in the nature of compensation.[28]

Stock Options

The valuation of a stock option can be highly subjective. The 2002 proposed regulations continue to provide for the use of the factors described in the 1989 proposed regulations.[29] In addition, the IRS has authority to provide methods for valuation of stock options through published guidance. Rev. Proc. 2002-13[30] provides several permissible valuation methods. One of the methods permitted is a simplified safe harbor approach modeled after the Black-Scholes valuation method. The safe harbor allows a corporation to establish a value for stock options based on spread at the time of the change in ownership or control, the remaining term of the option, and a basic assumption regarding the volatility of the underlying stock. Other factors relevant to the Black-Scholes valuation model, including a risk-free rate of return and dividend yield, are addressed in the table contained in the revenue procedure. The safe harbor valuation method provided in the revenue procedure may be used without regard to whether the underlying stock is publicly traded.[31]

Continuing Health Care Coverage

The second area of particular interest is health care or other insurance benefits that continue for a long period of time beyond the termination of employment of the disqualified individual, because these can be difficult to value. Here, proposed regulations provide useful guidance. Q/A-31 provides that the determination of the present value of an obligation to provide health care should be calculated in accordance with generally accepted accounting principles. It is permissible to measure this obligation by projecting the cost of premiums for purchased health care insurance, even if no health care insurance is actually purchased. If the obligation to provide health care is made in coordination with a health care plan that the corporation makes available to a group, then the premiums used for this purpose may be group premiums for purposes of determining whether there are excess parachute payments.

Premiums for health care insurance can be used for purposes of determining a corporation's loss of deduction or the excise tax obligation for a disqualified individual only to the extent such premiums are actually paid for health care insurance used to satisfy the corporation's obligation to provide health care.

Acceleration of Vesting or Payments of Deferred Compensation

In general, the full amount of any payment that is contingent on a change in control is a parachute payment. However, there are also issues of timing. Many employment agreements contain a provision for acceleration of vesting upon a change in control. In addition, there may be a provision for immediate payment of a vested amount that would otherwise be paid later (for example, on retirement).

Acceleration of Payment

The acceleration of a payment that would have been made in any event is treated as a parachute payment. The amount of the parachute payment is the value of the acceleration, using a discount factor equal to 120% of the applicable federal rate.[132] Generally, the rate used is the one in effect at the time the future payment is to be discounted (the earlier of the date of payment or the date of the change in control[133]), but the parties may agree in the contract that provides for the payment to use the rate in effect at the time the contract is executed.[134]

Acceleration of Vesting of Noncontingent Amounts

If the change in control accelerates vesting (for example, by causing a payment to be made that would only have been made three years later if the executive had continued to be employed until that time), the 2002 proposed regulations require consideration of two elements in computing the amount of a parachute payment: (1) the time value of money, as set forth in the preceding paragraph, and (2) the lapse of the requirement to perform additional services. The 2002 proposed regulations[35] provide that the amount reflecting the lapse of the obligation to continue to perform is 1% of the amount of the accelerated payment multiplied by the number of full months between the date that the individual's right to receive the payment is vested and the date that, absent the acceleration, the payment would have been vested. This rule also applies to the accelerated vesting of a payment in the nature of compensation even if the time at which the payment is made is not accelerated.

Example: X Corporation maintains a qualified plan and a nonqualified supplemental retirement plan ("SERP") for its executives. Benefits under the SERP are not paid to participants until retirement. E, a disqualified individual with respect to X, has a vested account balance of $500,000 under the SERP. A change in ownership or control of X occurs. The SERP provides that in the event of a change in ownership or control, all vested accounts will be paid to SERP participants. Because E was vested in $500,000 of benefits under the SERP prior to the change in ownership or control and the change merely accelerated the time at which the payment was made to E, only a portion of the payment is treated as contingent on the change. Thus, the portion of the payment that is treated as contingent on the change is the amount by which the amount of the accelerated payment ($500,000) exceeds the present value of the payment absent the acceleration.

If E would have been paid the $500,000 in three years time absent the change in control, and assuming that the applicable federal rate at the time of the change in control is 3.33%, then the amount of the parachute payment would be the difference between $500,000, and $444,498, which is the present value of $500,000 paid three years later, discounted at 4%. Therefore, the parachute payment is $55,502.

Now, suppose that the $500,000 would have been paid to E only if she continued her employment until July 1, 2006 and the change in control occurs on July 1, 2003. However, the change in control of R causes the payment to be made immediately. As before, $55,502 is a parachute payment. In addition, $180,000 (36 months times 1% times $500,000) is a parachute payment. Note that any additional amount paid that is contingent on a change in control would be a parachute payment, without any further computation. If the SERP provided that in addition to the vested account balance of $500,000 an additional $70,000 will be credited to E's account upon a change in control, the entire $70,000 payment is contingent on the change in ownership or control under Q/A-24 and is a parachute payment.[36]

Acceleration of Vesting of Equity-Based Compensation

The acceleration of vesting of stock, stock options, stock appreciation rights, and similar rights is determined by assuming that the stock would be worth at the time of vesting what it is worth at the time of the change in control. This allows the application of the principles applicable to accelerated vesting of amounts certain.

Example: E holds nonqualified stock options to purchase 100,000 shares of R at $5 per share. The stock is worth $10 per share at the time of the change in control. As a result of the change in control the options vest. Otherwise, they would all have vested three years later, assuming that E continued to be employed by R. Therefore, the 2002 proposed regulations assume that E would have received a payment of $500,000 (the spread) in three years, and the computation would be the same as in the preceding example.

Future Payment Not Ascertainable

The proposed regulations deal with the situation in which the executive is entitled not only to a basic amount of deferred compensation, but also to the earnings on that amount. If the amount of a payment without acceleration is not reasonably ascertainable (for example, because it includes future earnings at an indeterminate rate on a sum certain), and the acceleration does not significantly increase the value of the payment, then the present value of the payment absent the acceleration is deemed equal to the amount of the accelerated payment. As a result, the value of the accelerated payment is equal to the value of the payment absent acceleration and no portion of the payment is treated as contingent on a change in control.

If the value of a payment absent acceleration is not reasonably ascertainable and the acceleration significantly increases the value of the payment, the future value of the payment is equal to the amount of the accelerated payment. When the future value (as opposed to the present value) of the payment is deemed to be the amount of the accelerated payment, a portion of the payment is treated as contingent on the change.

Example: As a result of a change in the effective control of a corporation, a disqualified individual with respect to the corporation, D, receives accelerated payment of D's vested account balance in a nonqualified deferred compensation account plan. Actual interest and other earnings on the plan assets are credited to each account as earned before distribution. Investment of the plan assets is not restricted in such a manner as would prevent the earning of a market rate of return on the plan assets. The date on which D would have received D's vested account balance absent the change in ownership or control is uncertain, and the rate of earnings on the plan assets is not fixed. Thus, the amount of the payment absent the acceleration is not reasonably ascertainable.[37] Under these facts, acceleration of the payment does not significantly increase the present value of the payment absent the acceleration, and the present value of the payment absent the acceleration is treated as equal to the amount of the accelerated payment. Accordingly, no portion of the payment is treated as contingent on the change.[38]

Contingent Parachute Payments

There is a special rule for valuation of contingent payments. For example, a parachute payment might be a function of the value of stock at some future time, or of the amount of revenues or profits of the employer during some future period. The regulations introduce conventions in order to allow the computation of the amount of parachute payments.

Under Q/A-33 of the 2002 proposed regulations, if there is at least a 50% probability that a contingent payment will be made, the entire present value of that payment should be included for purposes of determining whether there are excess parachute payments. If there is less than a 50% probability of the payment, then the present value of that contingent payment is not included. When it becomes certain whether or not the payment will be made, the 3-times-base-amount test will be reapplied if the initial assumption of probability was incorrect. The main point here is that the payments are not discounted based on the probability of payment; either the entire payment (present valued) is included or it is not included at all.

If the inclusion or exclusion of the payment at the time of the change in ownership or control turns out to have been correct, there is no need to reapply the 3-times-base-amount test. In addition, if it is reasonably estimated that there is a less than 50% chance that the payment will be made and the payment is not included in the 3-times-base-amount test, but the payment is later made, the 3-times-base-amount test is not reapplied if the test without regard to the contingent payment resulted in a determination that the individual received (or would receive) excess parachute payments and no base amount is allocated to the contingent payment.

Note that if a payment is made that was not considered probable at the time of the change in control, the effect could be to cause past payments to be treated as excess parachute payments.

Therefore, the possibilities are as follows:

Probability	Full Payment Made	Full Payment Not Made
50% or More	Initial treatment unchanged	Recompute parachute payments; possible refunds
Less Than 50%; no excess parachute payments initially	Recompute parachute payments; possible excess parachute payments	Initial treatment unchanged
Less Than 50%; excess parachute payments initially	Entire contingent payment is an excess parachute payment	Initial treatment unchanged

Exceptions to the Golden Parachute Rules

Although there is no rule that specifically limits the application of the golden parachute rules to public companies, Congress was more concerned about them than about privately held companies, and the exceptions reflect this difference.

Shareholder Approval Requirements

The principal exception to the golden parachute rules in venture-backed companies allows for shareholder approval of what would otherwise be parachute payments. Under limited circumstances, the shareholders of a nonpublic company may approve payments that otherwise would be subject to Sections 4999 and 280G, and such approval will cause those sections not to apply. A company is not public if none of its stock (except preferred stock that would not be affected by a parachute payment) is readily traded on an established securities market or otherwise.[39] Section 280G(b)(5)(B) provides that the shareholder approval requirements are met if two conditions are satisfied:

1. First, the payment must be approved by a vote of the persons who owned, immediately before the change in ownership or control, more than 75% of the voting power of all outstanding stock of the corporation.

2. Second, there must be adequate disclosure to all shareholders of all material facts concerning all payments that (but for shareholder approval) would be parachute payments with respect to a disqualified individual.

Eligibility

A corporation cannot be treated as having no publicly traded shares if a substantial portion (at least one third) of its assets consist (directly or indirectly) of stock in another entity (or any ownership interest in such entity) that is publicly traded. Moreover, if a corporation is a member of an affiliated group (see Q/A-46), a shareholder vote will not solve the problem if any stock in any member of such group is readily tradeable on an established securities market or otherwise.

The following example illustrates the point that a public company can never avoid the golden parachute rules through the use of subsidiaries.

Example: Corporation P, whose stock is traded on a stock exchange, owns all of Corporation S; thus, the two corporations are affiliated and treated as a single corporation for purposes of the golden parachute rules. The S stock constitutes more than one third of P's assets. S makes severance payments to several of its disqualified individuals that are parachute payments. Because stock in P is readily tradable on an established securities market, the exception of section 280G(b)(5)(B) cannot apply, and therefore a shareholder vote approving the payments will not be effective to ward off sections 280G and 4999.[40]

It could be argued that the rule of Q/A-6(c) is overbroad. In the following example, the ownership of a relatively minor interest in a public company prevents the use of a shareholder vote on a disposition by a private company of an interest in another private company.

Example: P is not a public corporation. Most of the P stock is held by a venture capital partnership. P owns .7% of S, a public, Fortune 500 company. The S stock constitutes 35% of the fair market value of P's assets. P also owns 100% of the stock of T; therefore T and P are affiliated for purposes of the golden parachute rules. The T stock constitutes 57% of the fair market value of P's assets. In connection with a sale of 66% of the T stock by P to an unrelated corporation, T makes payments to certain of its disqualified individuals. A literal reading of the 2002 proposed regulations leads to the result that a shareholder vote will not be effective to ward off sections 280G and 4999 because (1) T and P are treated as a single corporation, and (2) more than one third of P's assets consist of stock of S, a public corporation.[41]

Mechanics of Shareholder Vote

Q/A-7 provides that stock held by a disqualified individual (or by certain entity shareholders) is not entitled to vote with respect to a payment to be made to any disqualified individual and that this stock is disregarded in determining whether the more than 75% approval requirement has been met. If disqualified individuals hold all the stock, then all the stock counts as outstanding and is entitled to vote.[42] For purposes of the 75% approval requirement, stock owned by a disqualified individual or a related person under section 318(a) is not treated as outstanding.[43]

It is permissible under the 2002 proposed regulations for only a portion of the payments that would otherwise be made to a disqualified individual to be subject to the shareholder vote.

Example: Assume that a disqualified individual with a base amount of $150,000 would receive payments that (but for the exemption for a corporation with no readily tradable stock) would be parachute payments including (i) a bonus payment of $200,000, (ii) vesting in stock options with a fair market value of $500,000, $200,000 of which is contingent on the change in ownership or control, and (iii) severance payments of $100,000. In this situation, assuming all of the payments are disclosed, the corporation may submit to the shareholders for approval (1) all of the payments, (2) any one of the three payments, or (3) $50,001 of any one of the payments (e.g., options with a value of $50,001). It is permissible that the shareholder vote can determine only whether the executive will receive payments that otherwise would be excess parachute payments.

This disclosure of information must be made to all shareholders entitled to vote, not just to shareholders with 75% of the voting power entitled to vote.[44] The issue submitted to a shareholder vote must be whether the payment will be made to the disqualified individual, not whether the corporation will be able to deduct the payment. In addition, the vote must be a separate vote of the shareholders. Therefore, if the merger, acquisition, or other transaction is conditioned on the shareholders' approval of the payment, the shareholder vote will not solve the golden parachute problem. On the other hand, different payments, including payments to different individuals, can be combined into a single vote that qualifies under the 2002 proposed regulations, if there is adequate disclosure of all material facts.

The shareholder approval requirements also require adequate disclosure of all material facts concerning the amount of all parachute payments. For this purpose, the 2002 proposed regulations state that the amount of all parachute payments to be made to each disqualified individual, and not just the amount of the payments subject to vote, is a material fact. The 2002 proposed regulations clarify that shareholders should be provided with basic information about the type of payments involved (e.g., vesting of stock options or severance payments).[45]

In practice, the documentation of the disclosure of all material facts to shareholders may fall short of what is required under the proposed regulations, or there will be no documentation at all. Although the IRS has not raised this issue in any decided case, inadequate disclosure could be a powerful weapon in the hands of a Revenue Agent. In most cases, the parties will want to tend to excessive disclosure to be on the safe side.

The Practical Problem with Shareholder Approval

In practice, the issue often arises in the following context. A key employee or officer already has an employment agreement or severance agreement that provides for a change of control payment that would be an excess parachute payment. In order to avoid the application of Sections 280G and 4999 the shareholder vote must actually determine the right of the employee to receive the payment;[46] otherwise, the vote is useless. Thus, the employee is asked to relinquish his or her legal right to the payment, based on a promise that the matter will be submitted for a vote of the shareholders.

Depending on the circumstances, the risk that the shareholders may not approve the payment may be quite acceptable, but in many cases the executive will balk. At this point, the parties may wish they had resolved this issue sooner. See below for some alternative means of dealing with this issue in employment or severance agreements.

Can the shareholders approve the payments in advance (e.g., when the parachute agreement is first executed)? Alternatively, can the shareholders agree today to vote in favor of the payment at some future time? The logical answer is no. First, it would be impossible to make adequate disclosure of all material facts until the change in control is about to occur. This is particularly true because most parachute-type payments are a function of some other factor that is not known at the time the initial contract with the executive is signed (e.g., the sale price of the company or the executive's salary during the period preceding the change in control). The amount of the parachute payment is a material fact that must be disclosed to the shareholders.[147] Second, the shareholders approving the payment must be the shareholders at the time of the change in control (or within three months thereof[148]). The shareholders may have changed by the time of the change in control.

Could each shareholder give to some person who is trusted by the executive a proxy to vote the shares on the single issue of whether to approve a parachute payment, but without any obligation to vote in a particular way? There is no authority directly in point[149]; all we can say is that the proposed regulations do not explicitly foreclose such a course of action. However, we can imagine the IRS taking the position that a shareholder vote means that the shareholders must themselves vote, following the literal language of section 280G(b)(5)(B)(i).

Votes by Entities

If a substantial portion (one-third or more) of the assets of an entity shareholder consists (directly or indirectly) of stock in the corporation undergoing the change in ownership or control, approval of the payment by that entity shareholder must be made by a separate vote of the persons who hold, immediately before the change in ownership or control, more than 75% of the voting power of the entity shareholder. No vote is required if the value of the stock of the corporation owned, directly or indirectly, by or for the entity shareholder does not exceed one percent of the total value of the outstanding stock of the corporation. Where approval of a payment by an entity shareholder must be made by a separate vote of the owners of the entity shareholder, the normal voting rights of the entity shareholder determine which owners shall vote.

In the venture context, the question often arises: who must vote upon the proposed payments? For example, if a limited partnership owns stock of the corporation about to be sold, must the limited partners vote? The answer is no, unless the partnership agreement so provides. The vote of the general partner will be sufficient.[50]

Corporations that Could Be or Are S Corporations

The golden parachute rules do not apply to any corporation that qualifies to be an S corporation (disregarding the requirement that the corporation not have a nonresident alien individual as a shareholder), whether or not it has elected to be an S corporation.[51] This raises the possibility that a corporation that has more than one class of stock could recapitalize immediately before a change in control to avoid the golden parachute rules. Generally, this should not be necessary because the shareholders could vote to approve the payment, but there may be cases in which it is easier to avoid the problem in another way.

Example: Corporation Y has as its shareholders only United States resident individuals. Two individuals, who together own 74.9%, and a trust that owns 25.1%, own the Y common stock. The trustee is 88 years old, suffers from gout and has not agreed to anything suggested by anyone since Reagan was president. Y also has outstanding 1,000 shares of nonvoting preferred stock, par value and fair market value $1000 per share. The company has received an offer of $20,000,000 for all of its stock. The common stock is worth $19,000,000. It should be possible to convert the preferred stock into $1,000,000 of common stock prior to the sale (ideally before the purchase and sale agreement is executed due to step transaction concerns[52]) and thus escape the golden parachute rules without a shareholder vote. It would also be possible to redeem the preferred stock with a note that would be paid as part of the sale proceeds.

Reasonable Compensation

Excess parachute payments do not include reasonable compensation for services actually performed. Section 280G(b)(4)(B) provides that, except in the case of securities violation parachute payments, the amount of an excess parachute payment is reduced by any portion of the payment that the taxpayer establishes by clear and convincing evidence is reasonable compensation for personal services actually rendered by the disqualified individual before the date of change in ownership or control.

The treatment of reasonable compensation for services rendered before the change in control is different from the treatment of reasonable compensation for services rendered after the change in control, although in both cases the taxpayer must show that the compensation was reasonable by clear and convincing evidence.[53] Reasonable compensation for services performed before the change in control reduces the amount of the excess parachute payment. Reasonable compensation for services performed after the change in control is not a parachute payment at all and is not subject to these rules.

The amount that the taxpayer shows is reasonable compensation is first applied against the portion of the base amount allocated to the parachute payment (and does not produce an offset in addition to the allocable base amount), as illustrated in the following example:

Example: Assume that a disqualified person receives a parachute payment of $1,000,000, to which there is allocable a base amount of $100,000; thus, there is an excess parachute payment of $900,000. The taxpayer can show by clear and convincing evidence that of the $1,000,000 payment, $800,000 is reasonable compensation for services performed before the change in control. The excess parachute payment is therefore reduced as follows: the first $100,000 of reasonable compensation is applied against the base amount, and the balance, $700,000, is applied against the excess parachute payment, reducing the amount of the excess parachute payment to $200,000.[54]

Clear and convincing evidence that a payment is reasonable compensation for services rendered after a change in ownership or control exists if the individual's annual compensation after the change in ownership or control (apart from normal increases) is not significantly greater then the individual's annual compensation before the change in ownership or control, provided that the individual's duties and responsibilities are substantially the same after the change in ownership or control as they were before the change in ownership or control. If the individual's duties and responsibilities have changed, then the clear and convincing evidence must demonstrate that the individual's annual compensation after the change in ownership or control is not significantly greater than the compensation customarily paid by the employer, or by comparable employers, to persons performing comparable services.

Payments under a covenant not to compete, if reasonable, are treated as payments for services. Under Q/A-42, a noncompete agreement qualifies if it is demonstrated with clear and convincing evidence that the agreement substantially constrains the individual's ability to perform services and there is a reasonable likelihood that the agreement will be enforced. Otherwise, the payments are treated as severance payments and are subject to the rules.

Under Q/A-44 severance payments cannot be reduced by reasonable compensation. A severance payment is a payment that is made to a disqualified individual on account of the termination of his or her employment prior to the end of a stated term, but does not include any payment that would have been made to such individual on the termination of his or her employment, whenever occurring.

Typical Terms of Golden Parachute Contracts

The manner in which the golden parachute rules are addressed in employment or severance agreements is generally a function of the amounts of leverage that can be exerted by the parties.

If the executive in question is highly prized by the company, he or she might be able to negotiate a gross-up parachute payment under which the company not only pays the 20% excise tax for the executive, but also makes a gross-up payment to the executive that leaves the executive in the same after-tax position as if the golden parachute rules had not been enacted. This may be a very expensive proposition for the company for two reasons. First, the company will lose the deduction for the excess parachute payment, which will include the entire amount of the gross-up. Second, the gross-up will be expensive.

Example: Assume that there is an excess parachute payment of $1,000,000, on which is imposed a 20% excise tax. The gross-up would not be $200,000; it would be the amount that, after income and excise taxes, equals $200,000. Assuming that the executive is in the 40% combined federal and state tax bracket, this would be $500,000. On the $500,000, there would be a 20% excise tax of $100,000, as well as income tax of 40% or $200,000. This leaves $200,000 to pay the excise tax on the original $1,000,000. Thus, the $1,000,000 turns into a $1,500,000 expense for the company, none of which is deductible.

This type of arrangement is very costly in taxes, but may be unavoidable. For example, the company may have several layers of venture preferred stock, much of which is under water. In such a case, the parties may believe that the common stock, and indeed some layers of the preferred stock, will never get anything. This makes equity incentives for executives unattractive, and a new CEO or other key person brought in to revive and sell the company will want a bonus (possibly computed as a percentage of the proceeds of a sale), rather than a traditional equity incentive. If the bonus is payable on a sale of the company, and the shareholder approval escape route is not available (and it will be available only if the executive is willing to waive at least some of the payment if it is not approved), the only alternative may be to accept the tax consequences of excess parachute payments.

More typically, the parties agree that the parachute payments cannot exceed 2.99 times the base amount and provide that each such payment (on a present value basis) will be reduced proportionately or in any other way the executive chooses. For example, the executive might prefer to have the initial cash payment reduced, but to keep the health insurance payments in full force. Generally, the parties agree that the determination as to whether the parachute payments exceed the limit will be made in an arbitration-type proceeding.[55]

There have been severance contracts in which the executive had considerable leverage and was able to negotiate a contract that allowed him or her to chose whether to take the excess parachute payment (but without a gross-up) or reduce the parachute payments to 2.99 times the base amount.

Example: Assume that the base amount is $250,000, so that the maximum parachute payments that can be received without the application of the excise tax is $749,999. Also, assume a 40% individual income tax rate. If the parachute payment without reduction would be $850,000, then the excess parachute payment would be $600,000; the excise tax would be $120,000 and the income tax would be $340,000, leaving the executive with $390,000. The executive is better off reducing the payment to $749,999, which would leave after tax proceeds of $449,400. On the other hand, if the parachute payment were $1,100,000 and the excess parachute payment therefore $850,000, the excise tax would be $170,000 and the income tax would be $440,000, leaving the executive with $490,000. In that case, the executive would be better off paying the excise tax. The employer, of course, would be better off reducing the payment so that it could take the deduction.

Timing of Payment of Excise Tax

The excise tax under section 4999 generally is payable at the time the disqualified individual is required to include it in gross income (for a cash method taxpayer, this is the time of payment)[56], and is subject to withholding as if it were an income tax.[57] The disqualified individual can elect to treat the payment as received at the time of the change in control, if this occurs before the actual payment.[58] Presumably, this election would also apply to the employer, but the Code does not say so.

In general, a transfer of property is considered a payment made (or to be made) in the taxable year in which the property transferred is includible in the gross income of the disqualified individual under section 83 and the regulations thereunder (that it, when it is vested). The amount of the payment is equal to the excess of the fair market value of the transferred property (determined without regard to any lapse restriction) at the time that the property becomes substantially vested, over the amount (if any) paid for the property. A "section 83(b) election" is ineffective to advance the time of inclusion for purposes of section 4999, and the value of the payment must be determined as of the date of actual vesting.[59]

An incentive stock option or nonqualified stock option is treated as property that is transferred not later than the time at which the option becomes substantially vested (whether or not the option has a readily ascertainable fair market value as defined in Reg. §1.83-7(b)). The vesting of such an option is treated as a payment in the nature of compensation. The amount of the payment is the fair market value of the option.

There may be circumstances in which it is not clear that the excise tax will be due, which places the parties in an awkward position.

Example: Corporation T employs disqualified individual Q as head of its valve division (known within the company as "Q Branch"). T also manufactures seals. Q Branch is worth 20% of the fair market value of all of T. Q's employment contract entitles him to a severance payment of more than three times his base amount if he is fired other than for cause. On January 3, 2004, T sells Q Branch, fires Q, and is ready to pay him his severance payment. However, T has also been in discussions with an investment banker regarding a possible sale of the T stock, or perhaps of the seal division. Thus far, no buyers have been identified.

It is true that Q Branch is not one third of the assets of T. Nothing else appearing, the payment to Q is not a parachute payment. On the other hand, if T sells the rest of its assets, or someone buys its stock, before January 3, 2005, then the payment to Q might be a parachute payment. After all, the payment is contingent on an event closely associated with a change in control (the termination of Q's employment), and if the change in control occurs within a year of the event, there will be a presumption that the payment to Q was contingent on the change in control. T and Q may be able to rebut the presumption by a showing that this payment would have been made even in the absence of the change in control, but the facts are not perfectly clear because at the time of Q's severance payment, T intended to enter into a transaction constituting a change in control.

Q and T ought to win this argument with the IRS, should it arise. Meanwhile, T does not want to take the risk that Q will no longer have the money to pay the tax, if it is assessed. Should T withhold 20% of Q's potential excess parachute payment? [60]

Conclusion

These complex and often frustrating rules cannot be justified as a matter of tax policy. They exist to modify behavior, not to raise taxes. In fact, sections 280G and 4999 have had the effect that Congress desired-a limit on golden parachute payments. Gross ups for the excise tax are very unusual, and the employers are loath to pay out compensation that they cannot deduct for tax purposes.

Nevertheless, having succeeded in their purpose, the golden parachute rules cost the government money because they limit the amount of compensation income of high-bracket individuals. For the past several years, the highest marginal bracket applicable to individuals has been higher than the highest bracket applicable to corporations. This means that the taxes paid by a disqualified individual as a result of receiving compensation income exceed the taxes saved by the corporate employer as a result of deducting the same amount. Moreover, compensation income generates employment taxes (the hospital insurance portion of FICA), and these, too, are lost to the government when compensation payments are limited. Thus, the government has made a considerable investment in these rules.

Whether shareholders actually have seen the benefit of these rules in terms of enhanced share values no one can tell. The only certain beneficiaries have been the tax lawyers who have to understand these rules, explain them to their dismayed clients, and draft employment and severance agreements that avoid them. In addition, accountants have to do complex computations to determine the allowable limits of parachute payments. It is nice to know that our elected representatives in Washington are looking out for us.

---

[1] REG-209114-90; 67 F.R. 7630-7656 (Feb. 20, 2002). The proposed regulations are organized in question and answer format, and citations to the 2002 proposed regulations appear herein as, for example, "Q/A 15." The 2002 proposed regulations were accompanied by an excellent explanation prepared by the Treasury and IRS, and this article draws freely upon it.

[2] It is not clear whether taxpayers can rely on the old regulations and new regulations selectively, question by question.

[3] Unless otherwise indicated, all statutory citations are to the Internal Revenue Code of 1986, as amended.

[4] There are no similar provisions for partnerships or limited liability companies that have not elected to be taxed as corporations. Generally, all corporations that form an affiliated group under section 1504 are considered as one corporation. Q/A-46.

[5] Section 280G(b)(2)(A). Section 280G(b)(2)(B) provides that the term parachute payment also includes any payment in the nature of compensation to, or for the benefit of, a disqualified individual if the payment is pursuant to an agreement that violates any generally enforced securities laws or regulation. See Q/A-37. Because this issue arises only rarely for tax purposes, we will mention it only in passing.

[6] Q/A-25.

[7] Q/A-26.

[8] Q/A 11.

[9] A/A-10.

[10] Section 280G(b)(3) and Q/A-34.

[11] Q/A-34(c).

[12] Section 280G(d)(2) and Q/A-35. Note that the year of the change in control is not included, which sometimes prevents increasing the executive's compensation immediately before the change in control in order to increase the base amount.

[13] Generally, purchasers in an initial public offering are not treated as a group, unless there is some other evidence of group activity. Q/A-27(b) and Q/A-28(d).

[14] Q/A 27(a).

[15] Q/A-28.

[16] Q/A-29.

[17] See, e.g., Florida Publishing Co. v. Commissioner, 64 T.C. 269, 280 (1975), aff'd. by unpublished order (5th Cir., Apr. 25, 1977).

[18] Section 280G(b)(1).

[19] Q/A-16.

[20] Section 280G(c).

[21] Q/A-18(a).

[22] Under the 1989 proposed regulations, an individual is a shareholder for purposes of section 280G if the individual, at any time during the disqualified individual determination period, owns stock of a corporation with a fair market value exceeding the lesser of $1 million or one percent of the total fair market value of the outstanding shares of all classes of the corporation's stock. The monetary test has been deleted in the 2002 proposed regulations.

[23] Q/A 20.

[24] Q/A-19.

[25] Q/A 22.

[26] Q/A 22(b)(3).

[27] Q/A 22(b)(1).

[28] Q/A 13. This is one case in which taxpayers may prefer to be subject to the old proposed regulations.

[29] See Q/A 13 of the 1989 proposed regulations.

[30] 2002-8 I.R.B. 549, modified by Rev. Proc. 2002-45, 2002-27 I.R.B. 1. For a further discussion of the option rules see M. Hevener, Golden Parachutes: New Exemptions for Some People and Some Deals but Bigger "Excess Parachutes" 96 J. Tax 261 (May, 2002); B. Salkin, Proposed Regulations Clarify and Revise Parachute Payment Rules, 68 Pract. Tax. Strategies 271 (May, 2002).

[31] The valuation of stock options is beyond the scope of this article. However, because the effects of the golden parachute rules can be so drastic, the use of stock options as parachute payments should be approached with caution, and in many cases ordinary prudence would require an appraisal by someone who is well versed in the field.

[32] Q/A-24(b).

[33] Q/A-31(a).

[34] Q/A-32.

[35] Q/A-24(c)(4).

[36] Q/A-24(f), Example 1.

[37] This might be the case if the plan called for the payment to be made when D retires, but not earlier than the date he attains age 60.

[38] Q/A-24(f), Example 2.

[39] Q/A6(a)(2)(i) and (d).

[40] Q/A-6(c) and 6(g), Example 3.

[41] The 1989 proposed regulations did not contain this rule, and so this is another case in which a taxpayer might prefer to rely on them.

[42] Q/A-7(b)(4) and (5).

[43] Q/A-7(b)(4). However, if all persons who hold voting power in the corporation are disqualified individuals or related persons, then stock owned by such persons is counted as outstanding stock.

[44] Q/A-7(e), Example 5.

[45] Q/A-7(c).

[46] Q/A-7(b)(1).

[47] Q/7-7(c).

[48] Q/A-7(b)(2).

[49] There is favorable analogous authority. For example, Rev. Rul. 84-79, 1984-1 C.B. 190, held that if a parent corporation transfers stock of a subsidiary to a voting trust, the two corporations will continue to be affiliated for purposes of the consolidated return rules, notwithstanding that the parent no longer possesses the voting power of the stock of the subsidiary.

[50] Q/A-7(b)(3), and (e), Example 2.

[51] Section 280G(b)(5); Q/A-6(a)(1) states that the corporation must be an S corporation "immediately before" the change in control.

[52] These concerns should not be overstated. The timing ought to matter only to the extent that small business corporation status is achieved before the change in control because that is all section 280G(b)(5)(A)(i) requires. The general rule in such matters is that if tax status is what required to achieve a desired result sanctioned under the Code, the taxpayer is entitled to take steps to achieve that status, even if motivated by tax reasons. See Rev. Rul. 70-238, 1970-1 C.B. 61; Rev. Rul. 76-363, 1976-2 C.B. 90; Modern Home Casualty and Fire Ins. Co. v. Commissioner, 54 T.C. 839 (1970), Acq., 1970-2 C.B. xx.

[53] See Balch v. Commissioner, 100 T.C. 331 (1993), where the taxpayer was unable to carry his burden of proof with respect to payments made after the change in control. It did not help that these payments were in substitution for payments that the parties realized would have been parachute payments if made at the time of the change in control, as originally contemplated. This situation is now covered by Q/A-23(b), Example 3.

[54] This disposes of the argument that the excess parachute payment is only $100,000, which would be the result if the excess parachute payment were first determined by subtracting the base amount from the parachute payment, and then subtracting the amount of reasonable compensation.

[55] In Cvelbar v. CBI Illinois Inc., 103 F.3d 1368 (7th Cir. 1997), the agreement provided that the determination would be made by the company's counsel in his sole discretion. When that discretion was exercised in favor of the employer, the executive brought suit. The court applied the "arbitrary

and capricious" standard to the exercise of discretion and held for the employer, while disclaiming any opinion of its own about the application of Section 280G.

[56] Q/A-11(b).

[57] Section 4999(c)(1).

[58] Q/A-11(b) and (c). The election is not available for certain deferred payments or for health benefits.

[59] Q/A-12.

[60] These facts are taken from an actual case. The parties decided to escrow the tax until the statute of limitations expired.

15

Nondeductibility of $1 Million Compensation

Until the Revenue Reconciliation Act of 1993,[1] corporations faced few restrictions on tax deductions taken for executive compensation payments. Compensation has been expected to be reasonable, but this standard has only found frequent use in limiting payments by closely held companies where dividends may be disguised as deductible compensation. To close off this unlimited tax benefit, I.R.C. § 162(m) holds the allowable deduction for the chief executive officer and the next four most highly compensated employees ("covered employees") of a publicly held corporation to no more than $1 million annually. Note that Section 162(m) does not apply to remuneration paid pursuant to a compensation plan or agreement that existed during the period in which the corporation was not publicly held.

A publicly held corporation includes an affiliated group of corporations filing a consolidated return and any of its foreign subsidiaries. If a covered employee is paid compensation in a taxable year by more than one member of an affiliated group, compensation paid by each member of the affiliated group is aggregated with compensation paid to the covered employee by all other members of the group. Any amount disallowed as a deduction by section 162(m) must be prorated among the payor corporations in proportion to the amount of compensation paid to the covered employee by each such corporation in the taxable year.[2]

A covered employee means any individual who, "on the last day of the taxable year," is the chief executive officer of the corporation or is acting in such capacity; or among the four highest compensated officers (other than the chief executive officer).[3] Thus, the total number of covered persons cannot exceed five. Whether a person is an officer and the amount of his or her compensation is determined under the rules applicable to filings with the SEC. The relevant date is the last day of the taxable year, so that anyone whose employment has terminated by that date is not a covered person.

Sections 162(m) and 280G can apply at the same time.[4] The $1,000,000 limitation in section 162(m) is reduced by the amount that would have been included in the compensation expense for payments to a covered employee for the taxable year but for being disallowed by reason of section 280G. For example, assume that during a taxable year a corporation pays $1,500,000 to a covered employee. Of the $1,500,000, $600,000 is an excess parachute payment, and as a result is not deductible. Because the excess parachute payment reduces the $1,000,000 limitation, the corporation can deduct $400,000, and $500,000 of the otherwise deductible amount is nondeductible by reason of section 162(m).

Regardless of the imposition of any penalty, interest on the unpaid tax will accrue from the date payment was due; interest will also accrue on any penalty imposed.[5] For the quarter of 2001 beginning April 1, for example, the rate is set at 8%.[6] The rate is adjusted periodically to reflect market conditions.

The $1 million limitation does not apply to compensation payments linked to productivity, such as remuneration payable on a commission basis and, most importantly, compensation tied to objective performance goals set by outside directors and approved in advance by the shareholders.[7] Stock options are the obvious answer; unlike restricted stock plans, stock options are not subject to the performance criteria.

[1] Omnibus Budget Reconciliation Act of 1993, § 13211.

[2] Treas. Reg. § 1.162-27(c)(1)(ii).

[3] Treas. Reg. § 1.162-27(c)(2).

[4] Treas. Reg. § 1.162-27(g).

[5] Section 6601(e)(2)(B).

[6] Rev. Rul. 2001-16, 2001-13 IRB (Mar. 9, 2001).

[7] The performance goal must be established in writing by the compensation committee not later than 90 days after the commencement of he services to which it relates and while the outcome is substantially uncertain (and in no event after 25% or more of the performance period has elapsed). Also, the performance goal must be stated in terms of an objective formula or standard. The goals can be based on business criteria that apply to the individual, a business, or the corporation as a while. Examples of valid criteria are: return on equity, sales, EPS, stock price, or market share. A performance goal does not have to be a positive result or increase - it may include maintaining a certain level of performance or limiting losses. A formula or standard is objective if a third-party having knowledge of the relevant performance could calculate the amount to be paid to the employee. The performance goal must also specify the individuals or class of employees eligible to receive compensation. *See generally* Chinn, *Impact of the Revenue Reconciliation Act of 1993 on Executive Compensation, in* 25th Ann. Inst. Sec. Reg. 255 (PLI Course Handbook Series No. B-827, 1993).

[8] §162(m)(4)(F).

16

Parachutes and the ERISA Trap

The problem arises from the fact that severance benefits fit the ERISA definition of the type of benefit which, if provided for in a "plan," requires certain formalities.[1] The issue is whether a given group of employment contracts should be considered a "plan" under ERISA. Most practitioners have generally approached the issue with a commonsense standard, taking into account what appeared to be the intent of the parties-the "looks like a duck, walks like a duck, quacks like a duck" theory. That is, if a group of individual contracts were funded like a deferred compensation plan, the benefits were bargained for in traditional ERISA mode and so on, the courts would be likely to apply ERISA requirements even though the plan consisted of separately negotiated contracts. However, a 1989 decision of a Pennsylvania U.S. district judge in *Purser v. Enron* Corp.[2] raises concerns in a nontraditional setting.

The *Purser* case involved contracts extended by a public company to more than 20 executives providing golden parachutes in the event of a hostile takeover. The court was not prepared to follow the "looks like duck" analysis. It had very little interest in the intent of the employer because, the court reasoned, the thrust of the statute could be defeated by wily employers simply using proper nomenclature, a revision perhaps to the old "Yellow

Dog" contracts used to defeat labor union organization prior to the advent of the Taft-Hartley Act. Instead, the court purported to follow an Eleventh Circuit holding, Donovan v. Dillingham,[3] and determined that a plan was established because, from the surrounding circumstances, a reasonable person could "ascertain the intended benefits, as class of beneficiaries, source of financing, and procedures for receiving benefits."

The practical problems with abandonment of the "looks like a duck" analysis, however, are apparent. How does one know, based on some sort of objective test, whether employment contracts are an ERISA "plan?" The Purser court went so far as to suggest that even one contract could constitute a plan in the appropriate circumstance.

---

[1] ERISA § 3(2)(A), 29 U.S.C. 186(c).

[2] Civ. No. 88-117 (W.D. Pa. 1989).

[3] 688 F.2d 1367 (11th Cir. 1982).

17

SEC Disclosure Rules

In 1992, the SEC adopted amendments to its disclosure requirements[1] in registration, periodic reporting and proxy statements which are designed to have behavior-modifying effects. Henceforth, the onus will be on the compensation committees of public companies to justify the relationship of key employee compensation to corporate performance and peer group indexes.[2] Stock option grants, heretofore deemed "free" in terms of compensation expense, must be valued according to, among other things, their "potential realized value."

In 2002, further disclosure requirements have been adopted by the SEC in '33 Act Rel. No. 33-8048, which now require a new table in the annual reports and the proxy statements in any year in which a compensation plan is submitted for shareholder action. The tables require information on compensation plans which (i) have been approved and (ii) have not been approved by the shareholders, the idea being to highlight those plans that have not yet been approved. In each category, the issuer has to disclose the number of shares to be issued, the weighted average exercise price of all outstanding options, warrants and rights, and the number of shares remaining available for future issuance under the equity compensation plan.

[1] The gist of the SEC's disclosure requirements appear in Item 402 of Regulation S-K.

[2] See Sec. Act Rel. No. 33-7009; Vlahakis, *Executive Compensation: The* Continuing Evolution, in I 25th Ann. Inst. Sec. Reg. 265 (PLI Course Handbook Series No. B-827, 1993).

18

'34 Act Section 16-Impact on Options

For many years, the "short swing" profits concept in § 16 of the '34 Act has caused mischief, particularly in relation to the issuance and exercise of stock options and other derivative securities.[1] The basic statutory scheme requires directors, officers and 10 percent holders of "any class" of a public issuer's equity to file a contemporaneous notice of purchases and sales deemed to be insider transactions.[2] Section 16(b)[3] requires the insider to disgorge any profits so-called "short swing" profits-made on sales and purchases (or vice versa) which can be matched in any six-month period. The profits are recoupable by the issuer, after counsel fees to those plaintiffs' lawyers (once led by one "16b Levy") who patrol the reports and bring the lawsuits.[4]

The statute has in the past posed a problem for optionees because, arguably, the award of an option is the purchase of either or both of the option and the option stock; the exercise of the option stock is a purchase of the option stock; and the sale of the option stock is, of course, a sale. Moreover, any one of the foregoing might be matched with an open market purchase. Further, option holders might also be participants in other types of stock purchase programs, pursuant to which purchasers or sales may occur without their direct intervention. Employees who have to raise the exercise price in order to obtain the option stock are often anxious to exercise and sell, if only by virtue of one of certain devices labeled "cashless exercise."[5] Section 16(b), thus, became a cottage industry for commentators and practitioners.

However, the SEC has mercifully simplified some of the complexities, and traps for the unwary, with the enactment of Rule 16b-3, which exempts certain transactions, including prominently the "purchase" which results from option exercise by officers and directors (not 10 percent holders) if (i) the employee benefit plan concerned sets forth the number of shares subject to the plan and the strike price[6] in writing, the option is nontransferable except in the case of death or divorce, the shareholders approved the plan, and the plan is administered (i.e., options granted) by disinterested directors; and (ii) the option has been owned for six months.[7] Once the exercise is out of the picture as a purchase, then the officer and/or director may sell the option stock free of short swing liability, provided the seller patrols the six month period prior to or succeeding sale of the option stock for other transactions which might qualify as a matching purchase.[8]

In the course of the SEC's revisions, other helpful changes and clarifications were made. Thus, the term "officer"[9] has been redefined; it closely parallels the definition of "executive officer" used elsewhere under the Exchange Act (such as for disclosure of compensation in proxy statements), and the term explicitly includes the principal financial officer, principal accounting officer or controller and officers of the issuer's parent who perform policy-making functions for the issuer (who in many cases would be considered "executive officers" anyway). Because the definition focuses on the function a person performs, rather than that person's title, a policy maker cannot avoid § 16 coverage by declining to take a particular title. Presumably, the persons listed in an issuer's Form 10-D as executive officers, together with any persons specified above, are "officers" for § 16 purposes.

In defining the term "beneficial owner," a person is considered to have an indirect pecuniary interest in all equity securities the person may acquire through the exercise or conversion of a derivative security, such as a stock option, whether or not presently exercisable or exercisable within 60 days. Consequently, one is required to report all securities covered by outstanding stock options, even though those stock options may not be presently exercisable. However, reporting the acquisition of those securities will often be deferred.[10]

The exercise of an out-of-the-money derivative security is not exempt under the new rules. The SEC's concern seems to be that, because the exercise of an out-of-the-money derivative security ordinarily makes no economic sense, an insider who exercises a derivative security that is out-of-the-money is more likely to be doing so based on nonpublic information.[11]

Problems continued and, accordingly, in 1996, the SEC adopted helpful revisions to Rule 16b-3, intending measures to streamline the Section 16 reporting and exemption scheme, particularly with respect to transactions between an issuer and its officers and directors, simplify the reporting system, broaden other exemptions from short-swing recovery, and codify Staff interpretative positions. The principal liberalization was to the prior requirement of shareholder approval. Under the new Rule, acquisitions by an officer or director of securities from the issuer are exempt if any of the following three conditions is met:

1. The issuer's board of directors or committee of two or more "Non-Employee Directors" approves the acquisition in advance. A "Non-Employee Director" is defined as a person who (i) is not currently an officer or employee of the issuer or a parent or subsidiary, (ii) does not receive compensation of more than $60,000 per year for services except as a director, and (iii) does not otherwise have transactions or business relationships with the issuer required to be disclosed under the proxy rules.

2. The issuer's shareholders approve the acquisition in advance or ratify it not later than the date of the next annual meeting of shareholders.

3. The director or officer holds the securities acquired for six months or, in the case of a derivative security (such as a stock option), at least six months elapse between the date of acquisition of the derivative security and the date of disposition of the underlying security.

If any of the three exemptions described above is met, the new Rule exempts the acquisition of the securities. In addition, the new Rule eliminates the following requirements of current Rule 16b-3:

1. The general written plan conditions, including the basis on which insiders may participate and the specification of the price or amount of securities offered.

2. The general prohibition against transfer of options and other derivative securities, other than by will, descent, or distribution or pursuant to a qualified domestic relations order.

3. The six-month holding period as a general condition for the Rule 16b-3 exemption for grants and awards (although holding the securities for six months is one of three ways in which a grant or award can be exempt).

4. The disinterested administration requirement for grant or award transactions (although approval by Non-Employee Directors is one of the three ways in which a grant or award can be exempt),

5. The requirement that shareholders approve the plan and any material amendments thereto (although shareholder approval of the transaction is one of the three ways in which a grant or award can be exempt).

6. The formula plan requirement (both as a substitute for disinterested administration and as a means by which administrators may receive securities while remaining disinterested).

7. The current public information, disinterested administration, window period and six-month holding period condition for the exercise of stock appreciation rights for cash.

The adopting Release indicates that both the shareholder approval exemption and the director approval exemption require that the specific grant (as opposed to the plan in general) be director approved or approved by shareholders. However, the adopting release indicates that a formula plan that is director approved or approved by shareholders does not require further exemptive relief for the grants made under such plan.

In addition to the three alternative exemptions described above for acquisition of securities by officers and directors, the new Rule exempts most routine transactions under plans that satisfy specified provisions of the Internal Revenue Code, such as thrift plans, stock purchase plans, and excess benefit plans, without needing to satisfy additional conditions. In that regard the new Rule broadly exempts from Section 16(b) liability any transactions in a "Tax-Conditioned Plan" (that is, a "Qualified Plan," "Excess Benefit Plan" or "Stock Purchase Plan") other than "Discretionary Transactions," discussed below. *Qualified Plan* is defined broadly to include: (1) an employee benefit plan that satisfies the broad-based coverage and participation requirements of IRC §§ 410 and 401(a)(26). *Excess Benefit Plan* is defined as any excess benefit (or mirror) plan operated in conjunction with a Qualified Plan that provides only the benefits that would have been provided under the Qualified Plan but for the contribution limitations of IRC §§ 40 1 (a)(I 7), 415, and similar IRC contribution limitations. A *Stock Purchase Plan* is defined as any employee benefit plan that satisfies the coverage and participation standards of IRC §§ 423(b)(3) and 423(b)(5) or § 410.

Employee thrift and stock purchase plans often permit a participant to choose one of several funds in which to invest (that is, an issuer stock fund, a money market fund, a bond fund, or an indexed fund). Plan participants typically are permitted to transfer assets from one fund to another and often have the right to withdraw their investments in cash from a fund containing equity securities of the issuer. These discretionary plan transactions involving an issuer's securities are defined under new Rule 16b-3 as

Discretionary Transactions. Under the new Rule, Discretionary Transactions are not automatically exempt. However, a Discretionary Transaction, including the switching of assets into or out of an issuer stock fund or withdrawing cash from an issuer stock fund regardless of whether or not the Discretionary Transaction is effected pursuant to a Tax-Conditioned Plan, will be exempt if the election by the officer or director to effect the Discretionary Transaction is made at least six months following any *opposite way* (a disposition in the case of an acquisition or an acquisition in the case of a disposition) election made under the plan in question or any other plan of the issuer. The definition of Discretionary Transaction excludes transactions that are incident to death, disability, termination of employment, or diversification elections required under ERISA.

The new Rule 16b-3 provides that any transaction (other than a Discretionary Transaction) involving a disposition of an equity security to the issuer is exempt from Section 16(b) liability if the disposition is approved in advance by the board of directors, by a committee of Non-Employee Directors, or by the stockholders (ratification by shareholders will not be sufficient). If the disposition is a Discretionary Transaction, to be exempt the transaction must satisfy the Rule 16b-3 conditions specifically applicable to Discretionary Transactions as described above. The specific terms of the disposition, including price, requires prior approval of either the full board, the committee of Non-Employee Directors, or shareholders. If shareholder approval is relied upon, both the proxy card and the proxy statement should provide that a vote in favor of the transaction also constitutes approval of the disposition of the equity securities to the issuer in connection with the transaction.

The new Rule is warmly welcomed by issuers (and their counsel) who have grappled with the unwieldy set of complicated rules and interpretations emanating from the 1991 revisions to the Section 16 reporting and exemptive scheme. The elimination of the disinterested administration, six-month holding period, shareholder approval, nontransferability of derivative securities, and other conditions of the current Rule 16b-3 help issuers avoid most of the pitfalls of current Rule 16b-3. It is relatively simple under the new Rule to craft an exemption from Section 16(b) liability for virtually all transactions between the issuer and its directors and officers, particularly when an otherwise non-exempt grant or award transaction is made exempt if the securities are simply held for six months by the insider. The emphasis under the new Rule 16b-3 has shifted from the content of the plan to the approvals obtained in connection with acquisitions of securities from, and dispositions of securities to, the issuer, whether or not pursuant to a formal plan.

The elimination of the current Rule 16b-3 six-month holding period permits greater flexibility for both issuers and insiders. For example, a director approved option is exercised (and the underlying securities sold) within six months of the grant of the option without the sale being matched with the grant of the option. As a result, monthly or quarterly vesting of such options no longer create a possible inadvertent § 16(b) violation in cases where the insider exercises the vested portion of an option in a brokers' cashless exercise within six months of the date of the option grant. Indeed, the new Rule eliminates the complicated web of the current Rule's participant-directed transaction requirements (other than the limited vestiges thereof included in the additional requirements for Discretionary Transactions).

Further, the elimination of the prohibition against transfers of options and other derivative securities increases estate planning opportunities for directors and officers. Although incentive stock options cannot retain their status as ISOs and be transferable, non-qualified stock options are not subject to those prohibitions.

One of the most welcome changes in the new Rule 16b-3 is the elimination of the current requirement that an exempt plan, and any material amendments to the plan affecting directors or officers, be approved by shareholders. However, shareholder approval of option and other plans and disinterested committees is required if grants of options or other securities intend to qualify as ISOs or "performance based compensation" under the $1 million deduction limit of IRC § 162(m). In addition, issuers may still find themselves constrained by the language of their current plans to effect certain amendments to those plans only with shareholder approval. Moreover, both for new plans and for amendments to those plans, issuers need to be cognizant of applicable rules of the Nasdaq National Market, the American Stock Exchange, and the New York Stock Exchange which generally require shareholder approval of stock option or other stock compensation plans or arrangements with officers and directors that are funded by newly-issued shares.

Finally, as the Adopting Release makes clear, directors who award themselves stock options or other forms of stock compensation are subject to state laws governing corporate self-dealing.

---

[1] While the definitions of *derivative securities* contains a number of exceptions, the term generally includes "any option, warrant, convertible security, stock appreciation right, or similar right with an exercise or conversion privilege at a price related to an equity security, [and] similar securities with a value derived from the value of an equity security." Among the exceptions is an exclusion for securities, such as some phantom stock plans, that may be redeemed or exercised only for cash and do not permit the receipt of equity securities in lieu of cash, if the securities either satisfy the conditions exempting grants or are exercisable only upon a fixed date or dates at least six months after the award, or upon death, retirement, disability or termination of employment.

[2] Holders must file a Form 3 disclosing their initial beneficial ownership upon becoming subject to Section 16 and a Form 4 to report transactions which effect a change in their beneficial ownership of the subject securities.

[3] Section 16(c) prohibits short sales, or sales "against the box" (in which the seller owns the security, but does not deliver it within a specified period) by statutory insiders, while § 16(d) and § 16(e) provide certain exemptions for dealers and arbitrageurs.

[4] Sec. Exh. Act Rel. No. 34-28869, issued on February 8. 1991, sets forth the new rules in their entirety as well as the new forms to be used by insiders for future reporting. The Release also includes a chart summarizing the changes in the staff interpretations contained in the SEC's 1981 question-and-answer interpretive release (Sec. Exch. Act Rel. No. 34-18114). Among other significant changes are (1) new definitions of "officer" and "beneficial owner," for purposes of determining which persons are subject to § 16 and what securities must be reported; and (2) revisions to Rule 16b-3, the

rule governing the exemptions for various transactions involving employee benefit plans, to cover broad-based, nondiscriminatory plans previously exempted under Rule 16a-8(b).

[5] Cashless exercise may mean (1) a short-term margin loan from a broker which enables the optionee to exercise and sell simultaneously, or (2) a swap of the option for stock which matches in current value the spread between the strike and trading prices, the latter not available to employees for Rule 144 purposes (see *Technology Funding*, SEC No-action Letter (avail. Nov. 19, 199 1)); and/or (3) a swap of publicly traded stock for shares equal in value to the spread.

[6] Or the formula by which the price is derived. Rule 16b-3(a).

[7] Or the option stock is held for six months.

[8] A useful, practical guide to the "dos and don'ts" is contained in Barnictiol, *The New Section 16 Rules: Compliance Procedures, in* 23d Ann. Inst. Sec. Reg. 735, 752 (PLI Course Handbook Series No. 755, 1991), where the author suggests illustrations helpful in understanding the new § 16 rules.

[9] The term *officer* means: an issuer's president, principal financial officer, or principal accounting officer (or, if there is no such accounting officer, the controller), any vice president of the issuer in charge of a principal business unit, division or function (such as sales, administration or finance), any other officer who performs a policy-making function, or any other person who performs similar policy-making functions for the issuer. Officers of the issuer's parent(s) or subsidiaries shall be deemed officers of the issuer if they perform such policy-making functions for the issuer. Rule 16a- 1 (f).

[10] In general, those transactions that are exempt from § 16(b) short-swing liability, such as acquisitions of stock options through a qualifying employee benefit plan, acquisitions through a dividend reinvestment plan, or acquisitions or dispositions of securities by gift, need not be reported on Form 4 but must then be reported annually on Form 5. However, a person may elect to report an exempt transaction on Form 4 immediately, rather than wait to include it on the next annual Form 5. By deferring the reporting of many transactions exempt from liability under § 16(b), the new reporting scheme attempts to ensure that the transactions reported on Form 4, which are presumably the ones of most interest to the financial community, are those which are subject to matching with another transaction within six months for purposes of imposing short-swing profit liability, Also to be reported on the new Form 5 are all holdings and transactions that should have been reported during the issuer's most recent fiscal year, but were not, and, in the case of the first Form to be filed, all holdings and transactions that should have been reported in each of the issuer's last two fiscal years, but were not.

The special rule applicable only to the exercise or conversion of derivative securities adds some complexity to the reporting scheme. Exercises or conversions of derivative securities, such as stock options, although exempt transactions under the new rules, must be reported on the next Form 4 that the reporting person is otherwise required to file or on the Form 5 for the fiscal year in which the exercise or conversion occurs, whichever is earlier.

[11] Although the desire to avoid the embarrassment of public disclosure will doubtless spur many previously delinquent insiders to file their reports in a more timely manner, perhaps a greater motivation will be the Securities Enforcement Remedies and Penny Stock Reform Act of 1990

(Enforcement Act). Under the Enforcement Act, the SEC has the power to seek civil fines through court proceedings (or through administrative proceedings if certain classes of regulated persons are involved) for the violation of most provisions of the Exchange Act or the rules thereunder, including the failure to file reports required by § 16. Such fines may not exceed, for each violation, the greater of (1) $5,000 for a natural person or $50,000 for any other person, or (2) the gross amount of pecuniary gain to the violator as a result of such violation. If the court finds that the violation involved fraud, deceit, manipulation, or deliberate or reckless disregard of a regulatory requirement, the foregoing amounts increase to $50,000 and $250,000, respectively.

19

Model Employment and Stock Purchase Agreement

Agreement made as of this 31st day of March 200_, by and among John Smith of New York City, New York ("Employee") and Newco, Inc. (the "Company").

PREAMBLE

The Board of Directors of the Company recognizes Employee's potential contribution to the growth and success of the Company and desires to assure the Company of Employee's employment in an executive capacity as Chief Executive and to compensate him therefore. Employee wants to be employed by the Company and to commit himself to serve the Company on the terms herein provided. In connection with his employment, Employee proposes to purchase and the Company to sell Restricted Stock on the terms herein provided, including particularly Employee's undertaking to remain loyal to the Company. Employee's duties will expressly include research and development of new technology and products, including the invention of novel items on behalf of and for the account of the Company.

NOW, THEREFORE, in consideration of the foregoing and of the respective covenants and agreements of the parties, the parties agree as follows:

1. Definitions

"Benefits" shall mean all the fringe benefits approved by the Board from time to time and established by the Company for the benefit of employees generally and/or for key employees of the Company as a class, including, but not limited to, regular holidays, vacations, absences resulting from illness or accident, health insurance, disability and medical plans (including dental and prescription drug), group life insurance, and pension, profit-sharing and stock bonus plans or their equivalent.

"Board" shall mean the Board of Directors of the Company, together with an executive committee thereof (if any), as same shall be constituted from time to time.

"Cause" for termination shall mean (i) Employee's final conviction of a felony involving a crime of moral turpitude, (ii) acts of Employee which, in the judgment of the Board, constitute willful fraud on the part of Employee in connection with his duties under this Agreement, including but not limited to misappropriation or embezzlement in the performance of duties as an employee of the Company, or willfully engaging in conduct materially injurious to the Company and in violation of the covenants contained in this Agreement, or (iii) gross misconduct, including but not limited to the willful failure of Employee either to (a) continue to obey lawful written instruction of the Board after thirty (30) days notice in writing of Employee's failure to do so and the Board's intention to terminate Employee if such failure is not corrected, or (b) correct any conduct of Employee which constitutes a material breach of this Agreement after thirty (30) days notice in writing of Employee's failure to do so and the Board's intention to terminate Employee if such failure is not corrected.[1]

"Chairman" shall mean the individual designated by the Board from time to time as its chairman.

"Change of Control" shall mean the occurrence of one or more of the following three events:

(1) After the effective date of this Agreement, any person becomes a beneficial owner (as such term is defined in Rule 13d-3 promulgated under the Securities Exchange Act of 1934) directly or indirectly of securities representing 33% or more of the total number of votes that may be cast for the election of directors of the Company;

(2) Within two years after a merger, consolidation, liquidation or sale of assets involving the Company, or a contested election of a Company director, or any combination of the foregoing, the individuals who were directors of the Company immediately prior thereto shall cease to constitute a majority of the Board; or

(3) Within two years after a tender offer or exchange offer for voting securities of the Company, the individuals who were directors of the Company immediately prior thereto shall cease to constitute a majority of the Board.

"Chief Executive Officer" shall mean the individual having responsibility to the Board for direction and management of the executive and operational affairs of the Company and who reports and is accountable only to the Board.

Optional Language: ["Disability" shall mean a written determination by a physician mutually agreeable to the Company and Employee (or, in the event of Employee's total physical or mental disability, Employee's legal representative) that Employee is physically or mentally unable to perform his duties of Chief Executive Officer under this Agreement and that such disability can reasonably be expected to continue for a period of six (6) consecutive months or for shorter periods aggregating one hundred and eighty (180) days in any twelve-(12)-month period.]

"Employee" shall mean John Smith and, if the context requires, his heirs, personal representatives, and permitted successors and assigns.

"Person" shall mean any natural person, incorporated entity, limited or general partnership, business trust, association, agency (governmental or private), division, political sovereign, or subdivision or instrumentality, including those groups identified as "persons" in §§ 13(d)(3) and 14(d)(2) of the Securities Exchange Act of 1934.

"Restricted Stock" shall mean the Company's Common Stock, $.01 par value.

"Reorganization" shall mean any transaction, or any series of transactions consummated in a 12-month period, pursuant to which any Person acquires (by merger, acquisition, or otherwise) all or substantially all of the assets of the Company or the then outstanding equity securities of the Company and the Company is not the surviving entity, the Company being deemed surviving if and only if the majority of the Board of Directors of the ultimate parent of the surviving entity were directors of the Company prior to its organization.

"Territory" shall mean any state of the United States and any equivalent section or area of any country in which the Company has revenue-producing customers or activities.

"Company" shall mean Newco, Inc., a Delaware corporation, together with such subsidiaries of the Company as may from time to time exist.

2. Position, Responsibilities, and Term of Employment

2.01 Position. Employee shall serve as Chief Executive Officer and in such additional management position(s) as the Board shall designate. In this capacity Employee shall, subject to the bylaws of the Company, and to the direction of the Board, serve the Company by performing such duties and carrying out such responsibilities as are normally related to the position of Chief Executive Officer in accordance with the standards of the industry. The Board shall either vote, or recommend to the shareholders of the Company, as appropriate, that during the term of employment pursuant to this Agreement: (i) Employee be nominated for election as a director at each meeting of shareholders held for the election of directors; (ii) Employee be elected to and continued in the office of President of the Company and such of its subsidiaries as he may select (and such other office, if any, as shall be denominated that of the Chief Executive Officer of the Company or such subsidiary in the Company's or such subsidiary's Bylaws or other constituent instruments); (iii) Employee be elected to and continued on the Board of each subsidiary of the Company, (iv) if the Board of the Company or any of its subsidiaries shall appoint an executive committee (or similar committee authorized to exercise the general powers of the Board), Employee be elected to and continued on such committee; and (v) neither the Company nor any of its subsidiaries shall confer on any other officer or employee authority, responsibility, powers or prerogatives superior or equal to the authority, responsibility, prerogatives and powers vested in Employee hereunder.

2.02 Best Efforts Covenant. Employee will, to the best of his ability, devote his full professional and business time and best efforts to the performance of his duties for the Company and its subsidiaries and affiliates.

2.03 Exclusivity Covenant. During the Agreement's term, Employee will not undertake or engage in any other employment, occupation or business enterprise other than a business enterprise in which Employee does not actively participate. Further, Employee agrees not to acquire, assume, or participate in, directly or indirectly, any position, investment, or interest in the Territory adverse or antagonistic to the Company, its business or prospects, financial or otherwise, or take any action towards any of the foregoing. The provisions of this Section shall not prevent Employee from owning shares of any competitor of the Company so long as such shares (i) do not constitute more than [1%] [5%] of the outstanding equity of such competitor, and (ii) are regularly traded on a recognized exchange or listed for trading by NASDAQ in the over-the-counter market.[2]

2.04 Post-Employment Noncompetition Covenant. Except with the prior written consent of the Board, Employee shall not engage in activities in the Territory either on Employee's own behalf or that of any other business organization, which are in direct or indirect competition with the Company for a period of one (1) year subsequent to Employee's voluntary withdrawal from employment with the Company (except for a termination pursuant to a Change in Control), or the Company's termination of Employee's employment for Cause. Employee and the Company expressly declare that the territorial and time limitations contained in this Section and the definition of "Territory" are entirely reasonable at this time and are properly and necessarily required for the adequate protection of the business and intellectual property of the Company. If such territorial or time limitations, or any portions thereof, are deemed to be unreasonable by a court of competent jurisdiction, whether due to passage of time, change of circumstances or otherwise, Employee and the Company agree to a reduction of said territorial and/or time limitations to such areas and/or periods of time as said court shall deem reasonable.

For a period of one year subsequent to Employee's voluntary withdrawal from employment with the Company (except for a termination pursuant to a Change in Control), or the Company's termination of Employee's employment for Cause, Employee will not without the express prior written approval of the Board (i) directly or indirectly, in one or a series of transactions, recruit, solicit or otherwise induce or influence any proprietor, partner, stockholder, lender, director, officer, employee, sales agent, joint venturer, investor, lessor, supplier, customer, agent, representative or any other person which has a business relationship with the Company or had a business relationship with the Company within the twenty-four-(24) month period preceding the date of the incident in question, to discontinue, reduce, or modify such employment, agency or business relationship with the Company, or (ii) employ or seek to employ or cause any business organization in direct or indirect competition with the Company to employ or seek to employ any person or agent who is then (or was at any time within six months prior to the date the Employee or the competitive business employs or seeks to employ such person) employed or retained by the Company. Notwithstanding the foregoing, nothing herein shall prevent the Employee from providing a letter of recommendation to an employee with respect to a future employment opportunity.

2.05 Confidential Information. Employee recognizes and acknowledges that the Company's trade secrets and proprietary information and know-how, as they may exist from time to time ("Confidential Information"), are valuable, special and unique assets of the Company's business, access to and knowledge of which are essential to the performance of Employee's duties hereunder. Employee will not, during or after the term of his employment by the Company, in whole or in part, disclose such secrets, information or know-how to any Person for any reason or purpose whatsoever, nor shall Employee make use of any such property for his own purposes or for the benefit of any Person (except the Company) under any circumstances during or after the term of his employment, provided that after the term of his employment these restrictions shall not apply to such secrets, information and know-how which are then in the public domain (provided that Employee was not responsible, directly or indirectly, for such secrets, information or processes entering the public domain without the Company's consent). Employee shall have no obligation hereunder to keep confidential any Confidential Information if and to the extent disclosure of any thereof is specifically required by law; provided, however, that in the event disclosure is required by applicable law, the Employee shall provide the Company with prompt notice of such requirement, prior to making any disclosure, so that the Company may seek an appropriate protective order. Employee agrees to hold as the Company's property all memoranda, books, papers, letters, customer lists, processes, computer software, records, financial information, policy and procedure manuals, training and recruiting procedures and other data, and all copies thereof and therefrom, in any way relating to the Company's business and affairs, whether made by him or otherwise coming into his possession, and on termination of his employment, or on demand of the Company at any time, to deliver the same to the Company. Employee agrees that he will not use or disclose to other employees of the Company, during the term of this Agreement, confidential information belonging to his former employers.

Employee shall use his best efforts to prevent the removal of any Confidential Information from the premises of the Company, except as required in his normal course of employment by the Company. Employee shall use his best efforts to cause all persons or entities to whom any Confidential Information shall be disclosed by him hereunder to observe the terms and conditions set forth herein as though each such person or entity was bound hereby.[3]

2.06 Nonsolicitation. Except with the prior written consent of the Board, Employee shall not solicit customers, clients, or employees of the Company or any of its affiliates for a period of twelve (12) months from the date of the expiration of this Agreement. Without limiting the generality of the foregoing, Employee will not willfully canvas, solicit nor accept any such business in competition with the business of the Company from any customers of the Company with whom Employee had contact during, or of which Employee had knowledge solely as a result of, his performance of services for the Company pursuant to this Agreement. Employee will not directly or indirectly request, induce or advise any customers of the Company with whom Employee had contact during the term of this

Agreement to withdraw, curtail or cancel their business with the Company. Employee will not induce or attempt to induce any employee of the Company to terminate his/her employment with the Company.

2.07 Records, Files. All records, files, drawings, documents, equipment and the like relating to the business of the Company which are prepared or used by Employee during the term of his employment under this Agreement shall be and shall remain the sole property of the Company.

2.08 Hired to Invent. Employee agrees that every improvement, invention, process, apparatus, method, design, and any other creation that Employee may invent, discover, conceive, or originate by himself or in conjunction with any other Person during the term of Employee's employment under this Agreement [that relates to the business carried on by the Company during the term of Employee's employment under this Agreement] shall be the exclusive property of the Company. Employee agrees to disclose to the Company every patent application, notice of copyright, or other action taken by Employee or any affiliate or assignee to protect intellectual property during the 12 months following Employee's termination of employment at the Company, for whatever reason, so that the Company may determine whether to assert a claim under this Section or any other provision of this Agreement.

2.09 Equitable Relief. Employee acknowledges that his services to the Company are of a unique character which give them a special value to the Company. Employee further recognizes that violations by Employee of any one or more of the provisions of this Section 2 may give rise to losses or damages for which the Company cannot be reasonably or adequately compensated in an action at law and that such violations may result in irreparable and continuing harm to the Company. Employee agrees that, therefore, in addition to any other remedy which the Company may have at law and equity, including the right to withhold any payment of compensation under Section 4 of this Agreement, the Company shall be entitled to injunctive relief to restrain any violation, actual or threatened, by Employee of the provisions of this Agreement.

3. Compensation

3.01 Minimal Annual Compensation. The Company shall pay to Employee for the services to be rendered hereunder a base salary at an annual rate of [_____] dollars ($_____) ("Minimum Annual Compensation"). There shall be an annual review for merit by the Board and an increase as deemed appropriate to reflect the value of services by Employee. At no time during the term of this Agreement shall Employee's annual base salary fall below Minimum Annual Compensation. In addition, if the Board increases Employee's Minimum Annual Compensation at any time during the term of this Agreement, such increased Minimum Annual Compensation shall become a floor below which Employee's compensation shall not fall at any future time during the term of this Agreement and shall become Minimum Annual Compensation.

Employee's salary shall be payable in periodic installments in accordance with the Company's usual practice for similarly situated employees of the Company.

3.02 Incentive Compensation. In addition to Minimum Annual Compensation, Employee shall be entitled to receive payments under the Company's incentive compensation and/or bonus program(s) (as in effect from time to time), if any, in such amounts as are determined by the Company to be appropriate for similarly situated employees of the Company. Any incentive compensation which is not deductible in the opinion of the Company's counsel, under § 162(m) of the Internal Revenue Code shall be deferred and paid, without interest, in the first year or years when and to the extent such payment may be deducted, Employee's right to such payment being absolute, subject only to the provisions of Section 2.09.

3.03 Participating in Benefits. Employee shall be entitled to all Benefits for as long as such Benefits may remain in effect and/or any substitute or additional Benefits made available in the future to similarly situated employees of the Company, subject to and on a basis consistent with the terms, conditions and overall administration of such Benefits adopted by the Company. Benefits paid to Employee shall not be deemed to be in lieu of other compensation to Employee hereunder as described in this Section 3.

3.04 Specific Benefits.[4]

During the term of this Agreement (and thereafter to the extent this Agreement shall require):

(a) Employee shall be entitled to five (5) weeks of paid vacation time per year, to be taken at times mutually acceptable to the Company and Employee.

(b) The Company shall provide fully paid accident and health insurance for Employee and his family with limits and extent of coverage similar to that provided by Employee's previous employer.

(c) The Company shall obtain at its expense (subject to Employee's insurability) an insurance policy on the life of Employee, subject to the last sentence of this Section 3.04(c), in the face amount of [$0,000,000] that provides it is fully funded after no more than five (5) years of premium payments. Employee shall have the exclusive right to designate the beneficiaries of such policy and change such beneficiaries from time to time. Such policy and the proceeds and cash value thereof shall be the sole property of Employee and the Company shall not retain any benefit therein. [The Company shall not be obligated to pay premiums for such insurance in excess of $15,000 per annum].

(d) Employee shall be entitled to sick leave benefits during the employment period in accordance with the customary policies of the Company for its executive officers, but in no event less than one (1) month per year. [In the event of Employee's Disability, disability insurance shall provide for the payment of Employee's Minimum Annual Compensation for a period of not less than one (1) year from the date of Disability.]

(e) In recognition of the necessity of the use of an automobile to the efficient and expeditious performance of Employee's services, duties and obligations to and on behalf of the Company, the Company shall provide to Employee, at the Company's sole cost and expense, a car to be chosen by Employee with an aggregate leasing cost to the Company of not more than $[ ] per month. In addition thereto, the Company shall bear the expense of insurance, fuel and maintenance therefor.

OR

(e) The Company will provide Employee with a new Company automobile of his choice provided that the cost of such automobile shall not, if purchased, exceed the list price or, if leased, exceed the lease price of a "fully equipped" 2000 Cadillac Seville. In addition, the Company will pay for the insurance, maintenance and monthly garaging expenses of the automobile for one garage, and the expenses of operating the automobile reasonably incurred by him in connection with the business of the Company during the term of this Agreement. Upon the termination of this Agreement for any reason other than termination for Cause, Employee may purchase from the Company or its agent the automobile provided to Employee at that time for the net book value of the automobile at that time.

(f) In addition to the vacation provided pursuant to Section 3.04(a) hereof, Employee shall be entitled to not less than ten (10) paid holidays (other than weekends) per year, generally on such days on which the New York Stock Exchange is closed to trading.

(g) Employee shall be entitled to receive prompt reimbursement for all reasonable expenses incurred by him (in accordance with the policies and procedures established by the Company or the Board for the similarly situated employees of the Company) in performing services hereunder.

OR

(g) Upon submission of travel and expense reports accompanied by proper vouchers, the Company will pay or reimburse Employee for all first class transportation, hotel, living and related expenses incurred by Employee on business trips away from the Company's principal office, and for all other business and entertainment expenses reasonably incurred by him in connection with the business of the Company and its subsidiaries during the term of this Agreement.

(h) The Company shall pay the reasonable costs of preparation, by a professional of Employee's choosing, of Employee's annual and estimated federal income tax and [New York City and State] income tax returns.

(i) The Company shall pay the reasonable costs of Employee's personal financial planning by a professional of Employee's choosing.

(j) Employee shall be eligible to participate during the Employment Period in Benefits not inconsistent or duplicative of those set forth in this Section 3.04 as the Company shall establish or maintain for its employees or executives generally.

4. Termination

4.01 Termination by Company for Other Than Cause. If during the term of this Agreement the Company terminates the employment of Employee and such termination is not for Cause, then, subject to the provisions of Section 2.09, the Company shall pay to Employee an amount equal to the monthly portion of Employee's Minimum Annual Compensation multiplied by the greater of twenty-four (24) or the number of months remaining in the term of this Agreement (the "Severance Period") until such time as Employee shall become reemployed in a position, in the [Borough of Manhattan, City of New York], consistent with Employee's experience and stature. If Employee obtains such a position but Employee's annual compensation shall be less than the Minimum Annual Compensation, then the difference shall be paid to Employee for the balance of the Severance Period. Such difference shall be calculated as follows: The difference between Employee's Minimum Annual Compensation for any year, or lesser period, in which this Agreement would have been in effect and the annualized compensation payable to Employee in his new position during such period shall be payable in the same manner as the Minimum Annual Compensation was paid prior to termination over the period of such reemployment during such period. If the Employee's employment in a new position shall terminate, then for the purposes of this Paragraph 4.01 Employee shall be entitled to continuation of the Minimum Annual Compensation until he shall again become reemployed, in which case only the difference shall be payable as aforesaid, and so on. [If the Employee's employment shall terminate as aforesaid or if the Employee's reemployment in a new position shall terminate, Employee shall use his best efforts to become reemployed as soon as reasonably possible in a position in the [Borough of Manhattan, City of New York] consistent with Employee's experience and stature.

Subject to the provisions of Section 2.09, the Company shall pay to Employee, in one lump sum as soon as practicable, but in no event later than sixty (60) days after the date of such termination, the Minimum Annual Compensation times the number of years, or portions thereof, remaining in the term of the Agreement [and discounted to present value using a capitalization rate of 10%].†

4.02 Constructive Discharge. If the Company fails to reappoint Employee to (or rejects Employee for) the position or positions listed in Section 2.01, fails to comply with the provisions of Section 3, or engages in any other material breach of the terms of this Agreement, Employee may at his option terminate his employment and such termination shall be considered to be a termination of Employee's employment by the Company for reasons other than "Cause."††

4.03 Termination by the Company for Cause. The Company shall have the right to terminate the employment of Employee for Cause. Effective as of the date that the employment of Employee terminates by reason of Cause, this Agreement, except for Sections 2.04 through 2.09, shall terminate and no further payments of the Compensation described in Section 3 (except for such remaining payments of Minimum Annual Compensation under Section 3.01 relating to periods during which Employee was employed by the Company, Benefits which are required by applicable law to be continued, and reimbursement of prior expenses under Section 3.04) shall be made.

4.04 Change in Control. If at any time during the term of this Agreement there is a Change of Control, the Company shall pay to Employee an amount equal to the monthly portion of Employee's Minimum Annual Compensation as in effect on the date Employee's employment terminated multiplied by thirty six (36). This amount shall be paid to Employee in one lump sum as soon as practicable, but in no event later than sixty (60) days, after the date of the Change in Control.

OR

If any time during the term of this Agreement there is a Change of Control and Employee's employment is terminated by the Company for reasons other than "Cause" within the greater of one (1) year following the "Change in Control" or the remaining term of this Agreement, the Company shall pay to Employee an amount equal to the monthly portion of Employee's Minimum Annual Compensation multiplied by thirty-six (36). This amount shall be paid to Employee in one lump sum as soon as practicable, but in no event later than sixty (60) days, after the date that Employee's employment terminated. To the extent that Employee is not fully vested in retirement Benefits from any pension, profit sharing or any other retirement plan or program (whether tax qualified or not) maintained by the Company, the Company shall pay directly to Employee the difference between the amounts which would have been paid to Employee had he been fully vested on the date that his employment terminated and the amounts actually paid or payable to Employee pursuant to such plans or programs.[5]

4.05 Termination on Account of Employee's Death.

(a) In the event of Employee's death during the term of this Agreement:

(1) This Agreement shall terminate except as provided in this Section; and

(2) The Company shall pay to Employee's beneficiary or beneficiaries (or to his estate if he fails to make such designation) an amount equal to the monthly portion of Employee's Minimum Annual Compensation as in effect on the date of his death multiplied by the greater of twenty-four (24) or the number of months which would have otherwise remained in the term of this Agreement had Employee not died. This amount shall be paid in one lump sum as soon as practicable after the date of his death.

(b) Employee may designate one or more beneficiaries for the purposes of this Section by making a written designation and delivering such designation to a Vice President or the Treasurer of the Company. If Employee makes more than one such written designation, the designation last received before Employee's death shall control.

4.06 Termination on Account of Employee's Disability. If Employee ceases to perform services for the Company because he is suffering from a medically determinable disability and is therefore incapable of performing such services, the Company shall continue to pay Employee an amount equal to two-thirds (2/3) of Employee's Minimum Annual Compensation as in effect on the date of Employee's cessation of services by reason of disability less any amounts paid to Employee as Workers Compensation, Social Security Disability benefits (or any other disability benefits paid to Employee as federal, state, or local disability benefits) and any amounts paid to Employee as disability payments under any disability plan or program for a period ending on the earlier of: (a) the date that Employee again becomes employed in a significant manner and on a substantially full-time basis; (b) the date that Employee attains normal retirement age, as such age is defined in a retirement plan maintained by the Company; or (c) Employee begins to receive retirement benefits from a retirement plan maintained by the Company.[6]

OR

4.06 Disability. If Employee shall sustain a Disability and be unable to perform his duties and responsibilities during the term of this Agreement, as shall have been certified by at least two (2) duly licensed and qualified physicians, one (1) approved by the Board of Directors of the Company and one (1) approved by Employee (the "Examining Physicians"), the Company shall continue to pay to Employee while such Disability continues the full amount of his Minimum Annual Compensation for the one-year period next succeeding the date upon which such Disability shall have been so certified. Thereafter, if Employee's Disability shall continue (as evidenced by the continued absence of Employee from his duties and by the certification of the Examining Physicians), the employment of Employee under this Agreement shall terminate and all obligations of Employee shall cease and Employee shall be entitled to receive only the Benefits, if any, as may be provided by any insurance to which he may have become entitled pursuant to Section 3.04 and the payment of any amounts then remaining to be paid under Section 4.01 and in such event the Company shall have no right to repurchase any shares of the Company's common stock as provided in Section 6. "Disability" means the complete and total disability of Employee resulting from injury, sickness, disease, or infirmity due to age, whereby Employee is unable to perform his usual services for the Company.[7]

5. Stock Options

5.01 Amount of Stock. In accordance with the provisions of the Company's _____ Incentive Stock Option Plan (the "Plan") and the specific authorization of the Board, the Company hereby grants to Employee, subject to all of the terms and conditions of the Plan and this Agreement, an option to acquire _____ shares of the Company's outstanding common stock ("Option Stock").

5.02 Vesting. The Option to acquire the Option Stock granted in Section 5.01 shall vest in _____ (__) equal, consecutive monthly increments of _____ shares each on the first day of each month beginning with April of 2000 and ending with September of 2004. Notwithstanding anything to the contrary contained in this Agreement, all Options to acquire Option Stock shall irrevocably vest thirty (30) calendar days prior to the scheduled consummation of a Change of Control.

5.03 Tax Changes. If any change(s) in the Federal income tax laws materially affect the tax treatment of Employee with respect to the Option or the Option Stock, the parties agree to negotiate in good faith to reach an agreement which will take advantage of, or minimize the disadvantages of, such changes.

6. Restricted Stock

6.01 Purchase of Restricted Stock; Section 83(b) Election. Employee shall, and does hereby, purchase and the Company shall, and does hereby, sell [ ] shares (the "shares") of Restricted Stock to Employee at $___ per share. Employee shall not file an election pursuant to § 83(b) of the Internal Revenue Code of 1954, as amended, unless Employee has agreed to an arrangement reasonably satisfactory to the Company to withhold sufficient amounts from Employee's compensation to enable the Company to deduct for federal tax purposes all compensation recognized by Employee. The Company is herewith paying Employee a bonus in the amount of $___, less withholding tax thereon, which net amount shall enable Employee to acquire the Restricted Stock.

For alternative language on the § 83(b) issue, consider:

6.01(a) Indemnification. Employee represents that he will file an election pursuant to § 83(b) of the Internal Revenue Code in connection with the purchase by Employee of the Shares. The parties agree that the value of the Shares is equal to the purchase price paid by Employee, and Employee will prepare his income tax returns to reflect such value of the Shares. If the value of the Shares at the time of their sale to Employee shall be redetermined for federal, state, or local income tax purposes to be higher than the purchase price paid by Employee, the Company shall upon demand pay Employee a bonus in an aggregate amount equal to the sum of: (i) an amount which, when multiplied by the difference between Employee's Tax Rate (as hereinafter defined) for the year in which such amount shall be payable to Employee and 100%, shall equal the additional income tax owing as result of such redetermination; and (ii) an amount which when multiplied by the difference between Employee's Tax Rate for the year in which such amount shall be payable to Employee and 100% shall equal the interest and penalties, if any, payable by Employee with respect to such redetermination. The term "Tax Rate" shall mean the sum of the following: (i) the highest federal income tax rate applicable to ordinary income of an individual taxpayer and (ii) the sum of the highest state and local tax rates for such ordinary income, multiplied by such federal tax rate. Employee shall give the Company notice of any proposed redetermination, but Employee shall be under no obligation to contest such proposed redetermination; provided, however, that Employee shall contest such proposed redetermination if requested to do so by the Company and at the sole cost and expense of the

Company. It is the intention of this Section 6.01 (a) to reimburse Employee for any additional income taxes (based upon the rates in effect for 2000), interest and penalties thereon arising from a redetermination of the value of Shares sold to Employee and for any tax on such reimbursement based upon tax rates in effect for the year of such reimbursement. The provisions of this Section 6.01 shall survive the termination of this Agreement for any reason whatsoever.

6.02 Right of Company of Repurchase Shares upon Death, Disability or Voluntary Termination of Employees.†††

(a) Call Option. If Employee shall at any time prior to the third anniversary of this Agreement voluntarily leave the employ of the Company for any reason whatsoever, or be terminated for Cause, the Company shall have the right and option (the "Call Option") to purchase any or all of the Shares from Employee at a price per Share equal to Fair Value (as defined below).

(b) Exercise of Call Option and Closing. The Company may exercise the Call Option by delivering to Employee written notice of exercise within 90 days after the termination of the employment of Employee giving rise to the Call Option. Such notice shall specify the number of Shares to be purchased. If and to the extent the Call Option is not so exercised within such 90-day period, the Call Option shall automatically expire and terminate effective upon the expiration of such 90-day period. Within 10 days after his receipt of the Company's notice of the exercise of the Call Option, Employee shall tender to the Company at its principal offices the certificate or certificates representing the Shares which the Company has elected to purchase, duly endorsed in blank by Employee or with duly endorsed stock powers attached thereto, all in form suitable for the transfer of such Shares to the Company.

Upon its receipt of such Shares, the Company shall deliver to Employee a check in the amount of the Fair Value of a Share multiplied by the number of Shares being purchased. The purchase price may be payable, at the option of the Company, in cancellation of all or a portion of any outstanding indebtedness of Employee to the Company or in cash (by bank or cashier's check) or both.

(c) No Stockholder Rights. After the time at which any Shares are required to be delivered to the Company for transfer to the Company pursuant to paragraph (b) above, the Company shall not pay any dividend to Employee on account of such Shares or permit Employee to exercise any of the privileges or rights of a stockholder with respect to such Shares, but shall, insofar as permitted by law, treat the Company as the owner of such Shares.

(d) Fair Value. For purposes of this Agreement, the Fair Value of a Share of Common Stock of the Company, as of any date by the Board of Directors, is as follows: if market quotations are readily available, a Share shall be valued at the last trade on the exchange on which such Shares are primarily traded or, if not traded on an exchange, at the closing bid price (or average of bid prices) last quoted by an established over-the-counter quotation service. If the Shares are not publicly traded, then a Share shall be valued by the Board of Directors, after considering all pertinent factors and all appropriate information and data, including liquidity; without limiting the generality of the foregoing, the Board of Directors shall consider and take into account published guidelines, including those sponsored by the National Venture Capital Association or any committee thereof. The Board of Directors may employ outside experts and independent consultants at the expense of the Company to assist in the valuation process; provided, however, that notwithstanding the above calculation, in no event will Fair Value of a Share of Common Stock be less than the par value of such Share.

6.03 Right of Employee to Sell Shares to the Company upon Death, Disability, or Involuntary Termination Without Cause.

(a) Put Option. If Employee at any time prior to the date three (3) years from the date of this Agreement shall die, become Disabled, or be terminated without Cause, Employee shall have the right and option (the "Put Option") to sell any or all of the Shares to the Company at a price per Share equal to Fair Value (as defined in Section 6.02(d) above).

(b) Exercise of Put Option and Closing. Employee may exercise the Put Option by delivering to the Company written notice of exercise within sixty days after the termination of the employment of Employee giving rise to the Put Option as set forth in Section 6.03(a) above. Such notice shall specify the number of Shares to be sold. If and to the extent the Put Option is not so exercised within such sixty-day period, the Put option shall automatically expire and terminate effective upon the expiration of such sixty days period. At the time of delivery of notice of the exercise of the Put Option, Employee shall tender to the Company at its principal offices the certificate or certificates representing the Shares which the Company is obligated to purchase, duly endorsed in blank by Employee or with duly endorsed stock powers attached thereto, all in form suitable for the transfer of such Shares to the Company.

Within ten (10) days of its receipt of the notice and such Shares, the Company shall deliver to Employee a check in the amount of the Fair Value of a Share multiplied by the number of Shares being sold. The purchase price may be payable, at the option of the Company, in cancellation of all or a portion of any outstanding indebtedness of Employee to the Company or in cash (by bank or cashier's check) or both.

(c) Right of Company to Delay Payment. If at any time the Company is unable to repurchase Shares pursuant to the provisions of this Section 6 or if it is determined by the Board of Directors of the Company in their good-faith judgment that the payment of the entire purchase price of such Shares pursuant to this Section 6 would be deleterious to the financial position of the Company, the Company may elect to defer payment of all or a portion of such purchase price (but not any amounts then payable by the cancellation of outstanding indebtedness of Employee to the Company). Such deferred portion of the purchase price shall thereafter be payable in five (5) equal annual installments beginning on the date on which such purchase price was to be paid but for the effect of this paragraph (c). The outstanding amount of such installments shall bear interest at a floating rate equal to 2% per annum plus the base rate announced from time to time by the [New York, New York office of Citibank, N.A.] as its base rate for commercial loans, and such interest shall be payable annually in arrears on each date that an installment of principal is owing. The Company may prepay its obligations under this paragraph (c) in whole or in part at any time, with such prepayments being applied first to interest accrued but unpaid to the date of such prepayment and thereafter to installments of principal in inverse order of their maturity. For so long as any interest or principal remains owing under this paragraph (c), the Company shall not make any distribution or dividend to the holders of its Common Stock.

6.04 Agreements Relating to Common Stock.

(a) No Issuances of Common Stock. The Company hereby represents that as of the date of this Agreement there are [ ] shares of Common Stock outstanding (including the Shares). The Company agrees that, pursuant to a Shareholders Agreement to be executed among Employee, the Company, and the Company's other stockholders, the Company will covenant with Employee that for so long as Employee owns any Shares, no additional shares of Common Stock or any voting securities of the Company or any security of the Company convertible into or exchangeable for Common Stock or other voting securities will be issued without the prior written consent of Employee.

(b) Termination of Call Option and Put Option. The Call Option and the Put Option shall terminate upon the closing of a sale of Common Stock registered pursuant to the Securities Act of 1933, as amended.

6.05 Restrictions on Transfer. Except as otherwise provided in this Section 6.05, Employee shall not, during the term of the Call Option, sell, assign, transfer, pledge, hypothecate or otherwise dispose of, by operation of law or otherwise (collectively "transfer"), any of the Shares, or any interest therein, unless and until such Shares are no longer subject to the Call Option. Notwithstanding the foregoing, Employee may transfer Shares to or for the benefit of any parent, parent-in-law, spouse, child, son-in-law, daughter-in-law or grandchild, or to a trust for their benefit; *provided* that such Shares shall remain subject to the provisions of this Agreement (including without limitation the restrictions on transfer set forth in this Section 6.05 and the Call Option and such permitted transferee shall, as a condition to such transfer, deliver to the Company a written instrument confirming that such transferee shall be so bound by all of such terms and conditions.

The Company shall not be required (i) to transfer on its books any of the Shares which shall have been sold or transferred in violation of any of the provisions set forth in this Agreement, or (ii) to treat as owner of such Shares or to pay dividends to any transferee to whom any such Shares shall have been sold or transferred.

6.06 Adjustments for Stock Splits, Stock Dividends, etc. If from time to time during the term of the Call Option or the Put Option, there is any stock split-up, stock dividend, stock distribution or other reclassification of the Common Stock of the Company, any and all new, substituted or additional securities to which Employee is entitled by reason of his ownership of the Shares shall be immediately subject to the Call Option and the Put Option, the restrictions on transfer and other provisions of this Section in the same manner and to the same extent as the Shares, and the Option Price and the exercise price for the Call Option and the Put Option shall be appropriately adjusted.

7. Miscellaneous

7.01 Assignment. This Agreement and the rights and obligations of the parties hereto shall bind and inure to the benefit of each of the parties hereto and shall also bind and inure to the benefit of any successor or successors of the Company in a reorganization, merger or consolidation and any assignee of all or substantially all of the Company's business and properties, but, except as to any such successor of the Company, neither this Agreement nor any rights or benefits hereunder may be assigned by the Company or Employee.

7.02 [Initial Term and Extensions. Except as otherwise provided, the term of this Agreement shall be three (3) years commencing with the effective date hereof. On the third anniversary of the effective date, and on each subsequent annual anniversary of the effective date thereafter, the Agreement shall be automatically extended for an additional year unless either party notifies the other in writing more than 90 days prior to the relevant anniversary date that the Agreement is no longer to be extended.][8]

7.03 Governing Law. This Agreement shall be construed in accordance with and governed for all purposes by the laws of the State of [New York].

7.04 Interpretation. In case any one or more of the provisions contained in this Agreement shall, for any reason, be held to be invalid, illegal or unenforceable in any respect, such invalidity, illegality or unenforceability shall not affect any other provisions of this Agreement, but this Agreement shall be construed as if such invalid, illegal or unenforceable provision had never been contained herein.

7.05 Notice. Any notice required or permitted to be given hereunder shall be effective when received and shall be sufficient if in writing and if personally delivered or sent by prepaid cable, telex or registered air mail, return receipt requested, to the party to receive such notice at its address set forth at the end of this Agreement or at such other address as a party may by notice specify to the other.

7.06 Amendment and Waiver. This Agreement may not be amended, supplemented or waived except by a writing signed by the party against which such amendment or waiver is to be enforced. The waiver by any party of a breach of any provision of this Agreement shall not operate to, or be construed as a waiver of, any other breach of that provision nor as a waiver of any breach of another provision.

7.07 Binding Effect. Subject to the provisions of Section 4 hereof, this Agreement shall be binding on the successors and assigns of the parties hereto.

All obligations of Employee with respect to any Shares covered by this Agreement shall, as the context requires, bind Employee's spouse and the divorce or death of such spouse shall not vitiate the binding nature of such obligation.

7.08 Survival of Rights and Obligations. All rights and obligations of Employee or the Company arising during the term of this Agreement shall continue to have full force and effect after the termination of this Agreement unless otherwise provided herein.

The Company

By_____

_____

Employee

_____

Spouse

[1] Most employment contracts, including those entered into by start-up firms, retain the concept of discharge for cause. It is seldom used in practice, however, because it is believed difficult, to the point of futility, for an employer to prove cause in all but the most grievous cases, for example, conviction of a felony or chronic alcoholism. "Cause" does, of course, include breach by the employee of the employment relationship, which guides this discussion into the issue of termination.

[2] Many desirable scientists are able (or willing) to work only part-time; they may want to retain their university affiliations to the extent possible and it may be in the best interests of the company that they do so. However, when allowing an employee to pursue outside interests, one must be cognizant of the consequences of that election on the employer's claims on inventions. If the individual is a consultant or independent contractor, it is harder to enforce a senior claim to the fruits of his inventive efforts. See Bartlett, Venture Capital: Law, Business Strategies, and Investment Planning, Ch. 16, §§ 16.7-16.9 (John Wiley & Sons, 1988).

[3] As if departing employees do not have enough trouble, they now have to cope (at least theoretically) with the Economic Espionage Act of 1996 (Pub. L. No. 104-294, 110 Stat. 3488 (1996)), which imposes criminal penalties for the theft of trade secrets. So far, the prosecutions have concerned faithless agents who were paid in fact to steal trade secrets. But the language of the Act is quite broad and could be construed as applicable to a departing employee who takes the trade secret to his new employer. The US. attorney general has recognized the potential danger of criminalizing the law of trade secrets and has insisted that her office specifically approve all prosecutions under the Act. Whether that leniency will apply if the employee winds up in the employ of a foreign (e.g., Chinese) competitor is open to question. See Reisner, Criminal Prosecution of Trade Secret Theft, N.Y.L.J. page 1 (Mar. 30, 1998).

[4] After the employee's salary and duties have been settled, counsel may tend to relax, passing over the sections on fringe benefits as routine. However, some "fringe benefits" can be quite expensive-medical and retirement plans, for example- particularly if the deductibility of the company's payments depends, under the Code, on compliance with a series of quite detailed requirements, including provisions calculated to ensure the benefits are extended in a nondiscriminating manner to most employees. See generally, on this issue, I.R.C. § 105(h)(medical plans) and, with respect to pension and profit-sharing Programs, I.R.C. §§ 401 (a)(3), 401 (a)(4), 401 (a)(5), and 410(b)(1). The onerous requirements are summarized in Buoymaster & Frank, Employee Benefit Plans, in Harroch, Start-Up Companies: Planning, Financing and Operating the Successful Business § 14.03 (1986). If the employee has the right to certain medical or retirement benefits, the company may find itself with a Hobson's Choice: either fund a special plan for the employee paid in after-tax dollars or increase everyone's benefits.

For mature corporations with resources to devote to the project, administering employee benefits can become an enormously complicated and sophisticated process, with full-time staff concentrating year round on the issues and paid consultants brought in to help make peer group surveys and provide notions on the state of the art. Start-ups ordinarily involve more primitive packages. For example, with the survival of the company in doubt during its early years, it is unlikely that much emphasis will be placed on retirement income and pension benefits. Nor will sophisticated side-benefits-below-market-rate loans, financial-consulting services, health clubs, and the like-be in the typical package. To the extent side benefits are involved, they will often have to do with the costs of housing and relocation, particularly for executives transferring to high-cost areas, such as Boston and San Francisco. On the other hand, life insurance on the lives of key employees is often taken out, but payable to the company in order to give the investors some opportunity to recoup their investment in the event the death of a critical officer, such as the founder, takes the company down with him. The proceeds of "key man" insurance, as it is called, may either be payable to the company's treasury and consumed in order to carry it over the rough spots caused by the founder's death, or rerouted, through some sort of trust device, to the repayment of investor debt or even the repurchase of stock. Query whether, even though the proceeds are paid to a trust which ostensibly exists outside the company's four walls, the issuer will have the power to redeem stock at a time when the company is shaky or whether the proceeds may nonetheless be viewed as "property of the debtor" under the Bankruptcy Code.

[5] In the Stock Purchase Agreement, the investors may believe they had dealt with the control question. The board is legally in charge of the company's affairs and the investors had paid for control of the board. They can become surprised and angry when they learn that, through the introduction of employment agreements, they have to pay for control a second time, buying out employment agreements.

[6] The discussion so far has proceeded on the theory that it is relatively clear whether the employee has voluntarily terminated his employment contract or has been involuntarily terminated -fired. There are interstitial issues that should be resolved, for example, if the employee dies or is disabled. Outside of the world of Agatha Christie, death is rarely an ambiguous event; the employee is dead or he is not. "Disability" is a more slippery concept. If the term is left undefined, it is open for the company to attempt to cut loose a given employee by alleging disability when none exists. On the other hand, impaired employees often have the ability to pull themselves together when the question of disability is being considered in a courtroom, particularly alcoholics and (now unfortunately) drug users. The typical provision on disability gives a period of time-three to six months-during which the employee is retained on the theory that the disability is (or may be, at least) temporary. At the conclusion of that period, the contract language often refers to medical advice, a doctor's certificate from the employee (or, if there is a dispute, an examination by a physician employed by the parties) that settles the issue of disability. It is interesting to note that, in the bargaining process, most key employees are concerned at giving the company untrammeled power to claim the employee is disabled if that conclusion enables the company to terminate the employment relationship without paying any of the penalties provided when the relationship is terminated in "breach" of the contract. The obvious contrast is to terminations in the public sector, where the terms of the collective

bargaining agreement and civil service regulations are such that many employees compete furiously for a holding that they are "disabled," enabling them to retire on a generous stipend.

If the employment relationship is terminated by death or disability, the norm is to provide that the equity emoluments vest (if the employee owns a large amount of stock, it may be necessary to recapture some portion in the event of his death in order to award the same to his successor); disability insurance proceeds are paid to the disabled employee; life insurance (to the extent not assigned to the company) is paid to the decedent's estate. There is on occasion a "put" in favor of the estate, entailing an obligation on the part of the company to buy back the equity interest at fair value so as to make the estate liquid. In the case of disability, some sort of salary continuation is often provided, to supplement or replace disability insurance for a period of time.

[7] One planning issue concerns whether to integrate the company's disability payments with Social Security insurance proceeds. The question presents issues well beyond the scope of the Text. The IRS's founding positions are set forth in Rev. Rul. 69-5, 1969-1 C.B. 125.

[8] Despite the general rule that all agreements should specify a term, this provision is not necessary. The contract may, and often does, states that either party can terminate at any time, on 30 days notice subject to certain specified consequences if an employee demands a "three-year" contract, that means either (i) he is promised a salary from, say, January 1, 2004, through December 31, 2006, meaning that the employee is contractually guaranteed a salary over an ever-decreasing amount of time; as of, say, October 1996, the salary protection has shrunk to a matter of months; or (ii) alternatively, a "three-year" contract means that the employee is hired on January 1, 1994, and is entitled to what amounts to three years' severance pay whenever he is terminated other than for cause or by his voluntary act. The employer, in effect, has issued an "evergreen" promise to pay him three years' salary regardless of when termination occurs, the day after he is employed or 10 years after. When considering the merits of each scenario, one has to go back to the point that the employment arrangement centers around the cost of buying out the employee's contract. With an evergreen provision, that cost is constant. Employment for a fixed term, on the other hand, makes it easier for the employee to be fired the longer he is with the company and thus fails to give the employee a fixed level of protection. Therefore, a multiyear employment contract usually refers to the evergreen arrangement; strictly speaking, the employee is terminable at will, subject to the severance arrangement. Assuming that the parties' minds have met on the term of the severance, the remaining issues concern price-what events give rise to the obligation of one or the other parties to pay a penalty, and in what amount?

†Note on Cause

Most employment contracts, including those entered into by start-up firms, retain the concept of discharge for cause. It is seldom used in practice, however, because it is believed difficult, to the point of futility, for an employer to prove cause in all but the most grievous cases, for example, conviction of a felony or chronic alcoholism. "Cause" does, of course, include breach by the employee of the employment relationship, which guides this discussion into the issue of termination.

Note on Severance

An employment contract reads as if Mr. Smith is being promised a long-term position with Start-up, Inc., for an annual salary plus, perhaps, equity in the firm, in consideration of Smith's promise to perform as, say, CEO for five years. Neither promise, however, is exactly what it seems. Realistically, Start-up's board of directors is saying to Smith, "If we want to fire you, we will pay you X dollars for your equity and Y dollars to buy out the remainder of your contract."[1] Smith is saying to Start-up, "If I decide to quit, you can get some of your stock back for nothing and the rest for Z dollars, plus a restraint to keep me out of your business for, say, one year."

The contract, in other words, is like a prenuptial agreement. As long as the parties are happily married, no one reads the document; the principal issues have to do with the payoff numbers when divorce ensues—what are the partners' remedies in the case of breach? Professor Harold Shepherd at Stanford Law School used to divide his course offerings on the law of contracts into two distinct sections: one having to do with the formulation of the agreement and its administration and the second, which he labeled "Remedies," having to do with the rights of the parties in the event of breach.[2] Employment agreements, because they are not specifically enforceable in the sense of requiring the parties to remain married,[3] become interesting when they fall into Shepherd's latter category: what to do in the case of breach.

This discussion started with a proposition that equitable relief is not generally available to compel a firm to continue to employ a given individual (versus paying his salary) for the agreed-upon period or to compel that individual to continue to report for duty at the firm. However, there are indirect ways of achieving that result, by working with the concept of damages. Thus, if an employment contract were to provide that, upon the early termination of a given employee, damages in the millions of dollars would be payable by the firm, that employee, in effect, would enjoy an insured lifetime position because he would be too expensive to fire. Alternatively, if an employee wishing to quit were faced with a provision in his contract that imposed on him an enormous penalty, then he (if able to respond in damages) would be indentured to the firm for the same reason. In fact, except in large public companies (where a multimillion award to a departing CEO may be immaterial to the annual financial results of the firm), huge penalty buyout provisions are uncommon. A start-up cannot afford to be locked into a seven-figure settlement amount for dismissing an individual. A typical provision contemplates that the employee will be paid the balance of his salary, either in a lump sum on a discounted basis or during the balance of the period remaining in the contract. And, from the company's perspective, while the employee's flight may in fact imperil enormous investments, it is questionable whether a court would enforce a huge liquidated damage provision against the employee.[4]

One of the principal reasons for stating the measure of damages is that the parties can, as they should, agree explicitly on the sticky issue of the employee's duty of "mitigation." If the contract is silent, it is not clear whether a given court will (or will not) find the terminated employee has an obligation to mitigate the employer's damages by finding other employment, setting off the employee's new salary against the employer's obligation to pay the old.[5] A duty to mitigate damages, whether express or implicit, includes subsidiary issues: What kind of position is the employee obligated to take? How much effort must he devote to looking for a new job? Where can he be required to take a job? In another city? When the issue is squarely addressed in a contract (as it should be), the possibilities to be covered in the drafting are lengthy. In addition to the ones mentioned, what if the employee elects, after termination, to manage his investments? If mitigation is contemplated, should the income from those investments be counted as if it were a salary? What if he is able to resell his vested equity in his old firm at a profit and then finds himself investing the proceeds in a new start-up, serving as chairman of the board of directors? Do director's fees count as salary, particularly if the former employee is devoting most of his time to the new company? The terminated founders of start-up companies are often young men who have *interesting business careers in front of them, albeit not of the conventional kind. It is tricky, therefore, to forecast all the kinds of income that should count against the obligation of their former company.

An extended payout to a terminated employee can give rise to another subsidiary issue. The employee is at risk if the start-up seeks some form of relief under the bankruptcy laws; he will bargain, therefore, for security and, failing that, the right to continue to receive financial reports concerning the solvency of his former firm, the former firm in turn being unwilling to give out any information to somebody whose loyalty is no longer reliable.

Another problem on termination, not cosmic but irritating, has to do with the continuation of certain fringe benefits. If the founder has been fired, it is usually agreed that only his base salary continues until the term expires. He no longer accrues any equity emoluments and bonuses are off the horizon. However, the outgoing employee may find it hard to equal the various benefits, such as medical and group life; the expense of obtaining that coverage independently can be quite substantial, particularly since corporations continue to be favored by the tax laws in this regard. The inclination of a firm to continue a fired employee in a group plan must be tempered by examination of the plan's eligibility requirements-is a former employee still an "employee" just because he is still being paid something?[6]

[1] This view is criticized by some commentators as unduly harsh on the employee because it gives the investors a "valuable option," the right to freeze out the founder/key employee upon the payment of money. Nusbaum & Weltman, employment Agreements, in Harroch, Start-Up Companies: Planning, Financing and Operating the Successful Business § 11.02[7] (1986) [hereinafter Nusbaum & Weltman]. Although the holdings are few and far between, a court adopting the partnership view of closely held corporations might restrain the recapture of the employee's equity. See the authorities collected in 1 O'Neal & Thompson, O'Neal's Oppression of Minority Shareholders Ch. 3 (2d ed. 1975).

[2] Long-term employment contracts, once viewed by the courts with suspicion, (see O'Neal, Close Corporations §§ 6.06-6.08 (1986)), are now generally deemed valid, the current exception being a result of the popular attack on "golden parachutes," severance pay agreements in publicly held companies for managers replaced as a result of a hostile takeover. Popular displeasure has been expressed in the Internal Revenue Code, which applies a penalty to "parachutes" in excess of three years' salary. I.R.C. § 280G.

[3] *Williston, Contracts § 1423A (3d ed. 1968).*

[4] *Nusbaum & Weltman, § 11.02(8), n.69. If no liquidated damage amount is set, most courts will stick to compensating the employer for the cost of hiring a replacement; there is authority for the proposition that damages may include lost profits. Id. at n.67.*

[5] *For the view that there is a duty to mitigate, see Nusbaum & Weltman § 20.02.*

[6] *The criteria are set out in Treas. Reg. 1.401-1(b)(4).*

††Note on Constructive Discharge

Absent an agreement to the contrary, the law contemplates that the board and/or its delegate, the CEO, tells the employee what to do. Under principles which were developed in an age when this branch of the law was labeled "master and servant," the employee is bound to follow lawful instructions or give up his job. Theoretically, an employment contract could confirm the ancient power relationship. Smith will do whatever Start-up, Inc. wants, wherever it wants the service to be performed, as long as Smith is paid $100,000 a year. In fact, however, such is not the typical case, at least in the case of key employees. Smith, if he is at all in demand, will want to specify in the agreement where he is to work and what duties and responsibilities he is to undertake-for example, chief financial officer and only chief financial officer. A clever board may in the future attempt to compel Smith to quit by demeaning him in subtle and not so subtle ways (taking away his support, bypassing him on important decisions, moving him to a smaller office, giving him routine, irksome tasks). This gambit involves the doctrine of constructive discharge[1] and raises significant drafting points. How specific should one write the clause denoting the scope of the employee's duties? Is it "petty" for the employee to insist on the use of a car, specific types of medical insurance, precise reporting channels?

For more specific language on this subject, consider the following:

Constructive Discharge

"Change in Duties" shall mean the occurrence, on the date upon which a Change in Control occurs or within two years thereafter, of any one or more of the following:

- *A significant reduction in the nature or scope of Executive's authorities or duties from those applicable to Executive immediately prior to the date on which a Change in Control occurs;*
- *A reduction in Executive's annual base salary or target opportunity under any applicable bonus or incentive compensation plan or arrangement from that provided to Executive immediately prior to the date on which a Change in Control occurs;*
- *A diminution in Executive's eligibility to participate in bonus, stock option, incentive award and other compensation plans which provide opportunities to receive compensation which are the greater of (A) the opportunities provided by the Company (including its subsidiaries) for*

executives with comparable duties or (B) the opportunities under any such plans under which Executive was participating immediately prior to the date on which a Change in Control occurs;

- *A diminution in employee benefits (including but not limited to medical, dental, life insurance, and long-term disability plans) and perquisites applicable to Executive from the greater of (A the employee benefits and perquisites provided by the Company (including its subsidiaries) to executives with comparable duties or (B) the employee benefits and perquisites to which Executive was entitled immediately prior to the date on which a Change in Control occurs; or*

- *A change in the location of Executive's principal place of employment by the Company by more than 50 miles from the location where Executive was principally employed immediately prior to the date on which a Change in Control occurs.*

[1] *Nusbaum & Weltman, § 20.02, n.2.*

†† **Note on Recall of Unvested Equity**

Often the most potent penalty imposed on a footloose employee is the recapture of nonvested equity, either options or cheap stock. If the draftsman employed by the company has kept the main chance in view, he will recall that the object of an employment agreement is multifaceted: to stimulate the employee's current performance and to keep out of his head visions of sugar plums dangled by competing firms. If valuable equity can be recaptured at a penalty price when the employee quits,[1] the term "golden handcuff" becomes apt. It is awkward to provide that the employee who terminates before his promised time has to pay a cash penalty back to the company; he usually does not have the resources to spare and it is more trouble than it is worth to the company to chase him for some sort of cash "cough-up," even though the injury to the investors may be substantial. On the other hand, the vanishing employee may cause the investors to lose their entire investment, perhaps running into millions. The better weapon used to avoid that unhappy result, therefore, is to string out the vesting of equity incentives as long as possible and to provide for forfeiture in the case of the employee's breach. It goes without saying that the employee's power to assign shares subject to forfeiture must be openly and notoriously restricted; otherwise, the possibility of forfeiture could be neutralized by a transfer to a bona fide purchaser whose lack of knowledge cuts off the forfeiture restraint. Further, it is customary to distinguish the level of equity recapture, depending on the occasion. If, as the earlier discussion assumes, the employee quits voluntarily-in the worst case, to join a competing firm-or is fired for cause, then the most severe recapture is called for. If the employee is fired for reasons other than cause, or dies, then either no provision is made or a modified quantum of nonvested stock is affected.

As a planning point, it may be useful to consider allocating the consideration to be paid to a departing employee among payments which do not generate tax deductions (for example, the repurchase of stock) and those that do, for example, consulting arrangements and covenants not to compete.

Employers must exercise caution in recapturing stock from employees in light of the Seventh Circuit, decision in Jordan v. Duff & Phelps.[2] *In that case, the employee held restricted stock pursuant to an agreement that it would be recaptured by the employer when the employee resigned.*[3] *The employee resigned, and the employer purchased the employee's stock. The employee, however subsequently claimed that the employer had a duty of disclosure. In fact, the employer was then in merger negotiations which proved to be favorable to the remaining stockholders. The employee was successful in seeking to rescind, based on the failure of the employer to make a disclosure which, the employee argued, would have caused him to reconsider the question whether he should resign or not.*

A recurring question in start-up companies, particularly those using restricted stock as a currency with which to pay employees, is whether the employer may manipulate the employee's term of employment so as to defeat the vesting of restricted stock or the exercise of stock options.[4] *The trick is, from the employer's point of view, to tie the recapture to an objectively verifiable event termination regardless of the reason. The issue will still remain, however, in liberal jurisdictions like California whether the employee's termination on the eve of vesting must be justified.*[5]

[1]*Historically, the law has not favored contractual provisions labeled as "penalties." However, the courts have generally upheld provisions recapturing an employee's cheap stock or options at cost, even though value is then well in excess of that figure. See, e.g., Allen v. Biltmore Tissue Corp., 2 N.Y.2d 534, 141 N.E.2d 812, 161 N.Y.S.2d 418 (1957).*

[2] *See Jordan v. Duff & Phelps, Inc., [1987 Transfer Binder] Fed. Sec. L. Rep. (CCH) 93,196 (7th Cir. 1987).*

[3] *Id. The case involved the acquisition of a closely held corporation by a publicly held corporation. When the employer resigned, the applicable agreement required the employee to sell his shares back to the closely held corporation at a price based on adjusted book value.*

[4] *The N.Y. Court of Appeals, applying literally the doctrine of employment-at-will, held that: "no duty of loyalty and good faith akin to that between partners, precluding termination except for cause, arises among those operating a business in the corporate form who have only the rights, duties and obligations of stockholders and not those of partners." Ingle v. Glamore Motor Sales, Inc., 73 N.Y.2d 183, 538 N.Y.S.2d 771, 535 N.E. 2d (1989); see also Ingle v. Glamore Motor Sales Co., 21 Sec. Reg. & L. Rep. (BNA) 392, 140 A.D.2d 493, 528 N.Y.S.2d 602 (1988). See Gallagher v. Lambert, 20 Sec. Reg. & L. Rep. (BNA) 1485 (Mar. 10, 1989), which considered the situation of an officer of Eastdil Realty who had entered into an agreement pursuant to which his stock was to be tendered to Eastdil at a penalty price unless he lasted in Eastdil's employment for a specified period of time. Twenty-one days before his stock would have vested, Eastdil fired him. Even though the circumstances of the firing appear to be suspicious, the court, despite a vigorous dissent, hewed to the letter of the agreement. There are special facts in the Ingle case which may distinguish it from cases to follow. However, the language in the court's opinion indicates that minority shareholders are not being treated as "partners" and that New York is not, to this extent, following the suggestion in the Massachusetts line of cases starting with Donohue v. Rodd Electrotype Co., 367 Mass. 578,*

328 N.E.2d 505 (1975), and Wilkes v. Springside Nursing Home, Inc., 370 Mass. 842, 353 N.E.2d 657 (1976).

[5]*See cases collected in Benton & Gunderson, Employee Stock Purchase Agreement, in 1 Halloran et al., Venture Capital and Public Offering Negotiation § 12.1 (2d ed.).*

20

Model Confidentiality and Non-Competition Agreement

Non-disclosure Agreements in Venture Capital Transactions

Occasionally a venture fund will receive a request from a potential portfolio company for the venture fund to sign a non-disclosure agreement prior to commencement of due diligence. The proposed non-disclosure agreement would commit the venture fund to maintaining the confidentiality of the company's information disclosed to the venture fund in the course of the due diligence investigation. Entering into non-disclosure agreements could restrict the future investing and disclosing activities of the venture fund or its principals.

Industry Custom

It is well established that for an initial meeting with a venture fund, a company seeking funding should not make any request for the venture fund to sign a non-disclosure agreement. Requesting a non-disclosure agreement for these meetings indicates that the company's technology is very weakly protected and that the company's field has low barriers to entry. In addition, the company's business plan should delineate what the company's technology does, not "how" the technology does what it does. The "how" should be protectable and may be the subject of a non-disclosure agreement at some later stage with the venture fund.

For later meetings with the full partnership of the venture fund and for most venture fund due diligence investigations, the custom in the venture capital industry has been, similarly, not to request a venture fund to sign a non-disclosure agreement. In return, a potential portfolio company would rely on the reputation of the venture fund and its principals that they have not in the past breached confidences of companies that they investigated. This custom is still the norm for virtually all initial meetings and presentations to venture funds. The rationale for this custom is threefold.

First, venture fund principals serve on corporate boards of many companies, and these principals have fiduciary duties as directors to these companies. If a venture capitalist, through his exposure to a new company's business plan or other disclosures, learns something material that is likely to affect a company on which he serves as a director, he would have a duty as a director to so inform his company, although he may choose not to reveal the source of the information. He naturally would not want to be conflicted because of a non-disclosure agreement to a company in which his venture fund has no investment.

Second, the mere funding by the venture fund of a company competing with the prospective portfolio company could be perceived by the prospective portfolio company as a breach of a non-disclosure agreement in that it may appear that the venture fund used the market information revealed in due diligence to evaluate another investment. Usually, non-disclosure agreements require that the recipient of the information use it only for evaluation of a business transaction with the company disclosing the information, not for evaluating another investment. Thus, the venture fund could be perceived as using the information for an impermissible purpose.

Third, venture funds and their principals have disclosure duties to their limited partners. That disclosure may involve information about a company or a market that was gleaned during a due diligence investigation. Some, but not all, of those disclosures to limited partners are themselves governed by a confidentiality agreement between the fund and the limited partners, but certain legal or regulatory duties may require the limited partners to disclose certain information they receive from the venture fund, and that could include information provided by a prospective or current portfolio company. Accordingly, the venture fund does not want to be restricted in its fundamental business by being bound by a variety of non-disclosure agreements.

Historically, though, there were certain exceptions to this custom. One exception was that carefully tailored non-disclosure agreements have been used with corporate venture capital funds where the corporation sponsoring the venture fund could be a competitor of the prospective portfolio company. Another exception was that, on occasion, a company could be restricted from disclosing a material contract because that contract requires that anyone reviewing that contract be subject to a non-disclosure agreement. Thus, a venture fund might sign a non-disclosure agreement in order to have access to that material agreement. A third exception was the "strong deal" exception. In a "strong deal," typically involving a veteran team of entrepreneurs, or a later-stage transaction with multiple interested investors, the venture fund after concluding preliminary due diligence and obtaining partner approval for the transaction, might agree to the non-disclosure agreement in order to finalize its due diligence prior to making the investment. In some instances, the company and the venture fund might agree that a third-party consultant hired by the venture fund would evaluate the sensitive technology or intellectual property (and this third-party would sign a non-disclosure agreement with the company), and the consultant would merely report summary information to the venture fund or merely confirm information that had already been provided to the venture fund not under a non-disclosure agreement.

Best Practices

No non-disclosure agreements should be needed for the initial meeting with the venture fund or for the review of the business plan. Consistent with this practice, the disclosing company should be careful about putting too much of how the technology works in the business plan. If a non-disclosure agreement is required to move the transaction forward after the initial meetings, then to insure that the venture fund has freedom to operate, the venture fund should insist on a limited non-disclosure agreement; that is, a non-disclosure agreement limited to a specific list of documents or information. This list should be comprised of only those documents and information that the potential portfolio company is required by law or by contract to keep confidential. This list of documents and information would be attached to the non-disclosure agreement.

The non-disclosure agreement should also be limited in other ways. If the agreements to be reviewed require confidential treatment only for a certain period of time, then the non-disclosure agreement should have the same limited term for its obligations of confidentiality. Also, the non-disclosure agreement should not contain a provision prohibiting solicitation of the potential portfolio company's employees, unless this provision is limited to just the venture fund and expressly excludes all affiliates of the venture fund. Affiliates of a venture fund could include the venture fund's portfolio companies, which, without the knowledge of the venture fund, might recruit and hire employees of the potential portfolio company. In addition, there should be an express acknowledgement that any provision in the non-disclosure agreement will in no way restrict the venture fund from evaluating or investing in any company including competitors or potential competitors of the potential portfolio company. Finally, the non-disclosure agreement should have a provision requiring confidential binding arbitration in the event of any disputes. This will prevent any disputes from being played out in public, and will be a faster, and therefore more efficient, route to a resolution of the dispute. The outcomes of arbitration are no better or no worse than those of a court, but the process can be confidential, and is speedier and therefore less expensive.

If a corporate venture capital investor is involved in the due diligence process, the potential portfolio company may desire a broader non-disclosure agreement with this investor. The corporate investor needs to insure that the obligations of confidentiality and non-solicitation of employees do not extend to the corporation at large, but apply just to the venture capital division (or corporate venture fund, depending on the business structure of the venture entity) involved in the transaction. At the same time, this venture capital division will be required to represent that any information received in due diligence will not be shared with the rest of the corporation.

Summary

In summary, non-disclosure agreements for venture funds should be discouraged by the funds, and for most transactions with established funds, the reputation of the fund and its treatment of entrepreneurs is a valuable asset, providing sufficient incentive to the fund and its principals to maintain the confidentiality of information disclosed by companies seeking funding. A non-disclosure agreement may also be a diversion or impede progress on the transaction. However, in those circumstances where a non-disclosure agreement is necessary or desirable, a venture fund or corporate venture fund usually can enter into an appropriately limited non-disclosure agreement that does not restrict the fund from carrying on its business.[†]

[†] The above was Contributed to VC Experts and Authored by: Thomas C. Klein, Member, Wilson Sonsini Goodrich & Rosati, P.C.

MODEL CONFIDENTIALITY AND NON DISCLOSURE AGREEMENT

THIS AGREEMENT is made by and between NEWCO, Inc., a Delaware corporation (the "Company") and John Smith ("Employee").

PREAMBLE

The Company desires to preserve the goodwill of its business and business relationships and to protect the details of its business and affairs from disclosure and unauthorized use and to ensure ownership of certain property. Employee recognizes and acknowledges that he shall have access to a variety of knowledge, information and property related to the Company's business or affairs and may have contact with the Company's customers, suppliers, other employees and similar persons and may assist in the creation and/or development of certain property; NOW, THEREFORE, in consideration of the terms and conditions set forth herein below, and for other good and valuable consideration, including the material benefits and training received as a result of his employment with the Company and the continuation thereof, the sufficiency of which is hereby acknowledged, and in reliance upon the recitals set forth above, which are fully made a part of this Agreement, the Company and Employee hereby agree as follows:

Confidential Information:

During the period of Employee's employment with the Company, and after the termination thereof for any reason, Employee agrees that, because of the valuable nature of the Confidential Information, he shall use his best efforts to maintain and protect the secrecy of the Confidential Information. Without in any manner limiting the generality of the foregoing obligation, Employee agrees that he shall not, directly or indirectly, undertake or attempt to undertake any of the following activities:

a. disclose any Confidential Information to any other person or entity;

b. use any Confidential Information for his own purposes;

c. make any copies, duplicates or reproductions of any Confidential Information;

d. authorize or permit any other person or entity to use, copy, disclose, publish or distribute any Confidential Information; or

e. undertake or attempt to undertake any activity the Company is prohibited from undertaking or attempting to undertake by any of its present or future clients, customers, suppliers, vendors, consultants, agents or contractors.

As used in this Agreement, the term "Confidential Information" means any knowledge, information or property relating to, or used or possessed by, the Company, and includes, without limitation, the following: trade secrets; patents, copyrights, software (including, without limitation, all programs, specifications, applications, routines, subroutines, techniques and idea for formulae); concepts, data, drawings, designs and documents; names of clients, customers, employees, agents, contractors, and suppliers; marketing information; financial information and other business records; and all copies of any of the foregoing, including notes, extracts, memoranda prepared or suffered or directed to be prepared by Employee based on any Confidential Information. Employee agrees that all information possessed by him, or disclosed to him, or to which he obtains access during the course of his employment with the Company shall be presumed to be Confidential Information under the terms of this Agreement, and the burden of proving otherwise shall rest with Employee.

Return of Confidential Information:

Upon termination of Employee's employment with the Company for any reason, Employee agrees not to retain or remove from the Company's premises any records, files or other documents or copies thereof or any other

Confidential Information whatsoever, and he agrees to surrender same to the Company, wherever it is located, immediately upon termination of his employment.

Assignment of Intellectual Property.

a. During the period of his employment with the Company, all processes, products, methods, improvements, discoveries, inventions, ideas, creations, trade secrets, know-how, machines, programs, designs, routines, subroutines, techniques, ideas for formulae, writings, books and other works of authorship, business concepts, plans, projections and other similar items, as well as all business opportunities, conceived, designed, devised, developed, perfected or made by the Employee, whether alone or in conjunction with others and whether or not during normal working hours or on the premises of the Company, and related in any manner to the actual or anticipated business of the Company or to actual or anticipated areas of research and development (the "Intellectual Property"), shall be promptly disclosed to and become the property of the Company, and Employee hereby assigns, transfers and conveys the Intellectual Property to the Company. Employee further agrees to make and provide to the Company any documents, instruments or other materials necessary or advisable to vest, secure, evidence or maintain the Company's ownership of the Intellectual Property, and patents, copyrights, trademarks and similar foreign and domestic property rights with respect to the Intellectual Property. The term "Intellectual Property" shall be given the broadest interpretation possible and shall include any Intellectual Property conceived, designed, devised, developed, perfected, or made by the Employee during off-duty hours and away from the Company's premises, as well as to those conceived, designed, devised, developed, perfected, or made in the regular course of Employee's performance.

b. Any Intellectual Property conceived, designed, devised, developed, perfected or made by the Employee within six (6) months after termination of his employment with the Company shall be conclusively presumed to have been conceived during such employment, and the burden of proving otherwise shall rest with Employee.

c. Without limiting the generality of the foregoing, in the performance of his/her duties as an employee of the Company, the undersigned may develop or assist in the development of computer programs or other works of authorship as defined in the Copyright Act of 1976, 197 U.S.C. Section 102 (hereinafter referred to as "Work"). Any original work of authorship fixed in any tangible medium of expression which the undersigned creates as a Company employee shall be considered a work made for hire pursuant to the copyright laws of the United States. Upon completion of any Work, and upon payment of any sums due to the undersigned, the Company shall have the sole and exclusive right, title and interest (including trade secret and copyright interests) in such Work. The undersigned hereby agrees to assign, and for no further consideration does assign, to the Company all of his/her worldwide right, title and interest in and to such Work, including trade secret and copyright interests. The undersigned agrees to assist the Company and its nominee, at any time, in the protection of the Company's worldwide right, title and interest in and to the Work and all rights of copyright therein, including, but not limited to, the execution of all formal assignment documents requested and prepared by the Company or its nominee and the execution of all lawful oaths and applications for registration of copyright in the United States and foreign countries.

Comment: *A number of agreements include a 'prior disclosure' concept, expressed along the following lines:*

Employee has set forth on the attached Prior Inventions Schedule a complete list of all Inventions that the Employee, alone or jointly with others, made prior to the commencement of my performance of services for the Company that the Employee considers to be his or her property or the property of third parties and that the Employee wishes to have excluded from the scope of this Agreement (collectively referred to as "Prior Inventions). If no such disclosure is attached, the Employee represents that there are no prior Inventions. If, in the course of the Employee's performance of services for the Company, the Employee incorporates a Prior Invention into a Company product, process or machine, the Company is hereby granted and shall have a nonexclusive, royalty-free, irrevocable, perpetual, worldwide license (with rights to sublicense through multiple tiers of sublicensees) to make, have made, modify, use and sell such Prior Invention. Notwithstanding the foregoing, the Employee agrees that he or she will not incorporate, or permit to be incorporated, Prior Inventions in any Company Inventions without the Company's prior written consent.

d. Any Intellectual Property conceived, designed, devised, developed, perfected or made by the Employee within six (6) months after termination of his employment with the Company shall be conclusively presumed to have been conceived during such employment, and the burden of proving otherwise shall rest with Employee.

Copyrightable Works:

Employee agrees that any copyrightable works made by him or her (solely or jointly with others) that are otherwise covered by the terms hereof and that are protectable by copyright, shall be deemed to be "works made for hire," as that term is defined in the United States Copyright Act (17 U.S.C. section 101). Accordingly, the Company shall be the sole and exclusive author and owner of all such copyrightable works and all right, title and interest therein and thereto, including, without limitation, all copyrights (and all renewals and extensions thereof). To the extent that any of such works are not determined to be a work for hire, the Employee hereby irrevocably, permanently, exclusively and absolutely assigns and grants to the Company all right, title and interest in and to such works, including, without limitation, all copyrights therein (and all renewals and extensions thereof.). The Company shall have the sole and exclusive right to use and exploit such works, in whole or in part, in any media or technology known or hereafter devised, in perpetuity. The Company's rights in and to such works may be assigned and licensed without limitation, and any such assignment or license shall be binding on he or she and shall inure to the benefit of such assignee or licensee. The Employee shall have no rights of consultation and/or approval with respect to the Company's exploitation, revision and/or use of such works. Moreover, the Employee hereby waives, forfeits, relinquishes and abandons all "moral rights" (as said term is commonly understood) and all rights of attribution and integrity that the Employee may otherwise have had with respect to such works through the universe, and all rights the Employee might otherwise have had under the Visual Artists Rights Act of 1990.

No Conflicting Obligation:

The Employee represents that his or her performance of all the terms of this Agreement as an employee, or otherwise, of the Company does not and will not breach any other agreement to keep in confidence information acquired by he or she in confidence or in trust prior to his or her performance of services for the Company. The Employee has not entered into, and agrees not to enter into, any other agreement whether written or oral in conflict herewith.

Noncompetition Agreement:

Employee acknowledges that the Company has provided and may provide additional special training (including, without limitation, training relating to programming of sophisticated computer programs) to Employee to enable Employee to perform his duties as an employee of the Company. As a result, Employee agrees that, during the term of his employment and for a period (the "Restricted Period") of two (2) years after the termination of the Employee's employment with the Company (whether such termination is with or without cause or results from Employee's resignation) Employee shall not, in the continental United States (the "Geographic Area") (i) directly or indirectly engage in, consult with, be employed by or be connected with any business or activity which directly or indirectly competes with the Company's business (a "Competing Business"), (ii) canvass, solicit or accept any business from any of the Company's current or former clients, (iii) own any interest in any Competing Business; (iv) assist others to open or operate any Competing Business; or (v) solicit, recommend or induce employees of the Company to terminate their employment with the Company. Employee agrees and acknowledges that the Geographic Area is reasonable in scope and that the two (2) year period is reasonable in length. Employee has agreed to the foregoing noncompetition agreement because (a) he recognizes that the Company has a legitimate interest in protecting the confidentiality of its business secrets (including the Confidential Information), (b) he agrees that such noncompetition agreement is not oppressive to him nor injurious to the public, and (c) the Company has provided specialized and valuable training and information to Employee.

During the Restricted Period, Employee will not without the express prior written approval of the Board of Directors of the Company (A) directly or indirectly, in one or a series of transactions, recruit, solicit or otherwise induce or influence any proprietor, partner, stockholder, lender, director, officer, employee, sales agent, joint venturer, investor, lessor, supplier, customer, agent, representative or any other person which has a business relationship with the Company to discontinue, reduce or modify such employment, agency or business relationship with the Company, or (B) employ or seek to employ or cause any competitive business to employ or seek to employ any person or agent who is then (or was at any time within six (6) months prior to the date the Executive or the competitive business employs or seeks to employ such person) employed or retained by the Company. Notwithstanding the foregoing, nothing herein shall prevent the Executive from providing a letter of recommendation to an employee with respect to a future employment opportunity; and general solicitations of employment published in a journal, newspaper or other publication of general circulation and not specifically directed towards such employees, consultants or independent contractors shall not be deemed to constitute solicitation for purposes of this Section 6.

Legal and Equitable Remedies:

Because the Employee's services are personal and unique, because the Employee has had and will continue to have access to and have become and will continue to become acquainted with the Proprietary Information of the Company and because any breach by the Employee of any of the restrictive covenants contained in this Agreement would result in irreparable injury and damage for which money damages would not provide an adequate remedy, the Company shall have the right to enforce this Agreement and any of its provisions by injunction, specific performance or other equitable relief, without bond and without prejudice to any other rights and remedies that the Company may have for a breach, or threatened breach, of this Agreement. The Employee agrees that in any action in which the Company seeks injunctive, specific performance or other equitable relief, the Employee will not assert or contend that any of the provisions of this Agreement are unreasonable or otherwise unenforceable.

Notices:

Any notices required or permitted hereunder shall be given to the appropriate party at the address specified below or at such other address as the party shall specify in writing. Such notices shall be deemed given upon personal delivery to the appropriate address or if sent by certified or registered mail, three (3) days after the date of mailing, or if sent by overnight courier upon written verification of receipt.

Services:

The Employee agrees and understands that nothing in this Agreement shall confer any right with respect to continuation of his or her performance of services for the Company, nor shall it interfere in any with the Employee's rights or the Company's right to terminate his or her performance of services for the Company at any time, for any reason.

United States Government and Other Obligations:

The Employee acknowledges that the Company from time to time may have agreements with other persons which impose obligations or restrictions on the Company regarding inventions made during the course of work under such agreements or regarding the confidential nature of such work. The Employee agrees to be bound by all such obligations and restrictions which are made known to me and to take all action necessary to discharge the obligations of the Company under such agreements.

General Provisions:

This Agreement will be governed by and construed according to the laws of the State of New York, as such laws are applied to agreements of this type. The Employee acknowledges and agrees that he or she has had an opportunity to seek advice of counsel in connection with this Agreement and that the covenants contained herein are reasonable in geographical and temporal scope and in all other respects. If any court or other decision-maker of competent jurisdiction determines that any of the Employee's covenants contained in this Agreement, or any part thereof, is unenforceable because of the duration or geographical scope of such provision, then, the duration or scope of such provision, as the case may be, shall be reduced so that such provision becomes enforceable and, in its reduced form, such provision shall then be enforceable and shall be enforced. In case any one or more of the provisions contained in this Agreement shall, for any reason, be held invalid, illegal or unenforceable in any respect, such invalidity, illegality or unenforceability shall not affect the other provisions of this Agreement, and this Agreement shall be construed as if such invalid, illegal or unenforceable provision had never been contained herein. This Agreement will be binding upon the Employee's heirs, executors, administrators, and other legal representatives and will be for the benefit of the Company, its successors, and its assigns. The provisions of this Agreement shall survive the termination of the Employee's performance of services for the Company and the assignment of this Agreement by the Company to any successor-in-interest or other assignee. No waiver by the Company of any breach of this Agreement shall be a waiver of any preceding or succeeding breach. No waiver by the Company of any right under this Agreement shall be construed as a waiver of any other right. The obligations pursuant to Sections __ and __ of this Agreement shall apply to any time during which the Employee was previously retained to perform services for the Company, or is in the future employed or retained to perform services for the Company, by the Company, including as a consultant, if no other Proprietary Information and Assignment Agreement governs nondisclosure and assignment of inventions during such period. This Agreement is the final, complete and exclusive agreement of the parties with respect to the subject matter hereof and supersedes and merges all prior discussions between us. No modification of or amendment to this Agreement, nor any waiver of any rights under this Agreement, will be effective unless in writing and signed by the party to charged. Any subsequent change or changes in my duties, salary or compensation will not affect the validity or scope of this Agreement.

Injunction:

Because the award of monetary damages would be an inadequate remedy, in the event of a breach or threatened breach by the Employee of any of the provisions of this Agreement, the Company shall be entitled to an injunction restraining the Employee from undertaking any such breach or threatened breach. Nothing herein shall be construed as prohibiting the Company from pursuing any other remedies available to it for such breach or threatened breach, including the recovery of damages from the Employee.

Amendment:

No amendment, whether express or implied, to this Agreement shall be effective unless it is in writing and signed by both parties hereto.

Waiver:

No consent or waiver, express or implied, by the Company to or of any breach or default by the Employee in the performance of his agreements hereunder shall operate as a consent to or waiver of any other breach or default in the performance of the same or any other obligations of the Employee hereunder. The Company's failure to complain of any such breach or default shall not constitute a waiver by the Company of its rights hereunder, irrespective of how long such failure continues.

Severability:

The invalidity or unenforceability of any provision hereof shall in no way affect the validity or enforceability of any other provision. In addition, should any time or area restriction contained herein be found by a court to be unreasonable, such restriction shall nevertheless remain as to the time or area such court finds reasonable, and as so amended, shall be enforced.

Miscellaneous:

This Agreement shall apply to all periods when the Employee is employed by the Company irrespective of whether or not this Agreement is reexecuted at the beginning of each such period. The title and paragraph headings of this Agreement are intended for reference only, and they shall not be construed as limiting or affecting any of the contents of this Agreement. This Agreement is binding upon and shall inure to the benefit of the parties' heirs, representatives, affiliates, successors or assigns. The use of any gender shall include all other genders.

EXECUTED this ＿＿ day of ＿＿＿＿＿＿＿＿＿, 200＿.

＿＿＿＿＿＿＿＿＿＿＿

＿＿＿＿＿＿＿＿＿＿＿

By: ＿＿＿＿＿＿＿＿＿

Title: ＿＿＿＿＿＿＿＿＿

Note on Non-Competition Covenants

The legal literature on occasion deals with certain promises between an employer and its employees-noncompetition, nondisclosure, and ownership of inventions-as if they were entirely separate arrangements, involving discrete legal principles and policy considerations. In fact, in the usual case, all three are closely interrelated, one might even say variations on a single theme. And, at the risk of some confusion for those accustomed to separate presentations, the discussion in the text will frequently treat them as if they were part of one whole.

The critical issues arise generally after the employment relationship is terminated. That is to say, if an individual is in fact a current employee, there is little controversy about an obligation, either expressly or by implication, not to compete and to maintain his employer's secrets in confidence. Once the employee is out on his own-either fired or by his voluntary act-how far can the employer impose restrictions on his subsequent behavior? Can the employer prevent him from joining or organizing a competitive firm and/or disclosing confidential information? Can a noncompete clause be considered a permissible surrogate for a nondisclosure obligation, on the theory that a ban on competition is the only way effectively to police the confidentiality undertaking? Can the employer assert ownership rights to inventions the employee comes up with, even those invented (at least ostensibly) after the relationship has been severed? Does it make a difference whether the employer is relying on common-law principles of unfair competition, a state statute (perhaps a version of the Uniform Trade Secrets Act) or express contractual provisions?

Depending on the state laws obtaining, it may be a bad idea to style any term of the employment arrangement baldly as a "covenant not to compete" (unless, as discussed below, the covenant is imposed in connection with the sale of a business or a significant stock position). Competition is the American way; labeling a restraint as anticompetitive is simply asking for some court to find a way around it in the clutch. Careful legal work, therefore, should start with the title of the section in the employment agreement, denoting what it is precisely that the company is trying to accomplish-a "covenant not to misappropriate proprietary information," perhaps, in which case the noncompete restriction is structured as a buttress, a way to enforce a nondisclosure obligation which cannot otherwise be realistically patrolled. In at least two states, New York and Illinois, federal courts have imposed post-employment restrictions even in the absence of a non-compete agreement on the theory that "ex-employees will inevitably disclose confidential information to new employers." See McMorris, "Judge Restricts Two Executives Despite Lack of Noncompete Pacts " Wall St. J,

Nov. 25, 1997, at B 12. It is interesting that the evidence in the New York case involved an Internet-related company called DoubleClick, Inc. The former employer was able to download e-mail from the laptop computer of one of the employees, which indicated the ex-employees had converted to their own use Double Click proprietary information.

Indeed, there are multiple reasons why courts and legislatures are hostile to noncompetition agreements.[1] Strictly enforced, the provisions could mean that the former employee cannot make a living in his field. Moreover, many of the most glamorous start-ups were the brain children of free spirits, who left giant oaks to plant little acorns. If IBM had elected to impose, and been allowed to enforce, noncompetitive clauses in every possible instance, one wonders what the computer industry in this country would look like today. Prudent counsel should start, therefore, with the presumption that a covenant not to compete may be unenforceable (pending, of course, a thorough review of state law). Instead of drafting language without substantive impact, the search should be for provisions which will survive, which have a fighting chance of accomplishing some corporate purpose when a valued employee leaves.

The issue, of course, can be serious. The flight of the scientific brains of the company into the arms of a competitor can be a death sentence. If a choice has to be made, the investors are well advised to let the provisions of, say, the registration rights agreement pass without negotiation, directing their counsel to focus in on this area. Given the high level of judicial and legislative hostility,[2] it is sensible to "frame each contract individually, tailor-made to the particular employee and the threat he poses, once on the loose, to his former employer's prosperity. If he is to serve as the marketing manager, the agreement should zero in on avoiding the harm that an individual in that post can do; perhaps a prohibition on the former employee aiding another firm in contacting customers he cultivated while in the plaintiff's employment. A court is much more likely to enforce a restraint if it is carefully limited to the potential injury facing the employer; this requires that thought be given to each individual case. Off-the-shelf provisions are unlikely to accomplish their stated objective.

It should be noted that emotions run extremely high in these disputes. The work atmosphere in a high-tech firm is often intense;[3] the key officers work so feverishly and such killing hours in the development of a new technology that their bond is as close as the marriage sacrament. When one of them decides he owes it to himself to strike out on his own, the emotions can be extremely bitter, the investors and officers of the earlier firm viewing the defection as hideously unfair if the defector is able to parlay his knowledge and experience into the building of a competitor, as is so often the case. Tying employees to a firm for life may be good and accepted practice in Japan but it conflicts with the mobility built into U.S. society. On the other hand, for investors and employees of a given firm to see their hard-earned secrets walk out the door and form the basis for a clone across the street is unfair competition of the most exasperating kind.

The precedents are hard to align into a body of black letter rules because the states have adopted quite different approaches to the issues involved, either through the common law of unfair competition and trade secret protection as interpreted by judges and/or because legislation has been enacted. The rights of the two contesting parties-employer and former employee-will often depend on where the action is brought and which state law the court elects to apply. Without attempting to review the authorities,[4] certain general propositions can be extracted, with the caveat that they are just that-general in nature and subject to local exceptions:

First, an obvious point: If the employer, the boss, breaches the employment contract, the employee is released from at least his noncompetition and probably his nondisclosure promises. (In a given context, the obligation to respect trade secrets may exist independent of contract.) The situation dealt with in this section is termination of the relationship because the employee quits, either in breach of his agreement or because the agreement no longer requires him to stay on.

Secondly, if a post-employment constraint is connected with the sale of a business, courts are more likely to enforce a noncompetition provision.[5] Assume Smith, the sole owner of Widget, Inc., sells all his stock to Jones. Smith agrees to stay on for a period as a consultant and, for two years thereafter, to stay out of the widget business. If Smith attempts to violate his promise, a court will justify intervention by construing the restraint as protection for the goodwill that Jones has just bought.[6] In this instance, the noncompetition covenant need not be tied to the unfair use of proprietary. The investor has bargained for certain assets from the issuer, including the issuer's promise to stay out of the business. (It is not clear why investors purchasing a partial interest in Smith's company are entitled to any less consideration if Smith elects to quit. The goodwill is dissipated in either event.)

Allied to the "sale of the business" concept is the notion that, if the noncompetition restraint is created in connection with the resale of significant equity position back to the company, the liveliness of the restraint is enhanced. As a planning point, therefore, it makes sense from the issuer's vantage point to tie the restraint to a buy/sell arrangement respecting the employee's equity. (If the repurchase is at a penalty price-e.g., the employee's cost-or for a de minimis amount of stock, common sense would suggest that the stock transaction should lend little help to the restraint's validity.) The two provisions should be expressly tied together, maybe even contained in the same numbered paragraph.[7] The linkage device is not, of course, foolproof. As is the case generally in this area, courts in various states and at various stages approach the issues variously. Some will invent ways to ignore the equity side of the transactions and invalidate the restraint, reasoning that, for example, the price does not reflect a sale of goodwill.

The repurchase-of-equity provisions create a further opportunity for the firm to escape the negative implications of a "covenant not to compete." If the employer is located in a state hostile to post-employment restraints, one possibility is to string out certain benefits for the employee-for example, payment for the stock or deferred salary-and then provide for forfeiture if the employee winds up working for a competitor.[8]

Alternatively, the former employer can sue the new employer, not the employee, for tortious interference, coupled with an allegation of wrongful misappropriation of proprietary information; the remedy sought in such a case is damages but the object of the exercise is equitable in nature, to intimidate the competitor and/ or the potential investors so that they refrain from infringing the former employer's domain.[9] To repeat a prior point, the plaintiff's claim is that noncompetition restraints are generally justified as necessary to enforce in the real world the underlying obligation not to misappropriate the employer's rights to its proprietary information.[10] The idea is that, once the employee has been allowed to form a rival firm, the damage has been done, the horse is out of the barn.

The gloss of "reasonableness" colors the discussion and holdings, meaning that the judges are consulting what they perceive to be the equities and common sense of the situation. Thus, the longer the employee has been employed and/or the higher his station in the company, the more likely a restraint will be enforced. A narrowly focused restraint will be more successful than one which bars the employee from working in any competitive job anywhere in the world."[11] The more sensitive the data to which the employee is privy, the likelier an injunction becomes. Indeed, injunctive relief is possible even in the absence of a contract if the secrets are particularly critical[12] but the failure of the employer to insist on a contract can be highly dangerous; the employer's lassitude cheapens its later assertions that the information is vital and may, in fact, constitute a lack of vigilance which negates the employer's rights under the law of trade secrets.[13]

The discussion to this point is focused on the language the employer should bargain for in the employment contract to protect itself. Venture finance, as indicated, involves the converse view, the flip side so to speak. When a start-up is in the process of organization, it is often the case that its founder and his colleagues are vulnerable to attack from the earlier employer, and the planning points have to do with mitigating the chances of that contingency. Thus, if the founder of Start-up, Inc. plans to take with him the members of his entire team at Goliath, Inc., common sense dictates that the departures be staggered, rather than all at once. If the founder plans to leave first, he should wait until he is no longer on the job before soliciting his colleagues. The departing employee should leave all documents behind and take only what can be carried in his own mind; as one noted venture capital attorney likes to advise his clients, employees should walk out the door naked as the day they were born.[14] An offer to pay to the former employer a royalty for a license of disputed technology is ambiguous; it may demonstrate the good faith of those ship (or, of course, may be construed as an admission of liability).

---

[1] The Restatement of Contracts stresses that covenants not to compete are "often the product of unequal bargaining power and – the employee is likely to give scant attention to the hardship he may suffer later on." Restatement (Second) of Contracts § 188 cmt. g(1981).

[2] See generally Nusbaum & Weltman, § 11.02[6].

[3] See Kidder, The Soul of a New Machine (1981).

[4] The principles involved are discussed at length in Restatement (Second) of Contracts § 188, Comment and Reporter's Note (1981). Section 188 would invalidate covenants not to compete if the restraint is "greater than needed" or the employer's need for the restraint is "outweighed" by harm to the employee and "likely injury to the public." Id. § 188(1).

[5] Id. § 188(2)(a) cmt. Courts also may be more disposed to enforcement of agreements in the sale of business" context because the seller of a business usually has more bargaining power than an employee and is receiving consideration other than wages for the covenant. See Business Records Corp. v. Lueth, 981 F.2d 957 (7th Cir. 1992); O'Sullivan v. Conrad, 358 N.E.2d 926, 929 (Ill. App. Ct. 1976); Blake, Employee Agreements Not to Compete," 73 Harv. L. Rev. 625, 646-647 (1960); Note, The Validity of Covenants Not to Compete: Common Law Rules in Illinois Law, 1978 Ill. L.F. 249,253.

Most (but not all) states allow "blue penciling" of covenants, meaning covenants will be enforced only to the extent necessary to protect the interests of the employer and may be narrowed by judicial ruling. See Wells v. Wells, 9 Mass. App. Ct. 321, 400 N.E.2d 1317 (1980). Drafting strategy will obviously be different in a state that does not allow "blue penciling," since excessive zeal may result in complete rejection of the covenant, while a more modest covenant might have survived.

[6] If the sale price is equal to net tangible book value, some courts may be prone to find no purchase of goodwill and, therefore, no consideration for the promise. For a general discussion, see Reed Roberts Assocs., Inc. v. Strauman, 40 N.Y.2d 303, 305, 353 N.E.2d 590, 583 386 N.Y.S.2d 677, 679 (1976).

[7] See Nusbaum & Weltman, § 11.02[6](b). The covenant should "clearly state that it relates to the sale of the founder's shares." Id.

[8] For a case upholding this arrangement, see Diakoff v. American Re-insurance Co., 492 F. Supp. 1115 (S.D.N.Y. 1980). Some courts would treat a forfeiture restriction as if it were a covenant not to compete. Rochester Corp. v. Rochester, 450 F.2d 118 (4th Cir. 1971).

[9] There is some authority for the proposition that the officers and directors of the company which entrances the employee to leave with misappropriated intellectual property under his arm may be liable. Coolley, *Personal Liability of Corporate Officers and Directors for Infringement of Intellectual Property*, 68 J. Pat. & Trademark Off. Soc'y 228 (1986).

[10] There are cases which will enforce the covenant even in the absence of trade secret concerns if the employee's services are "special, unique or extraordinary." Purchasing Assocs., Inc. v. Weitz, 13 N.Y.2d 267, 196 N.E.2d 245, 246 N.Y.S.2d 600 (1963), *discussed in* Restatement (Second) of Contracts § 188 note, cmt. g.

[11] The extent of the restraint is a critical factor in determining its reasonableness." Restatement (Second) of Contracts § 188 cmt. (d).

[12] The foundation case is Lumly v. Wagner, 1 De G. M. & G 604, 42 Eng. Rep. 687 (Cf. 1852)

[13] See Bartlett, Venture Capital: Law, Business Strategies, and Investment Planning § 16.5 (John Wiley & Sons, 1988).

[14] The vivid phrase was coined by the late Richard Testa of Testa, Hurwitz & Thibault.

21

Model Form: Employee NDA (covering: Noncompetition, Confidentiality and Inventions)[3]

NONCOMPETITION/CONFIDENTIALITY/INVENTIONS
AGREEMENT

THIS AGREEMENT made this ___ day of _____, ___, by and between ACME INC.a Delaware corporation ("the Company"), with a principal place of business at One Chestnut Street, Nashua, New Hampshire 03060, and _____ (the "Employee"), with a mailing address of _____.

WHEREAS, Employee is currently employed by the Company in the position of _____ [-or- the Company desires to employ Employee, and Employee desires to perform the duties required by the Company]; and WHEREAS, the Company and Employee acknowledge that Employee is [-or- will be] employed at the will of the Company, in a position of trust and confidence in which Employee learns of, has access to and will continue to develop [-or- may hereafter learn of, have access to, and develop] proprietary, confidential and trade secret information of the Company; and

---

[3] **Contributed by VC Experts Editor**: Zach Shulman of Cornell University, Johnson School of Business

WHEREAS, the Company desires to protect any rights it may have in such proprietary, confidential and trade secret information that Employee may acquire in connection with his\her employment for the Company.

NOW, THEREFORE, the Company and Employee, in consideration of Employee's employment by the Company and the mutual promises contained herein, agree as follows:

1. Definitions.
As used herein the following capitalized terms shall have the following meanings:

1.1 "Confidential Information" shall include, without limitation, whether tangible or intangible (i) all information relating to intellectual property, including, without limitation, licenses, patents, trademarks, tradenames, servicemarks and copyrights, (ii) trade secret data and related information, (iii) all information relating to the development, research, testing, manufacturing and marketing activities and techniques of the Company, (iv) all information relating to the products manufactured, sold or distributed by the Company, (v) all information relating to the raw materials, costs, sources of supply and strategic plans of the Company, (vi) all information relating to the identity of special needs of the customers of the Company, (vii) all information relating to the persons and organizations with whom the Company has or has had business relationships, including, without limitation, customer lists, (viii) all information relating to the identity of prospective customers of the Company and (ix) all other information which the Company deems confidential and proprietary in its sole discretion.

1.2 "Invention or Inventions" shall include, without limitation, all tangible and intangible concepts, ideas, creations, developments, designs, discoveries, processes, methods, formulae, techniques and work product, whether patentable or not, and all enhancements, modifications and improvements thereof or thereto.

2. Non-disclosure of Confidential Information.

2.1 Employee acknowledges that the Company has invested and will continue to invest considerable resources in the research, development and advancement of Company's business, which investment has or will result in the generation of Confidential Information. Employee acknowledges and agrees that it would be unlawful for Employee to appropriate, to attempt to appropriate or to disclose to anyone such Confidential Information.

2.2 Employee agrees, therefore (i) to hold in confidence all Confidential Information received, acquired, produced or developed by Employee in the course of the performance of Employee's employment with the Company and (ii) not to use, disclose, reproduce or dispose of such Confidential Information in any manner except as required by applicable law or in connection with the performance of his\her duties and responsibilities to the Company. Employee expressly agrees and understands that the restrictions contained in this Section 2.2 shall continue to apply after Employee's employment with the Company terminates, regardless of the reason for such termination.

2.3 Employee agrees to comply with all security regulations established by law, the Company, the Company's current and prospective customers, contractors and other third parties for the purpose of protecting Confidential Information.

2.4 Employee expressly agrees and understands that all Confidential Information is the property of the Company regardless if Employee is directly or indirectly involved in the development or creation of such Confidential Information.
2.5 Notwithstanding anything in this Agreement to the contrary, the obligations of confidentiality are nonexistent with respect to all or any particular portion of the Confidential Information if:

(a) it was in the public domain at the time of the Company's communication thereof to Employee;

(b) it entered the public domain through no fault of Employee subsequent to the time of the Company's communication thereof to Employee; or

(c) it was rightfully communicated to Employee free of any obligation of confidence subsequent to the time of the Company's communication thereof to Employee.

3. Ownership of Inventions.

3.1 During the term of Employee's employment with the Company, Employee shall maintain accurate records of any and all work related to Inventions and shall, upon request, promptly disclose said records to the Company and keep the Company informed from time to time of any Inventions made by him\her, in whole or in part, or conceived by him\her along or with others, as the result of any work for or at the request of the Company, or which relates to activities, products, services or processes of the Company.

3.2 All Inventions required to be disclosed to the Company pursuant to Section 3.1 above, shall be and remain the sole property of the Company, and Employee shall assign all his\her right, title and interest therein to the Company and execute, acknowledge and deliver to the Company instruments confirming the complete ownership by the Company of such Inventions.

3.3 The Company acknowledges and agrees that all Inventions produced by Employee prior to his\her employment with the Company shall not be the property of the Company provided such Inventions are identified to the Company on Exhibit 3.3 hereto. Employee agrees that all Inventions not identified on Exhibit 3.3 shall be deemed to have been made subsequent to the commencement of Employee's employment with the Company.

3.4 Employee shall assist the Company to obtain patents for any Invention, at the request and sole expense of the Company, provided, however, that the Company shall be under no obligation to commence or continue any patent applications hereunder.

4. Covenant Not To Compete; No Solicitation.

4.1 Employee agrees that some restrictions on his\her activities during and after his\her employment with the Company are necessary to protect the goodwill, Confidential Information, Inventions and other legitimate business interests of the Company. In recognition thereof, while he\she is employed by the Company and for a period of two (2) years thereafter, Employee shall not, without the written consent of the Company, (i) directly or indirectly, whether as owner, partner, investor, consultant, agent, employee, or otherwise, engage in any business in competition with the business of the Company as conducted at any time during Employee's employment with the Company, and (ii) directly or indirectly attempt to hire any employee of the Company, assist in such hiring by any other person, encourage any such employee to terminate his\her relationship with the Company, or solicit or encourage any customer or vendor of the Company to terminate its relationship with the Company or to conduct with any person any business or activity which such person conducts or could conduct with the Company. The foregoing restriction shall not prevent Employee from owning 5% or less of the equity securities of any publicly traded company.

4.2 Employee acknowledges that the broad geographic scope of the covenants contained in Section 4.1 may be required because the Company is likely to build and maintain a business which is international in scope. Employee acknowledges that, under current business conditions, Employee's education would likely enable Employee to obtain employment in many different areas of his\her field, and to work for different types of employers, so that, under such conditions, it is not foreseeable at the execution of this

Agreement that Employee would need to violate the provisions of Section 4.1 this Agreement in order to remain economically viable.

5. Surrender of Confidential Information and Inventions. Employee will surrender to the Company upon termination of Employee's employment with the Company for any reason, all written or otherwise tangible documentation, in whatever form, representing or embodying Confidential Information or Inventions or copies thereof, whether or not prepared by Employee or another, in Employee's possession or control. Nothing in this Section 5 shall be interpreted to imply that Employee is authorized to have in Employee's possession any of the Confidential Information or Inventions.

6. Proprietary Rights Indemnification. Employee agrees to defend, indemnify and hold the Company harmless from and against all loss, damage and expense, including reasonable attorney's fees and expenses, and amounts paid in settlement arising from the claim that any confidential, proprietary, trade secret or similar information that Employee uses in the course of his\her employment with the Company and which was not obtained from the Company or with the Company's consent infringes any patent, copyright, trade secret or other proprietary rights of any third party.

7. Survival; Relief. The provisions of this Agreement shall independently survive the termination of Employee's employment by the Company and be separately enforceable by the Company in any court of competent jurisdiction. Employee acknowledges that a violation of the provisions of this Agreement by Employee may result in irreparable harm to the Company. Therefore, Employee agrees that the Company shall be entitled to preliminary and permanent injunctive relief against any breach by Employee of the provisions of this Agreement, without having to post bond; provided, that nothing in the foregoing clause shall limit the Company's right to seek monetary damages, including, without limitation, attorney's fees, costs and disbursements, as it may have sustained in the event of the violation by Employee of any of the provisions of this Agreement. The existence of any

claim, dispute or cause of action of Employee against the Company, whether predicated upon this Agreement or otherwise, will not constitute a defense to the enforcement by the Company of any provision of this Agreement.

8. Severability and Reformation.

8.1 In the event that any portion or provision of this Agreement shall be determined by a court of competent jurisdiction to be unlawful or unenforceable, then the remainder of this Agreement, or the application of such portion or provision in circumstances other than those as to which it is so declared unlawful or unenforceable, shall not be affected thereby, and the remaining portions and provisions of this Agreement shall remain in full force and effect.

8.2 In furtherance and not in limitation of the foregoing Section 7.1, should any restriction imposed on Employee by this Agreement be found by any court of competent jurisdiction to be overly broad, Employee and the Company intend that such court enforce this Agreement in any less broad manner that the court may find appropriate by construing such overly broad provisions to cover only that restriction on activities which may be enforceable. The parties acknowledge the possible uncertainty of the law in this respect and expressly agree that this Agreement be given the construction that renders its provisions valid and enforceable to the maximum extent permitted by law in order to effectuate the intentions of the Company and Employee evidenced by this Agreement.

9. Miscellaneous.

9.1 Waiver. No waiver of any provision hereof shall be effective unless made in writing and signed by the waiving party. The failure of either party to require the performance of any term or obligation of this Agreement, or the waiver by either party of any breach of this Agreement, shall not prevent any subsequent enforcement of such term or obligation or be deemed a waiver of any subsequent breach.

9.2 Assignment; Binding Effect. The Company, but not Employee, may assign or transfer any right under this Agreement or any interest herein, by operation of law or otherwise, without the prior consent of Employee. This Agreement shall inure to the benefit of and be binding upon the Company and Employee, their respective successors, executors, administrators, heirs and permitted assigns.

9.3 Governing Law. This Agreement will be governed and construed in accordance with the laws of the State of New Hampshire without regard to the conflict of laws principles thereof.

9.4 Amendments. This Agreement may be amended or modified only by a written instrument signed by Employee and a duly authorized representative of the Company.

9.5 Entire Agreement. This Agreement constitutes the entire understanding between Employee and the Company and supersedes all prior oral or written communications, proposals, representations, warranties, covenants, understandings or agreements between Employee and the Company relating to the subject matter of this Agreement.

9.6 Notices. All notices, demands or other communications under this Agreement shall be in writing and shall be deemed to have been duly given when personally delivered or mailed by United States registered or certified first class mail (or, where appropriate, international mail), return receipt requested, postage prepaid, to the addresses set forth at the beginning of this Agreement or such other addresses as either party may have furnished to the other in accordance herewith.

9.7 Employee Acknowledgment. Employee acknowledges that he\she has carefully read and fully understands all of the provisions of this Agreement and that Employee, in consideration of his\her employment with the Company, is voluntarily entering into this Agreement. Employee represents and acknowledges that in executing this Agreement, Employee does not rely and has not relied upon any representation or statement made by the Company with regard to the subject matter, basis or effect of this Agreement, other than those contained in this Agreement.

IN WITNESS WHEREOF, this Agreement has been executed as a sealed instrument by the Company, by its duly authorized officer, and by Employee as of the day and year first above written.

ACME INC.BROADBAND SYSTEMS, INC.

_____

By:

_____

Employee

EXHIBIT 3.3
INVENTIONS OWNED BY EMPLOYEE

22

Model Form: Mutual Non-Disclosure Agreement[4]

MUTUAL NONDISCLOSURE AGREEMENT

This Nondisclosure Agreement (this "Agreement") is dated as of _____, 200__, between ACME Systems Inc., a Delaware corporation having a principal place of business at One Technology Park, Nashua, NH 03060 ("ACME"), and _____, with a place of business at _____ ("Company").

ACME INC. and Company hereby agree as follows:

1. Confidential Information. As used in this Agreement, "Confidential Information" means all information of either party that is not generally known to the public, whether of a technical, business or other nature (including, without limitation, trade secrets, know-how and information relating to the technology, customers, business plans, promotional and marketing activities, finances and other business affairs of such party), that is disclosed by one party (the "Disclosing Party") to the other party (the "Receiving Party") or that is otherwise learned by the Receiving Party in the course of its discussions or business dealings with, or its physical or electronic access to the premises of, the Disclosing Party, and that has been identified

[4] **Contributed by VC Experts Editor**: Zach Shulman of Cornell University, Johnson School of Business

as being proprietary and/or confidential or that by the nature of the circumstances surrounding the disclosure or receipt ought to be treated as proprietary and confidential. Confidential Information also includes all information concerning the existence and progress of the parties' dealings.

2. Use and Ownership of Confidential Information. The Receiving Party, except as expressly provided in this Agreement, will not disclose Confidential Information to anyone without the Disclosing Party's prior written consent. In addition, the Receiving Party will not use, or permit others to use, Confidential Information for any purpose other than the following:

_____

[NOTE: If the foregoing is left blank, then it shall be understood to be completed by the following phrase: "to further the mutually beneficial business opportunities contemplated by both parties."]

The Receiving Party will take all reasonable measures to avoid disclosure, dissemination or unauthorized use of Confidential Information, including, at a minimum, those measures it takes to protect its own confidential information of a similar nature. All Confidential Information will remain the exclusive property of the Disclosing Party, and the Receiving Party will have no rights, by license or otherwise, to use the Confidential Information except as expressly provided herein.

3. Exceptions. The provisions of Section 2 will not apply to any information that (i) is or becomes publicly available without breach of this Agreement; (ii) can be shown by documentation to have been known to the Receiving Party prior to its receipt from the Disclosing Party; (iii) is rightfully received from a third party who did not acquire or disclose such information by a wrongful or tortious act; or (iv) can be shown by documentation to have been developed by the Receiving Party without reference to any Confidential Information.

4. Disclosures to Courts and Governmental Entities. If the Receiving Party becomes legally obligated to disclose Confidential Information by any court or governmental entity with jurisdiction over it, the Receiving Party will give the Disclosing Party prompt written notice to allow the Disclosing Party to seek a protective order or other appropriate remedy. Such notice must include, without limitation, identification of the information to be so disclosed and a copy of the order. The Receiving Party will disclose only such information as is legally required and will use its reasonable best efforts to obtain confidential treatment for any Confidential Information that is so disclosed.

5. Compliance with Laws; Exportation/ Transmission of Confidential Information. Both parties will comply with all applicable federal, state, and local statutes, rules and regulations, including, but not limited to, United States export control laws and regulations as they currently exist and as they may be amended from time to time.

6. Receiving Party Personnel. The Receiving Party will restrict the possession, knowledge, development and use of Confidential Information to its employees, agents, subcontractors and entities controlled by or controlling it (collectively, "Personnel") who have a need to know Confidential Information in connection with the purposes set forth in Section 2. The Receiving Party's Personnel will have access only to the Confidential Information they need for such purposes. The Receiving Party will ensure that its Personnel comply with this Agreement and will promptly notify the Disclosing Party of any breach of this Agreement.

7. Return of Confidential Information. Upon the Disclosing Party's written request, the Receiving Party promptly will return or destroy (or, in the case of electronic embodiments, permanently erase) all tangible material embodying Confidential Information (in any form and including, without limitation, all summaries, copies and excerpts of Confidential Information) in its possession or under its control.

8. Independent Development. The Disclosing Party acknowledges that the Receiving Party may currently or in the future be developing information internally, or receiving information from other parties, that is similar to the Confidential Information. Accordingly, nothing in this Agreement will be construed as a representation or agreement that the Receiving Party will not develop or have developed for it products, concepts, systems or techniques that are similar to or compete with the products, concepts, systems or techniques contemplated by or embodied in the Confidential Information, provided that the Receiving Party does not violate any of its obligations under this Agreement in connection with such development.

9. Injunctive Relief. The Receiving Party acknowledges that disclosure or use of Confidential Information in violation of this Agreement could cause irreparable harm to the Disclosing Party for which monetary damages may be difficult to ascertain or an inadequate remedy. The Receiving Party therefore agrees that the Disclosing Party will have the right, in addition to its other rights and remedies, to injunctive relief for any violation of this Agreement without posting bond, or by posting bond at the lowest amount required by law.

10. Limited Relationship. This Agreement will not create a joint venture, partnership or other formal business relationship or entity of any kind, or an obligation to form any such relationship or entity. Each party will act as an independent contractor and not as an agent of the other party for any purpose, and neither will have the authority to bind the other.

11. Cumulative Obligations. Each party's obligations hereunder are in addition to, and not exclusive of, any and all of its other obligations and duties to the other party, whether express, implied, in fact or in law.
12. Entire Agreement; Amendment. This Agreement constitutes the entire agreement between the parties relating to the matters discussed herein and supersedes all prior oral and written understandings with respect to any information disclosed or received under this Agreement. This Agreement

may be amended or modified only with the mutual written consent of the parties.

13. Term and Termination. This Agreement is intended to cover Confidential Information disclosed or received by either party prior or subsequent to the date of this Agreement. Unless otherwise earlier terminated, this Agreement automatically will expire five (5) years from the date first written above; provided, however, that each party's obligations with respect to the other party's Confidential Information disclosed or received prior to termination or expiration will survive for three (3) years following the expiration or termination of this Agreement.

14. Nonwaiver. Any failure by either party to enforce the other party's strict performance of any provision of this Agreement will not constitute a waiver of its right to subsequently enforce such provision or any other provision of this Agreement.

15. No Warranty. The Receiving Party acknowledges that Confidential Information may still be under development, or may be incomplete, and that such information may relate to products that are under development or are planned for development. THE DISCLOSING PARTY MAKES NO WARRANTIES, EXPRESSED OR IMPLIED, INCLUDING ANY IMPLIED WARRANTIES OF MERCHANTABILITY AND FITNESS FOR A PARTICULAR PURPOSE IN CONNECTION WITH ANY CONFIDENTIAL INFORMATION WHICH IT DISCLOSES IN CONNECTION WITH THIS AGREEMENT. The Disclosing Party accepts no responsibility for any expense, losses or action incurred or undertaken by the Receiving Party as a result of the Receiving Party's receipt or use of Confidential Information.

16. Governing Law; Etc. This Agreement will be governed by internal laws of the State of New Hampshire, without reference to its choice of law rules, may be executed in counterpart copies, and, in the absence of an original signature, faxed signatures will be considered the equivalent of an original

signature. If a provision of this Agreement is held invalid under any applicable law, such invalidity will not affect any other provision of this Agreement that can be given effect without the invalid provision. Further, all terms and conditions of this Agreement will be deemed enforceable to the fullest extent permissible under applicable law, and, when necessary, the court is requested to reform any and all terms or conditions to give them such effect.

The parties have executed this Agreement on the date first written above.

ACME INC.BROADBAND SYSTEMS, INC.

By:_____

Print Name:_____

Title:_____

[FILL IN NAME OF OTHER PARTY]

By:_____

Print Name:_____

Title:_____

23

Model Stock Incentive Plan

Purposes of the Plan:

The purposes of this Stock Incentive Plan are to attract and retain the best available personnel, to provide additional incentive to Employees, Directors and Consultants and to promote the success of the Company's business.

Definitions:

As used herein, the following definitions shall apply:

"Administrator" means the Board or any of the Committees appointed to administer the Plan.

"Applicable Laws" means the legal requirements relating to the administration of stock incentive plans, if any, under applicable provisions of federal securities laws, state corporate and securities laws, the Code, the rules of any applicable stock exchange or national market system, and the rules of any foreign jurisdiction applicable to Awards granted to residents therein.

"Award" means the grant of an Option, Restricted Stock, SAR, Dividend Equivalent Right, Performance Unit, Performance Share, or other right or benefit under the Plan.

"Award Agreement" means the written agreement evidencing the grant of an Award executed by the Company and the Grantee, including any amendments thereto.

"Board" means the Board of Directors of the Company.

"Cause" means, with respect to the termination by the Company or a Related Entity of the Grantee's Continuous Service, that such termination is for "Cause" as such term is expressly defined in a then-effective written agreement between the Grantee and the Company or such Related Entity, or in the absence of such then-effective written agreement and definition, is based on, in the determination of the Administrator, the Grantee's: (i) refusal or failure to act in accordance with any specific, lawful direction or order of the Company or a Related Entity; (ii) unfitness or unavailability for service or unsatisfactory performance (other than as a result of Disability); (iii) performance of any act or failure to perform any act in bad faith and to the detriment of the Company or a Related Entity; (iv) dishonesty, intentional misconduct or material breach of any agreement with the Company or a Related Entity; or (v) commission of a crime involving dishonesty, breach of trust, or physical or emotional harm to any person. At least 30 days prior to the termination of the Grantee's Continuous Service pursuant to (i) or (ii) above, the Company shall provide the Grantee with notice of the Company's or such Related Entity's intent to terminate, the reason therefor, and an opportunity for the Grantee to cure such defects in his or her service to the Company's or such Related Entity's satisfaction. During this 30 day (or longer) period, no Award issued to the Grantee under the Plan may be exercised or purchased.

"Code" means the Internal Revenue Code of 1986, as amended.

"Committee" means any committee appointed by the Board to administer the Plan.

"Common Stock" means the common stock of the Company.

"Company" means Company Name, a State corporation.

"Consultant" means any person (other than an Employee or a Director, solely with respect to rendering services in such person's capacity as a Director) who is engaged by the Company or any Related Entity to render consulting or advisory services to the Company or such Related Entity.

"Continuous Service" means that the provision of services to the Company or a Related Entity in any capacity of Employee, Director or Consultant, is not interrupted or terminated. Continuous Service shall not be considered interrupted in the case of (i) any approved leave of absence, (ii) transfers among the Company, any Related Entity, or any successor, in any capacity of Employee, Director or Consultant, or (iii) any change in status as long as the individual remains in the service of the Company or a Related Entity in any capacity of Employee, Director or Consultant (except as otherwise provided in the Award Agreement). An approved leave of absence shall include sick leave, military leave, or any other authorized personal leave. For purposes of each Incentive Stock Option granted under the Plan, if such leave exceeds ninety (90) days, and reemployment upon expiration of such leave is not guaranteed by statute or contract, then the Incentive Stock Option shall be treated as a Non-Qualified Stock Option on the day three (3) months and one (1) day following the expiration of such ninety (90) day period.

"Corporate Transaction" means any of the following transactions to which the Company is a party:

a merger or consolidation in which the Company is not the surviving entity, except for a transaction the principal purpose of which is to change the state in which the Company is incorporated;

the sale, transfer or other disposition of all or substantially all of the assets of the Company (including the capital stock of the Company's subsidiary corporations);

approval by the Company's shareholders of any plan or proposal for the complete liquidation or dissolution of the Company;

any reverse merger in which the Company is the surviving entity but in which securities possessing more than fifty percent (50%) of the total combined voting power of the Company's outstanding securities are transferred to a person or persons different from those who held such securities immediately prior to such merger; or

acquisition by any person or related group of persons (other than the Company or by a Company-sponsored employee benefit plan) of beneficial ownership (within the meaning of Rule 13d-3 of the Exchange Act) of securities possessing more than fifty percent (50%) of the total combined voting power of the Company's outstanding securities, but excluding any such transaction that the Administrator determines shall not be a Corporate Transaction.

"Director" means a member of the Board or the board of directors of any Related Entity.

"Disability" means a Grantee would qualify for benefit payments under the long-term disability policy of the Company or the Related Entity to which the Grantee provides services regardless of whether the Grantee is covered by such policy. If the Company or the Related Entity to which the Grantee provides service does not have a long-term disability plan in place,

"Disability" means that a Grantee is permanently unable to carry out the responsibilities and functions of the position held by the Grantee by reason of any medically determinable physical or mental impairment. A Grantee will not be considered to have incurred a Disability unless he or she furnishes proof of such impairment sufficient to satisfy the Administrator in its discretion.

"Dividend Equivalent Right" means a right entitling the Grantee to compensation measured by dividends paid with respect to Common Stock.

"Employee" means any person, including an Officer or Director, who is an employee of the Company or any Related Entity. The payment of a director's fee by the Company or a Related Entity shall not be sufficient to constitute "employment" by the Company.

"Exchange Act" means the Securities Exchange Act of 1934, as amended.

"Fair Market Value" means, as of any date, the value of Common Stock determined as follows:

Where there exists a public market for the Common Stock, the Fair Market Value shall be (A) the closing price for a Share for the last market trading day prior to the time of the determination (or, if no closing price was reported on that date, on the last trading date on which a closing price was reported) on the stock exchange determined by the Administrator to be the primary market for the Common Stock or the Nasdaq National Market, whichever is applicable or (B) if the Common Stock is not traded on any such exchange or national market system, the average of the closing bid and asked prices of a Share on the Nasdaq Small Cap Market for the day prior to the time of the determination (or, if no such prices were reported on that date, on the last date on which such prices were reported), in each case, as reported in *The Wall Street Journal* or such other source as the Administrator deems reliable; or

In the absence of an established market for the Common Stock of the type described in (i), above, the Fair Market Value thereof shall be determined by the Administrator in good faith.

"Good Reason" means the occurrence after a Corporate Transaction of any of the following events or conditions unless consented to by the Grantee:

(A) a change in the Grantee's status, title, position or responsibilities which represents an adverse change from the Grantee's status, title, position or responsibilities as in effect at any time within six (6) months preceding the date of a Corporate Transaction or at any time thereafter or (B) the assignment to the Grantee of any duties or responsibilities which are inconsistent with the Grantee's status, title, position or responsibilities as in effect at any time within six (6) months preceding the date of a Corporate Transaction or at any time thereafter;

reduction in the Grantee's base salary to a level below that in effect at any time within six (6) months preceding the date of a Corporate Transaction or at any time thereafter; or

requiring the Grantee to be based at any place outside a [50]-mile radius from the Grantee's job location [or residence] prior to the Corporate Transaction except for reasonably required travel on business which is not materially greater than such travel requirements prior to the Corporate Transaction.]

"Grantee" means an Employee, Director or Consultant who receives an Award under the Plan.

"Immediate Family" means any child, stepchild, grandchild, parent, stepparent, grandparent, spouse, former spouse, sibling, niece, nephew, mother-in-law, father-in-law, son-in law, daughter-in-law, brother-in-law, or sister-in-law, including adoptive relationships, any person sharing the

Grantee's household (other than a tenant or employee), a trust in which these persons (or the Grantee) have more than fifty percent (50%) of the beneficial interest, a foundation in which these persons (or the Grantee) control the management of assets, and any other entity in which these persons (or the Grantee) own more than fifty percent (50%) of the voting interests.

"Incentive Stock Option" means an Option intended to qualify as an incentive stock option within the meaning of Section 422 of the Code

"Non-Qualified Stock Option" means an Option not intended to qualify as an Incentive Stock Option.

"Officer" means a person who is an officer of the Company or a Related Entity within the meaning of Section 16 of the Exchange Act and the rules and regulations promulgated thereunder.

"Option" means an option to purchase Shares pursuant to an Award Agreement granted under the Plan.

"Parent" means a "parent corporation," whether now or hereafter existing, as defined in Section 424(e) of the Code.

"Performance Shares" means Shares or an Award denominated in Shares which may be earned in whole or in part upon attainment of performance criteria established by the Administrator.

"Performance Units" means an Award which may be earned in whole or in part upon attainment of performance criteria established by the Administrator and which may be settled for cash, Shares or other securities or a combination of cash, Shares or other securities as established by the Administrator.

"Plan" means this 200_ Stock Incentive Plan.

"Registration Date" means the first to occur of (i) the closing of the first sale to the general public of (A) the Common Stock or (B) the same class of securities of a successor corporation (or its Parent) issued pursuant to a Corporate Transaction in exchange for or in substitution of the Common Stock, pursuant to a registration statement filed with and declared effective by the Securities and Exchange Commission under the Securities Act of 1933, as amended; and (ii) in the event of a Corporate Transaction, the date of the consummation of the Corporate Transaction if the same class of securities of the successor corporation (or its Parent) issuable in such Corporate Transaction shall have been sold to the general public pursuant to a registration statement filed with and declared effective by the Securities and Exchange Commission under the Securities Act of 1933, as amended, on or prior to the date of consummation of such Corporate Transaction.

"Restricted Stock" means Shares issued under the Plan to the Grantee for such consideration, if any, and subject to such restrictions on transfer, rights of first refusal, repurchase provisions, forfeiture provisions, and other terms and conditions as established by the Administrator.

"SAR" means a stock appreciation right entitling the Grantee to Shares or cash compensation, as established by the Administrator, measured by appreciation in the value of Common Stock.

"Share" means a share of the Common Stock.

"Subsidiary" means a "subsidiary corporation," whether now or hereafter existing, as defined in Section 424(f) of the Code.

Stock Subject to the Plan:

Subject to the provisions of Section 10(a) below, the maximum aggregate number of Shares which may be issued pursuant to all Awards (including

Incentive Stock Options) is [____] Shares. The Shares may be authorized, but unissued, or reacquired Common Stock.[1]

Any Shares covered by an Award (or portion of an Award) which is forfeited or canceled, expires or is settled in cash, shall be deemed not to have been issued for purposes of determining the maximum aggregate number of Shares which may be issued under the Plan. Shares that actually have been issued under the Plan pursuant to an Award shall not be returned to the Plan and shall not become available for future issuance under the Plan, except that if unvested Shares are forfeited, or repurchased by the Company at their original purchase price, such Shares shall become available for future grant under the Plan.

Administration of the Plan:

Plan Administrator. With respect to grants of Awards to Employees, Directors, or Consultants, the Plan shall be administered by (A) the Board or (B) a Committee (or a subcommittee of the Committee) designated by the Board, which Committee shall be constituted in such a manner as to satisfy Applicable Laws. Once appointed, such Committee shall continue to serve in its designated capacity until otherwise directed by the Board. The Board may authorize one or more Officers to grant Awards subject to such limitations as the Board determines from time to time.

Multiple Administrative Bodies. The Plan may be administered by different bodies with respect to Directors, Officers, Consultants, and Employees who are neither Directors nor Officers.

Powers of the Administrator. Subject to Applicable Laws and the provisions of the Plan (including any other powers given to the Administrator hereunder), and except as otherwise provided by the Board, the Administrator shall have the authority, in its discretion:

to select the Employees, Directors and Consultants to whom Awards may be granted from time to time hereunder;

to determine whether and to what extent Awards are granted hereunder;

to determine the number of Shares or the amount of other consideration to be covered by each Award granted hereunder;

to approve forms of Award Agreements for use under the Plan;

to determine the terms and conditions of any Award granted hereunder;

to establish additional terms, conditions, rules or procedures to accommodate the rules or laws of applicable foreign jurisdictions and to afford Grantees favorable treatment under such rules or laws; provided, however, that no Award shall be granted under any such additional terms, conditions, rules or procedures with terms or conditions which are inconsistent with the provisions of the Plan;

to amend the terms of any outstanding Award granted under the Plan, provided that any amendment that would adversely affect the Grantee's rights under an outstanding Award shall not be made without the Grantee's written consent;

to construe and interpret the terms of the Plan and Awards, including without limitation, any notice of Award or Award Agreement, granted pursuant to the Plan; and

to take such other action, not inconsistent with the terms of the Plan, as the Administrator deems appropriate.

Eligibility. Awards other than Incentive Stock Options may be granted to Employees, Directors and Consultants. Incentive Stock Options may be granted only to Employees of the Company, a Parent or a Subsidiary. An

Employee, Director or Consultant who has been granted an Award may, if otherwise eligible, be granted additional Awards. Awards may be granted to such Employees, Directors or Consultants who are residing in foreign jurisdictions as the Administrator may determine from time to time.

Terms and Conditions of Awards:

Type of Awards. The Administrator is authorized under the Plan to award any type of arrangement to an Employee, Director or Consultant that is not inconsistent with the provisions of the Plan and that by its terms involves or might involve the issuance of (i) Shares, (ii) an Option, a SAR or similar right with a fixed or variable price related to the Fair Market Value of the Shares and with an exercise or conversion privilege related to the passage of time, the occurrence of one or more events, or the satisfaction of performance criteria or other conditions, or (iii) any other security with the value derived from the value of the Shares. Such awards include, without limitation, Options, or sales or bonuses of Restricted Stock, SARs, Dividend Equivalent Rights, Performance Units or Performance Shares, and an Award may consist of one such security or benefit, or two (2) or more of them in any combination or alternative.

Designation of Award. Each Award shall be designated in the Award Agreement. In the case of an Option, the Option shall be designated as either an Incentive Stock Option or a Non-Qualified Stock Option. However, notwithstanding such designation, to the extent that the aggregate Fair Market Value of Shares subject to Options designated as Incentive Stock Options which become exercisable for the first time by a Grantee during any calendar year (under all plans of the Company or any Parent or Subsidiary) exceeds $100,000, such excess Options, to the extent of the Shares covered thereby in excess of the foregoing limitation, shall be treated as Non-Qualified Stock Options. For this purpose, Incentive Stock Options shall be taken into account in the order in which they were granted, and the

Fair Market Value of the Shares shall be determined as of the grant date of the relevant Option.

Conditions of Award. Subject to the terms of the Plan, the Administrator shall determine the provisions, terms, and conditions of each Award including, but not limited to, the Award vesting schedule, repurchase provisions, rights of first refusal, forfeiture provisions, form of payment (cash, Shares, or other consideration) upon settlement of the Award, payment contingencies, and satisfaction of any performance criteria. The performance criteria established by the Administrator may be based on any one of, or combination of, increase in share price, earnings per share, total stockholder return, return on equity, return on assets, return on investment, net operating income, cash flow, revenue, economic value added, personal management objectives, or other measure of performance selected by the Administrator. Partial achievement of the specified criteria may result in a payment or vesting corresponding to the degree of achievement as specified in the Award Agreement.

Acquisitions and Other Transactions. The Administrator may issue Awards under the Plan in settlement, assumption or substitution for, outstanding awards or obligations to grant future awards in connection with the Company or a Related Entity acquiring another entity, an interest in another entity or an additional interest in a Related Entity whether by merger, stock purchase, asset purchase or other form of transaction.

Deferral of Award Payment. The Administrator may establish one or more programs under the Plan to permit selected Grantees the opportunity to elect to defer receipt of consideration upon exercise of an Award, satisfaction of performance criteria, or other event that absent the election would entitle the Grantee to payment or receipt of Shares or other consideration under an Award. The Administrator may establish the election procedures, the timing of such elections, the mechanisms for payments of, and accrual of interest or other earnings, if any, on amounts, Shares or other consideration so deferred, and such other terms, conditions, rules and procedures that the Administrator deems advisable for the administration of any such deferral program.

Award Exchange Programs. The Administrator may establish one or more programs under the Plan to permit selected Grantees to exchange an Award under the Plan for one or more other types of Awards under the Plan on such terms and conditions as determined by the Administrator from time to time.

Separate Programs. The Administrator may establish one or more separate programs under the Plan for the purpose of issuing particular forms of Awards to one or more classes of Grantees on such terms and conditions as determined by the Administrator from time to time.

Early Exercise:

The Award Agreement may, but need not, include a provision whereby the Grantee may elect at any time while an Employee, Director or Consultant to exercise any part or all of the Award prior to full vesting of the Award. Any unvested Shares received pursuant to such exercise may be subject to a repurchase right in favor of the Company or a Related Entity or to any other restriction the Administrator determines to be appropriate.

Term of Award. The term of each Award shall be the term stated in the Award Agreement, provided, however, that the term of an Incentive Stock Option shall be no more than ten (10) years from the date of grant thereof. However, in the case of an Incentive Stock Option granted to a Grantee who, at the time the Option is granted, owns stock representing more than ten percent (10%) of the voting power of all classes of stock of the Company or any Parent or Subsidiary, the term of the Incentive Stock Option shall be five (5) years from the date of grant thereof or such shorter term as may be provided in the Award Agreement.

Transferability of Awards. Incentive Stock Options may not be sold, pledged, assigned, hypothecated, transferred, or disposed of in any manner other than by will or by the laws of descent or distribution and may be exercised, during the lifetime of the Grantee, only by the Grantee; provided, however, that the Grantee may designate a beneficiary of the Grantee's Incentive Stock Option in the event of the Grantee's death on a beneficiary designation form provided by the Administrator. Other Awards shall be transferred by will and by the laws of descent and distribution, and during the lifetime of the Grantee, by gift and or pursuant to a domestic relations order to members of the Grantee's Immediate Family to the extent and in the manner determined by the Administrator.

Time of Granting Awards. The date of grant of an Award shall for all purposes be the date on which the Administrator makes the determination to grant such Award, or such other date as is determined by the Administrator. Notice of the grant determination shall be given to each Employee, Director or Consultant to whom an Award is so granted within a reasonable time after the date of such grant.

Award Exercise or Purchase Price, Consideration and Taxes:

Exercise or Purchase Price. The exercise or purchase price, if any, for an Award shall be as follows:
In the case of an Incentive Stock Option:
granted to an Employee who, at the time of the grant of such Incentive Stock Option owns stock representing more than ten percent (10%) of the voting power of all classes of stock of the Company or any Parent or Subsidiary, the per Share exercise price shall be not less than one hundred ten percent (110%) of the Fair Market Value per Share on the date of grant; or

granted to any Employee other than an Employee described in the preceding paragraph, the per Share exercise price shall be not less than one hundred percent (100%) of the Fair Market Value per Share on the date of grant.

In the case of a Non-Qualified Stock Option, the per Share exercise price shall be not less than [eighty-five percent (85%)] of the Fair Market Value per Share on the date of grant unless otherwise determined by the Administrator.[2]

In the case of other Awards, such price as is determined by the Administrator.

Notwithstanding the foregoing provisions of this Section __, in the case of an Award issued pursuant to Section ___, above, the exercise or purchase price for the Award shall be determined in accordance with the principles of Section 424(a) of the Code.

Consideration. Subject to Applicable Laws, the consideration to be paid for the Shares to be issued upon exercise or purchase of an Award including the method of payment, shall be determined by the Administrator (and, in the case of an Incentive Stock Option, shall be determined at the time of grant). In addition to any other types of consideration the Administrator may determine, the Administrator is authorized to accept as consideration for Shares issued under the Plan the following, provided that the portion of the consideration equal to the par value of the Shares must be paid in cash or other legal consideration permitted by the Delaware General Corporation Law:

- cash;
- check;
- delivery of Grantee's promissory note with such recourse, interest, security, and redemption provisions as the Administrator determines as appropriate;

- if the exercise or purchase occurs on or after the Registration Date, surrender of Shares or delivery of a properly executed form of attestation of ownership of Shares as the Administrator may require (including withholding of Shares otherwise deliverable upon exercise of the Award) which have a Fair Market Value on the date of surrender or attestation equal to the aggregate exercise price of the Shares as to which said Award shall be exercised (but only to the extent that such exercise of the Award would not result in an accounting compensation charge with respect to the Shares used to pay the exercise price unless otherwise determined by the Administrator);

- with respect to Options *(with the new FASB rules, the parenthetical will be superfluous)*, if the exercise occurs on or after the Registration Date, payment through a broker-dealer sale and remittance procedure pursuant to which the Grantee (A) shall provide written instructions to a Company designated brokerage firm to effect the immediate sale of some or all of the purchased Shares and remit to the Company, out of the sale proceeds available on the settlement date, sufficient funds to cover the aggregate exercise price payable for the purchased Shares and (B) shall provide written directives to the Company to deliver the certificates for the purchased Shares directly to such brokerage firm in order to complete the sale transaction; or

- any combination of the foregoing methods of payment.

Taxes. No Shares shall be delivered under the Plan to any Grantee or other person until such Grantee or other person has made arrangements acceptable to the Administrator for the satisfaction of any foreign, federal, state, or local income and employment tax withholding obligations, including, without limitation, obligations incident to the receipt of Shares or the disqualifying disposition of Shares received on exercise of an Incentive

Stock Option. Upon exercise of an Award the Company shall withhold or collect from Grantee an amount sufficient to satisfy such tax obligations.

Exercise of Award:

Procedure for Exercise; Rights as a Stockholder.

Any Award granted hereunder shall be exercisable at such times and under such conditions as determined by the Administrator under the terms of the Plan and specified in the Award Agreement.

An Award shall be deemed to be exercised when written notice of such exercise has been given to the Company in accordance with the terms of the Award by the person entitled to exercise the Award and full payment for the Shares with respect to which the Award is exercised, including, to the extent selected, use of the broker-dealer sale and remittance procedure to pay the purchase price as provided in Section _____. Until the issuance (as evidenced by the appropriate entry on the books of the Company or of a duly authorized transfer agent of the Company) of the stock certificate evidencing such Shares, no right to vote or receive dividends or any other rights as a stockholder shall exist with respect to Shares subject to an Award, notwithstanding the exercise of an Option or other Award. The Company shall issue (or cause to be issued) such stock certificate promptly upon exercise of the Award. No adjustment will be made for a dividend or other right for which the record date is prior to the date the stock certificate is issued, except as provided in the Award Agreement or Section ____, below.

Exercise of Award Following Termination of Continuous Service.

An Award may not be exercised after the termination date of such Award set forth in the Award Agreement and may be exercised following the termination of a Grantee's Continuous Service only to the extent provided in the Award Agreement.

Where the Award Agreement permits a Grantee to exercise an Award following the termination of the Grantee's Continuous Service for a specified period, the Award shall terminate to the extent not exercised on the last day of the specified period or the last day of the original term of the Award, whichever occurs first.

Any Award designated as an Incentive Stock Option to the extent not exercised within the time permitted by law for the exercise of Incentive Stock Options following the termination of a Grantee's Continuous Service shall convert automatically to a Non-Qualified Stock Option and thereafter shall be exercisable as such to the extent exercisable by its terms for the period specified in the Award Agreement.

Conditions Upon Issuance of Shares:

Shares shall not be issued pursuant to the exercise of an Award unless the exercise of such Award and the issuance and delivery of such Shares pursuant thereto shall comply with all Applicable Laws, and shall be further subject to the approval of counsel for the Company with respect to such compliance.

As a condition to the exercise of an Award, the Company may require the person exercising such Award to represent and warrant at the time of any such exercise that the Shares are being purchased only for investment and without any present intention to sell or distribute such Shares if, in the opinion of counsel for the Company, such a representation is required by any Applicable Laws.

Adjustments Upon Changes in Capitalization:

Adjustments upon Changes in Capitalization. Subject to any required action by the stockholders of the Company, the number of Shares covered by each outstanding Award, and the number of Shares which have been authorized for issuance under the Plan but as to which no Awards have yet been granted or which have been returned to the Plan, the exercise or purchase price of each such outstanding Award, as well as any other terms that the Administrator determines require adjustment shall be proportionately adjusted for (i) any increase or decrease in the number of issued Shares resulting from a stock split, reverse stock split, stock dividend, combination or reclassification of the Shares, or similar transaction affecting the Shares, (ii) any other increase or decrease in the number of issued Shares effected without receipt of consideration by the Company, or (iii) as the Administrator may determine in its discretion, any other transaction with respect to Common Stock to which Section 424(a) of the Code applies or a similar transaction; provided, however that conversion of any convertible securities of the Company shall not be deemed to have been "effected without receipt of consideration." Such adjustment shall be made by the Administrator and its determination shall be final, binding and conclusive. Except as the Administrator determines, no issuance by the Company of shares of stock of any class, or securities convertible into shares of stock of any class, shall affect, and no adjustment by reason hereof shall be made with respect to, the number or price of Shares subject to an Award.[3]

Corporate Transaction:

Except as provided otherwise in an individual Award Agreement, in the event of a Corporate Transaction:

(A) to the extent an Award either is (x) assumed by the successor corporation or Parent thereof or replaced with a comparable Award with respect to shares of the capital stock of the successor corporation or Parent thereof or (y) replaced with a cash incentive program of the successor corporation which preserves the compensation element of such Award existing at the time of the Corporate Transaction and provides for subsequent payout in accordance with the same vesting schedule applicable to such Award, then such Award (if assumed), the replacement Award (if replaced), or the cash incentive program automatically shall become fully vested, exercisable and payable and be released from any restrictions on transfer (other than transfer restrictions applicable to Options) and repurchase or forfeiture rights, immediately upon termination of the Grantee's Continuous Service (substituting the successor employer corporation for "Company or Related Entity" for the definition of "Continuous Service") if such Continuous Service is terminated by the successor company without Cause or voluntarily by the Grantee with Good Reason within twelve (12) months of the Corporate Transaction; or

(B) in the event an Award which is at the time outstanding under the Plan is not assumed by the successor corporation or the Parent thereof, each such Award shall automatically become fully vested and exercisable and be released from any restrictions on transfer (other than transfer restrictions applicable to Incentive Stock Options) and repurchase or forfeiture rights, immediately prior to the specified effective date of such Corporate Transaction, for all of the Shares at the time represented by such Award.

The determination of Award comparability above shall be made by the Administrator, and its determination shall be final, binding and conclusive.

Effective Date and Term of Plan. The Plan shall become effective upon the earlier to occur of its adoption by the Board or its approval by the stockholders of the Company. It shall continue in effect for a term of ten (10) years unless sooner terminated. Subject to Section __, below, and Applicable Laws, Awards may be granted under the Plan upon its becoming effective.

Amendment, Suspension or Termination of the Plan:

The Board may at any time amend, suspend or terminate the Plan. To the extent necessary to comply with Applicable Laws, the Company shall obtain stockholder approval of any Plan amendment in such a manner and to such a degree as required.

No Award may be granted during any suspension of the Plan or after termination of the Plan.

Any amendment, suspension or termination of the Plan (including termination of the Plan under Section __, above) shall not affect Awards already granted, and such Awards shall remain in full force and effect as if the Plan had not been amended, suspended or terminated, unless mutually agreed otherwise between the Grantee and the Administrator, which agreement must be in writing and signed by the Grantee and the Company.

Reservation of Shares:

The Company, during the term of the Plan, will at all times reserve and keep available such number of Shares as shall be sufficient to satisfy the requirements of the Plan.

The inability of the Company to obtain authority from any regulatory body having jurisdiction, which authority is deemed by the Company's counsel to be necessary to the lawful issuance and sale of any Shares hereunder, shall relieve the Company of any liability in respect of the failure to issue or sell such Shares as to which such requisite authority shall not have been obtained.

No Effect on Terms of Employment/Consulting Relationship:

The Plan shall not confer upon any Grantee any right with respect to the Grantee's Continuous Service, nor shall it interfere in any way with his or her right or the Company's right to terminate the Grantee's Continuous Service at any time, with or without cause.

No Effect on Retirement and Other Benefit Plans:

Except as specifically provided in a retirement or other benefit plan of the Company or a Related Entity, Awards shall not be deemed compensation for purposes of computing benefits or contributions under any retirement plan of the Company or a Related Entity, and shall not affect any benefits under any other benefit plan of any kind or any benefit plan subsequently instituted under which the availability or amount of benefits is related to level of compensation. The Plan is not a "Retirement Plan" or "Welfare Plan" under the Employee Retirement Income Security Act of 1974, as amended.

Stockholder Approval:

The grant of Incentive Stock Options under the Plan shall be subject to approval by the stockholders of the Company within twelve (12) months before or after the date the Plan is adopted excluding Incentive Stock Options issued in substitution for outstanding Incentive Stock Options pursuant to Section 424(a) of the Code. Such stockholder approval shall be obtained in the degree and manner required under Applicable Laws. The Administrator may grant Incentive Stock Options under the Plan prior to approval by the stockholders, but until such approval is obtained, no such Incentive Stock Option shall be exercisable. In the event that stockholder approval is not obtained within the twelve (12) month period provided above, all Incentive Stock Options previously granted under the Plan shall be exercisable as Non-Qualified Stock Options.[4]

Note on Stock Incentive Plans

When option plans first became popular, they typically permitted the grant of options to purchase shares, but not other types of share awards or equity-related incentives. More recently, it has become common to adopt broadly based incentive plans that permit the issuance of shares pursuant to options, the "award" or direct issuance of shares or phantom stock interests (sometimes called "units"), the grant of stock appreciation rights (SARs) and similar features (sometimes called "stock-based awards") that create a potential economic benefit related in whole or in part to the market value of the company's shares. An SAR may be granted in tandem with an option, or it may be freestanding. The tandem interests may be awarded simultaneously or at different times. An option may include dividend equivalent rights that entitle the exercising optionee to a cash or stock benefit equivalent to the dividends paid on the underlying shares during the period the option was held. A plan may entitle a participant to a "tax benefit right," or a cash payment equal to the tax the participant must pay under defined circumstances in connection with the exercise of an option or a disposition of the underlying shares. The plan participants may have the right to defer the receipt of various benefits.

Shares issued or granted pursuant to a direct award may be transferred to the recipient with or without consideration paid by the recipient, and with or without conditions on the recipient's right to retain the shares. (Theoretically, the type of universal plan discussed herein can be used for a broad-based employee stock purchase plan that qualifies for favorable tax treatment under I.R.C. § 423. However, plans designed to comply with this section generally have different characteristics from those discussed herein, and might be adopted more appropriately as separate plans.) Awards of restricted shares often have conditions attached. For example, the recipient may be required to forfeit the shares or transfer them back to the company in return for a refund of any consideration paid if the recipient's employment or service with the company terminates. Typically, the obligation to return the shares lapses, either entirely or in progressive installments, after a stated period or periods of continuing employment; that is, unrestricted and unconditional ownership of the shares "vests" in the recipient when the period of continued employment is satisfied. The vesting of unrestricted shares also may be conditioned upon meeting performance targets. Award shares typically have voting and dividend rights, but are not transferable until the forfeiture conditions lapse. Payment of dividends may be deferred until the restrictions lapse. The committee often reserves the right to waive restrictions or vesting conditions.

By accepting a grant or award under a plan (or possibly by exercising an option), the recipient may assume an obligation to remain in the company's employ for a specified period. Such employment obligation normally is to serve at the employer's pleasure, and many grant and award documents disclaim any employer obligation to provide continued employment.

Typically, the board of directors or a board-appointed committee of directors administers the plan and has full authority to determine the precise terms of specific options and awards, limited only by the terms of the plan itself. (For convenience, the discussion in the text refers to a committee as the administrator of the plan. Such reference includes the full board for those plans that the board itself administers. Some plans contain indemnity and exculpatory provisions for committee members protecting them from liability, comparable to the indemnity provisions found in governing documents to protect directors. Plans may permit the committee to delegate part of its responsibility to other employees or committees.) Unless there is a specific reason to limit flexibility in a particular case, companies typically adopt "universal" or "omnibus" plans that are as open-ended and non-restrictive as possible, containing only the minimal limitations necessary to satisfy basic tax and securities laws requirements as well as limitations considered necessary as a matter of shareholder relations. Within these broad parameters, the committee will fix the variables for each participant in the documents relating to the specific grant or award.

If desired, certain matters, such as those relating to the vesting pattern of options, may be addressed in the plan with default provisions that apply only if the committee does not specify otherwise in a particular option document. Default provisions simplify the documentation for individual grants and awards, which would be required to address the particular variable covered by the plan only when the default provision was not intended to apply.

Most plans permit the grant of options that qualify as ISOs under the Code and also options that do not so qualify, non-qualified stock options (NSOs). Maximum flexibility arises from plans that give the power to grant both ISOs and NSOs. (If the plan and the option itself meet the ISO tests, the option will qualify for ISO treatment whether or not the plan or the option refers to ISO treatment under the Code, unless the option states affirmatively that it is not intended to be an ISO. However, it is recommended that if ISOs are intended to be granted, the plan and the particular option document should reflect that fact. The company may have an affirmative reason to want an option treated as an NSO, even if it meets the Code's test for an ISO.)

Most companies want at least some of their plans to be designed so that directors and officers will avoid "short-swing profit" recapture liability under the '34 Act § 16(b), and also will desire that certain benefits under their plans be "performance based" for purposes of I.R.C. § 162(m) (the $1 million cap on deductibility of certain types of compensation, which cap does not apply to certain performance-based items). The compensation committee reports of some companies indicate that compliance with I.R.C. § 162(m) is not a significant consideration in formulating compensation policies. Some companies are so large that the deduction potentially lost is immaterial. Some companies believe that there will be no member of senior management whose annual compensation is likely to exceed the cap in the foreseeable future (although it should be noted that the option itself may contribute a significant amount over time to the employee's compensation).

Simpler plans specify a finite number of authorized but unissued shares and/or treasury shares that are issuable under the plan, which number usually is subject to adjustment under an anti-dilution provision in circumstances such as stock splits. Plans should make clear that the anti-dilution provisions apply not only to the total number of shares covered by the plan, but also to any other plan references to share numbers, such as provisions limiting the number of options that any optionee may receive per year or setting the formula for automatic annual grants to plan administrators. Anti-dilution provisions may also cover mergers, spinoffs, and similar events as well as ordinary dividends. So-called evergreen plans specify that the number of shares issuable under the plan shall be increased at stated times (for example, each fiscal year end) by an amount equal to a stated percentage of the number of shares outstanding at a given time. To meet the Code requirement for a plan permitting ISOs, an overall outer limit on the number of shares must be set forth in the plan but (subject only to shareholder relations considerations) such limit can be a very high one that the issuer does not expect to reach for many years.

Evergreen formulations vary widely. The following provision reflects the evergreen approach:

The aggregate maximum number of shares for which awards or options may be granted pursuant to the plan is 1,000,000 (subject to anti-dilution adjustments set forth elsewhere herein), increased on December 31 of each year from and including December 31, 200* by a number of shares equal to one percent (1%) of the number of shares of Common Stock outstanding on such date; provided, however, that any such increase shall be made only to the extent that the company has sufficient authorized and unreserved Common Stock for such purpose; and further provided that the maximum aggregate number of shares to be issued under the plan shall not exceed 3,000,000 (subject to anti-dilution adjustments set forth elsewhere herein). Such increase shall be made each December 31, regardless of the number of shares remaining available for issuance under the plan on such date.

Under I.R.C. § 422(b)(1) and Prop. Treas. Reg. § 1.422A-2(b)(3)(i) and (ii), an evergreen formula that does not have a fixed maximum limit would not meet the requirement for a plan under which ISOs may be granted.

An alternative is to establish a share limit that applies only to ISOs. Plans typically specify that shares underlying lapsed options and award shares reacquired by the company remain available for reissue under the plan.

A plan may provide for various methods by which an option may be exercised. These include payment of the exercise price in cash, payment in the form of previously owned shares surrendered to the company (typically valued at current fair market value and possibly excluding restricted shares still subject to a risk of forfeiture) if permitted by state law, or payment to the optionee of the option's 'in-the-money value' (that is, the excess of the current fair market value of the shares covered by the option over the option exercise price) in either shares or cash upon relinquishment of the option. The company may require that shares surrendered must have been held by the optionee for a specified minimum period (that is, "matured").

The company may accept the optionee's note as payment for shares, or installment payments may be accepted, if permitted by the applicable state law provision on the acceptable forms of consideration for a purchase of shares (which may differ if treasury rather than authorized but unissued shares are delivered on the option exercise), and subject to the limits of the Federal Reserve Board's Margin Rules. It may be possible for the company to assist the optionee financially by making a loan or guaranteeing a third-party loan, even if it cannot accept a note in payment for shares. See Herbert Kraus, Executive Stock Options and Stock Appreciation Rights, § 2.05 (Law Journal Seminars-Press, 1994).

If an option permits exercise by surrendering previously owned shares, the optionee may receive the full "in-the-money value" of the option in the form of shares without significant cash outlay through "pyramiding."

Illustration: Assume the fair market value of the shares is twice the option exercise price of a 51,000 share option. By surrendering 100 pre-owned shares (or shares acquired by exercising the option to the extent of 100 shares), the optionee can get 200 shares. Then the 200 can be exchanged for 400, which can be exchanged for 800, and so forth. With relatively few turns, this geometric progression will permit a very large number of shares to be acquired. If the optionee owned the first 100 shares, after eight sequential exercises, 100 pre-owned shares would grow to 25,600 fully paid shares and the option would have been exercised to the full extent of 51,000 shares with no cash outlay.

Companies may grant "reload" or "restoration" options when shares are used, or a portion of the option is surrendered, to pay the exercise price, with the new options covering the number of shares or options surrendered. In addition, the reload options may have an exercise price equal to the market value on the exercise date of the earlier option and the same expiration date as the options exercised. In general, a reload feature allows the optionee to lock in a gain in the option and still have the upside potential on the total number of shares covered by the original option. The exercise of a reload option may or may not trigger further reloads, either indefinitely or with a fixed number of reloads.

Various techniques can be used to encourage continued exposure to equity risk and/or continued employment when reload options are granted. For example, the company may restrict resale of the shares issued on the exercise of the original option for a specified time, and the exercisability of the reload option may be deferred or conditioned on continued employment.

A "cashless exercise" may be permitted so that an optionee may arrange, on the date of the option exercise, for a broker to sell a portion of the shares acquired on exercise, and for the broker to then pay the option exercise price to the company from the sale proceeds. Under such arrangements, the company may not receive the exercise price of the option from the broker until the settlement date on the sale, a few days after the exercise notice is given by the optionee. A plan or option form that requires the exercise price to accompany the exercise notice would seem to preclude this method of exercise if applied strictly. A cash loan can be made from the broker to pay for the shares on the date the exercise notice is given, which may require the optionee to pay interest until the sale proceeds repay the loan. The requirements of the Federal Reserve Board's Regulations T and G should be considered in connection with any extension of credit by brokers or the company. Under the margin rules, if an optionee transmits to a broker an irrevocable notice to exercise an option and an order to sell the shares immediately, the broker's loan of the sale proceeds is not considered an extension of margin credit, the broker (although not required) generally will charge interest on the loan, and the transaction may be completed in a cash account. See Corporate Counsel 8 (Sept.-Oct. 1987).

Consideration should be given to whether the option is to be deemed exercised and the shares acquired on the date the optionee gives an exercise notice or the date the company receives payment, an issue that can affect the amount of withholding tax, holding periods, the right to receive dividends if the record date falls between the dates of the exercise notice and the payment, and so forth. Corporate Executive 6 (Nov.-Dec. 1994) suggests that the plan avoid specificity on this subject and that the committee resolve the issue. It would be desirable to have a plan provision giving the committee the right to waive defects in the exercise procedure.

A plan may disclaim the company's obligation to create a separate fund for the performance of its cash payment obligations, thereby making the participants unsecured general creditors. The committee may be given the discretion to create a trust fund or similar arrangement for such purpose.

Prior to a recent change in the law, it was customary to require the company to retain the right to withhold sufficient shares, valued at current fair market value, to cover withholding tax that is payable at the time an employee (but not an outside director) exercises an NSO (Corporate Counsel I (Mar.-Apr. 1992) discusses various withholding issues in depth) or receives a share award, unless the optionee supplies cash equal to the necessary withholding. The plans may give the company the right to deduct the amount of the withholding due on the exercise of an option from salary or other payments due or becoming due from the company to the optionee.

Originally, it was common for plans to provide that, as set forth in the ISO rules (I.R.C. § 422(b)), options were not transferable by the optionee other than as transfers at death in accordance with the laws of descent and distribution. NSOs may be transferable, however, and there may be considerable tax planning advantages when optionees transfer options to family members. See Priv. Ltr. Rul. 9349004 and 9350016. See also Corporate Executive I (Oct.-Nov. 1993), 1 (Mar.-Apr. 1994), and I (May-June 1997). Companies vary in their approach to permitted transfers. Some permit option transfers without payment of consideration only to family members in defined relationships to the optionee, trusts for family members and partnerships composed only of family members, or transfers pursuant to a "qualified domestic relations order" as that term is defined under the Code and ERISA. Some plans include charities or non-profit organizations as permitted transferees. It is also possible to permit transfers more broadly.

Traditionally, the right to exercise options terminated at or shortly after the termination of the optionee's employment with the company. A typical pattern, which meets the ISO requirement, permits the exercise of the option (to the extent it was exercisable by the optionee at the termination of employment) for one year after employment terminates as a result of the optionee's death (Note: ISOs may survive death to the end of the original term of the option, and need not expire in one year, but it is common to impose some limit on carryover after death.) or disability, or three months after employment terminates for any other reason, but in no event after the option's stated expiration date. Plans may address the extent to which a leave of absence constitutes a termination of employment for this purpose.

There is no generally applicable legal requirement for an NSO to terminate with the termination of employment. Accordingly, some companies take the view that the then-exercisable portion of an NSO should be considered earned at the date employment terminates, and the option should remain exercisable, to the extent exercisable when employment terminates, until the end of its stated term irrespective of continued employment. Other companies may permit options to continue vesting according to the original schedule during the post-employment period, at least for specified classes of optionees such as retirees. There also may be special circumstances when it is appropriate to permit additional installments to become exercisable at the committee's discretion in accordance with the original vesting schedule (or even to permit vesting to accelerate) during the post-employment period. For example, such a provision could make it much more attractive for an optionee to accept an early retirement proposal that the company is anxious to have accepted.

The right to exercise an option during the permitted period after termination of employment may be subject to conditions, such as compliance with non-competition, non-disclosure, non-disparagement, or non-solicitation provisions as long as such provisions comply with applicable labor laws. A provision limiting post-employment exercise can be supplemented by a separate agreement that if the option is first exercised and thereafter, within a restricted period that may extend beyond the option's post-employment exercisability period, the optionee engages in prohibited activities, the optionee will repay the amount of the spread to the company. Additionally, the option, or a separate agreement, may give the company an express right of offset, reducing its obligation under the option by any obligations of the optionee to the company. Matters relating to forfeiture are discussed in Corporate Executive 4-5 (Sept.-Oct. 1995), (Nov.-Dec. 1995), and 7 (May-June 1997); N.Y. Times, Oct. 22, 1995, § 3, at 11. 1

Traditional options are "time-vested"; that is, they become exercisable, in full or in stated installments, with the passage of time (if they were not fully exercisable at the time of grant). It is also possible to issue "performance-based" options that condition exercisability on the achievement of some performance target. If the number of shares covered or the exercise price of a performance-based option cannot be determined on the grant date, the option would not be deemed granted for purposes of I.R.C. § 16, nor would it be a "derivative security" under Rule 16a- I (c)(6), until both variables become fixed. Certilman Balin Adler & Hyman, letter dated Apr. 6, 1992, Fed. Sec. L. Rep. (CCH) 176,144. A target may relate to the market price of the company's stock; for example, the option becomes exercisable only if the market price reaches (and, if desired, sustains) a specified level. The performance target may relate to the company's net income, pre-tax income, operating income, return on equity, return on assets, or any other company-specific ratio or formula that is less subject to the vagaries of the public stock market price.

Performance provisions may provide for partial exercisability if goals are met partially, or they may be on an all-or-none basis. The committee may reserve the right to modify the performance targets in the light of unexpected circumstances.

As variations on the theme, optionees may be promised options that will not be granted unless a performance goal is met, or the options may terminate early, before they become fully exercisable, if a performance goal is not met (sometimes called "truncating" options). In addition to performance-based options that are exercisable by the optionee's payment of consideration in cash or shares, performance-based incentives may be created that entitle the holder to receive shares (sometimes called "deferred shares"), without payment of any consideration by the holder, if a predetermined performance goal is met.

Most options have a fixed exercise price. Fixed-price options may be a very inefficient device to serve as an incentive and reward for good performance, because there may be little correlation between the performance of the company (or the optionee) and the market price for the stock in turbulent markets. There may be considerable value in options of poorly performing companies during bull markets. Conversely, options in companies that outperform their peers may be valueless in down markets.

To better correlate the value of an option to the company's relative performance, the option exercise price can be variable. Options that do not have a fixed price initially are not "derivative securities" under § 16 or Rule 16a-1(c)(6) until the price becomes fixed. See also Rule 16b-6(a). However, an option with a price variable in accordance with a formula that can be determined in advance (for example, 5 percent each year) would be a derivative security. See Sec. Act Rel. No. 34-28869, n. 134. So-called index options vary the exercise price based on the company's relative performance compared to a stock market index such as the S&P 500, a relevant index for the company's industry, or possibly a company-specific ratio such as return on capital. Alternatively, the option price can increase each year by a fixed dollar amount or a fixed percentage. The option price may also vary by the extent to which the return received by the company's shareholders exceeds some other standard, such as the risk-free Treasury Bond rate. In applying the index, adjustments may be made for dividends paid by the company and/or issuers in the index. The exercise price may be the lower of the market price on the grant date or a specified discount from the market price on the exercise date. An ISO may have a variable price provided that the exercise price can never be below the fair market value on the grant date.

The exercise price may be structured to change only upward. For example, the exercise price may increase by the interest rate an investor might have received by investing in a Treasury Bond or might increase by a company-specific ratio such as a return on equity, reflecting the rate of return that shareholders must realize before the options are in-the-money. Alternatively, the exercise price may be subject to adjustment in both directions. Downward adjustments may be based on absolute changes in the index; for example, if the relevant stock market price index decreases, the option exercise price decreases by the same percentage. Or decreases may be made only if the company outperforms the relevant index; for example, in a down market, the option price decreases only if the company's stock either decreases less than the relevant index or increases. Obviously, if the concept of a variable price option is accepted, there are unlimited variations that can be adopted.

The same general principle can be applied to the grant of new options under plans contemplating annual or other periodic grants. Under such an arrangement, each year after the base year the option exercise price will be fixed, but will change from the exercise price in the base year option in proportion to the change in the index. Thus, if the company's stock has risen more (or fallen less) than the index from the base date, the next option exercise price will be below the company's stock market price, reflecting the company's outperformance of the index. Conversely, the next option price will be above the market price if the company's stock has risen less (or fallen more) than the index.

Most options are exercisable at the fair market value on the grant date. Some companies, however, have adopted compensation strategies of granting NSOs exercisable at a discount well below the market price on the grant date ("deep-in-the-money options").

Options also may have exercise prices at a premium over the grant date market price ("out-of-the-money options"). Such options serve as a clear incentive for the optionee to work toward performance that justifies a market price increase for the shares. Premium options probably have been used most frequently in connection with very large grants ("megagrants") to very senior executives, sometimes coupled with other options that are exercisable at the market.

Companies also may wish to grant options that are exercisable at a trailing average of the market price, for example, the average market price between the grant date and a specified prior date such as one month or one year earlier. One purpose of this approach is to minimize the possible impact of aberrational market price fluctuations on the grant date. The trailing market average approach seems especially appropriate for options that are issued automatically (such as formula options or options under plans that call for annual grants), where the committee does not act to fix the price of the options at the time of assurance. The foregoing principle also can be applied, with an adjustment in either absolute dollar terms or percentage terms, to options intended to be at a premium over or discount to the current market price.

Options granted in connection with an initial public offering of stock may be granted at the price the company receives for the shares net of the underwriters' discount. A company that sells its shares at a slight discount through a dividend reinvestment plan might offer the same discount in pricing its options. In either case, the rationale of the discount would be that the company need not receive a greater net price from its optionees than it would receive from others.

There is no generally applicable legal requirement that a plan must have a fixed duration. However, an ISO may not be granted more than 10 years after the earlier of the date the plan is adopted or approved by the shareholders. If the ISO is granted during the life of the plan, the option itself may expire after the life of the plan.

In addition to directors and employees of the issuer (or "key" employees, which term may or may not be defined), plans may cover employees of companies that are affiliated with the issuer as well as their respective consultants, advisers, and others who stand in a defined relationship such as vendors, customers, independent contractors/agents, and franchisees. ISOs may be granted only to employees. If the plan is too expansive in its eligibility, it may cease to be an "employee benefit plan" as defined under 1933 Act Rule 405, which could have the consequence of making the underlying shares ineligible for '33 Act registration on Form S-8. Because of the interrelationship of the definition of "employee benefit plan" in Rule 405 and the eligibility requirements in General Instruction A(l)(a) in Form S-8 as discussed below, companies may wish to include the qualification embodied in Rule 405 that consultants and advisors be limited to those providing a bona fide service not related to the sale of securities in capital-raising transactions.

Although a universal or omnibus plan may be administered to grant options to anyone covered by its eligibility provisions, some companies tailor special plans to narrower groups such as senior executives or non-employee directors. Alternatively, an omnibus plan may also contain provisions for specific grants pursuant to a formula to defined classes of persons, such as outside directors.

Change of control often triggers accelerated vesting of optionee, either by a change of control having occurred (a "single trigger"), or by a change of control having occurred, subsequent to which either (1) the employment of the option or award holder is terminated either by the employee for good reason (as defined) or by the employer without cause (as defined), or (2) such person's compensation or authority is reduced (a "double trigger").

A plan may call for automatic formula grants for certain persons, such as all outside directors. Clearly, the formula in the plan should fix the key option variables such as the number of shares, exercise price, term, vesting provisions, and so forth. The formula may vary the number of options granted based on objective criteria such as length of service or the company's return on equity. Kent Electronics, letter dated Dec. 20, 199 1, CCH 76,046; Cooper Tire & Rubber Co., letter dated May 11, 1992, CCH 76,154. To eliminate any question about the adequacy of the formula, it is desirable that the formula address all of the variables that might relate to the option, including such matters as whether the option accelerates upon a change of control, available methods of exercise, and so forth. (See Ropes & Gray, letter dated Dec. 1, 1992, CCH 176,400, stating that an automatic acceleration on a change of control, defined by objective criteria, would not be inconsistent with a formula option or affect the status of an otherwise disinterested director. See also prior Rule 16b-3(c)(2). The correspondence raises the suggestion that a discretionary acceleration would be inappropriate for a formula option.)

On the scheduled grant date for a formula option, there may be material non-public information that would be expected to affect the market price of the company's stock on disclosure. A formula plan may permit delay of grants until after the disclosure, if the general counsel determines that there is material non-public information on the scheduled grant date. Merck & Co., letter dated Jan. 16, 1992. In this case, the basic formula price was the higher of the average of the high and low prices for the day or the last sale price for the day.

Because repricing options is currently unpopular, the opprobrium may be obviated by a provision that options will terminate automatically if they have been out-of-the-money by a specified amount over a specified period of time. This technique can cause valueless options to self-destruct.

Plans may reserve to the committee the right to modify outstanding options and awards in any respect that is not adverse to the option or award holder, including particularly the right to accelerate the option's exercisability (such an acceleration is not a "modification" under I.R.C. § 424(h)(3)(C); however, it may be a modification for accounting purposes), and to waive minor conditions or requirements. The holder is unlikely to object to such a provision. The purpose of such a provision is to help support the position (which may or may not prevail, depending on specific factual context) that a change favorable to the holder need not be treated as a new grant or award for tax, disclosure, accounting or other relevant purposes. It also serves to eliminate questions about the adequacy or timing of an exercise that might fail to comply with a technicality in the plan or the option.

A provision that authorizes the committee to interpret the plan and to adopt rules and regulations for its administration is also useful. Such a provision empowers the committee to resolve ambiguities and adopt operating procedures without the need for a formal plan amendment.

Form S-8 is ordinarily used to register shares underlying a plan if the company is subject to Exchange Act reporting and has filed all reports required during the preceding 12 months. The form is available to register shares underlying an "employee benefit plan" as defined in 1933 Act Rule 405, which definition includes a wide range of written plans (including individual agreements) "solely" for the benefit of employees, directors, and other categories, including consultants and advisors, provided that bona fide services must be rendered by consultants or advisors and such services must not be in connection with the offer or sale of securities in a capital-raising transaction. For purposes of Form S-8, the term "employee" includes former employees as well as successors on death.

Form S-8 can be used for transferable options held by current employees. However, Form S-8 can be used for sales to former employees and successors on death only if the options are non-transferable, except under the laws of descent and distribution. (See General Instruction A(l)(a) to Form S-8.) If an employee with a transferable option is about to terminate his or her employment and values the liquidity of Form S-8 registration more than the transferability feature, an irrevocable undertaking by the optionee to eliminate the transferability feature should be effective to preserve the availability of Form S-8 registration of the underlying shares.

A registration statement for shares underlying an option plan typically covers the specific number of shares covered by the plan (subject to anti-dilution adjustments as permitted by Rule 416). Questions arise about how the count is made. If the plan provisions permit shares reacquired on a forfeiture to be resold under the plan, must the second sale count for purposes of using up the amount registered? If an option is exercised for shares by the delivery of previously owned shares, does such exercise use up the gross or the net increase in the number of shares outstanding? The staff of the SEC has declined to give guidance on this subject. The consequence may be that in certain circumstances the number of shares registered may be fully used even though additional shares may remain available under the terms of the plan. The most conservative approach is to count each separate issuance for Form S-8 purposes: for example, if shares issued under the plan are reacquired on a forfeiture and reissued, as permitted under the plan, both issuances would reduce the number of shares remaining available under the Form S-8; if an SAR granted in tandem with an option is exercised, the exercise uses up the number of SARs and options surrendered, not the net number of shares issued. It might be desirable (although no examples of the technique being used can be cited) for companies to increase the filing fee by a relatively small amount and to register a larger number of shares than the number covered by the terms of the plan, so that the count required by the plan will not exceed the count required by Form S-8. By contrast, the SEC has taken a much more liberal approach, essentially deferring to the company's own count, for purposes of a prior version of Rule 16b-3, in determining whether the number of shares issued exceeds the amount approved by the shareholders. On counting for Form S-8 purposes, see Corporate Counsel 3 (July-Aug. 1994); on counting for former Rule 16b-3 purposes, see Release No. 34-34514 at n. 69; and Corporate Executive 8 (Sept.-Oct. 1995).

If there are circumstances in which Form S-8 cannot be used to register shares underlying a plan, an issuer eligible to use Form S-3 should consider registration on the latter form. It may be possible for the company to use Form S-3 even if it does not have a sufficient market float to use the form for normal primary sales.

If the company meets the generally applicable requirements for the use of Form S-3 for primary offerings, including a $75 million market float of its securities, Form S-3 is available unquestionably to register shares underlying an option plan. Form S-3 may be used for securities issued on the exercise of transferable "warrants" (a term not defined in the form) by issuers that need not meet the market float requirement. (See General Instruction B4 of Form

S-3.) Arguably, an option that is transferable by its original terms, or is made transferable by amendment, would qualify as a "warrant" for this purpose.

If shares are awarded to a participant under the plan without payment of consideration, the transaction would not constitute a sale by the company and, therefore, the initial issuance of the shares would not require Securities Act registration. The same result may follow if, for state law or other reasons, the shares were sold for a nominal consideration such as $.01.

If registered shares are issued under a plan, participants who are not affiliates receive stock that can be resold freely without further registration, and affiliates receive shares that can be resold under Rule 144 without a holding period. The SEC has determined, as a matter of policy, that if unregistered shares are issued directly to a participant under a plan, the same pattern applies with respect to resales without registration if three conditions are met: (1) the company is subject to Exchange Act reporting, (2) the stock being distributed is actively traded in the open market, and (3) the number of shares being distributed is relatively small in relation to the number of shares of the class issued and outstanding (and for this purpose I percent can be viewed as a safe harbor). Sec. Act Rel. No. 33-6281 (Jan. 15, 198 1), § IIIB; Rubbermaid, Inc., letter available June 5, 1989.

An option clearly is a security for federal securities law purposes, and a "derivative security" under Exchange Act § 16. The grant of an option is generally not considered to be a sale under such laws. However, the exercise of an option and the sale of restricted securities under a plan are sales that must be registered unless an exemption applies.

Many options condition their exercise on continued employment but do not as such require continued employment. (Indeed, the option form often negates any obligation to continue the optionee's employment.) If the acceptance of an option obligated the optionee to a term of continued employment, the argument could be made that the option was sold in a transaction that requires '33 Act registration or an applicable exemption, but this has not been the prevailing interpretation. (Compare '33 Act Rule 144(d)(3)(iii).)

It is possible that the grant of an option, and it is highly likely that the exercise of an option or the sale of restricted shares, constitutes a sale of a security under applicable state blue sky laws. For most public companies, state securities laws provisions (other than anti-fraud and filing fee provisions) probably are preempted by federal law, by virtue of '33 Act § 18. To the extent not preempted, state laws may apply in states where the optionee or purchaser resides, and possibly also laws of the state from which the company handles the transaction as well as the state in which the optionee or purchaser handles the transaction, if different from the state of residence. Companies should consider the blue sky laws in administering their plans. For blue sky purposes, the company must also consider the broker dealer and agent or salesman licensing requirements. Kraus, Executive Stock Options and Stock Appreciation Rights, §§ 5.01 et seq. and 9.02 [2] (Law Journal Seminars-Press, 1994) has an extensive survey of blue sky law provisions dealing with options and related matters.

Note on Merger Effects

This is usually the most difficult and contentious provision in the entire Plan. There are five common alternatives, summarized as follows, and these alternatives can be modified to suit the particular circumstances of the company (please read the actual text of the Plan for a more detailed explanation of each alternative):

- Alternative 1 - Automatic Termination Unless Assumed: All outstanding options under the Plan automatically terminate upon the consummation of a Corporate Transaction unless they are assumed by the successor corporation. Note that there is no need to assume or terminate options upon a Change in Control.

- Alternative 2 - Automatic Acceleration Regardless of Assumption: All outstanding options under the Plan automatically become fully vested and exercisable immediately prior to a Corporate Transaction or Change in Control. Upon the consummation of the Corporate Transaction, all outstanding options terminate unless assumed by the successor corporation.

- Alternative 3 - Automatic Acceleration Unless Assumed: All outstanding options under the Plan automatically become fully vested and exercisable immediately prior to the Corporate Transaction unless they are assumed or replaced with a comparable award by the successor corporation.

- Alternative 4 - Automatic Acceleration Unless Assumed or Terminated After Assumption: All outstanding options under the Plan automatically become fully vested and exercisable immediately prior to the Corporate Transaction unless they are assumed or replaced with a comparable award by the successor corporation. Assumed options or replacement options automatically become fully vested and exercisable if the grantee is terminated by the successor company without cause or voluntarily by the grantee for good reason within 12 months of the Corporate Transaction or a Change in Control.

- Alternative 5 - Discretionary Acceleration: The Administrator of the Plan has the authority at any time while an option is outstanding, to provide for the full automatic vesting and exercisability of one or more outstanding unvested awards under the Plan.

Choice 1 is often used in high tech companies because the companies have value in the employee pool and acceleration can make a company a less attractive takeover candidate because the employees will need to be further compensated to remain after the Corporate Transaction; acceleration also creates parity issues. Many companies choose Choice 1 and provide acceleration in individually negotiated agreements for certain executives in which the Double Trigger at Choice 4 is becoming popular. Note that, under current accounting conventions, a portion of the purchase price is assigned to the "value" of the vesting restriction on assumed stock awards, confirming the idea that value is lost if all awards are accelerated.

Choice 2 - Acceleration of vesting regardless of assumption (less commonly used than Choice 1, 3 or 4). Except as provided otherwise in an individual Award Agreement, in the event of any Corporate Transaction, each Award shall automatically become fully vested and exercisable and be released from any restrictions on transfer (other than transfer restrictions applicable to Options) repurchase or forfeiture rights, immediately prior to the specified effective date of such Corporate Transaction, for all of the Shares at the time represented by such Award.

Choice 3 - Single Trigger - Acceleration of vesting if not assumed or substituted Except as provided otherwise in an individual Award Agreement, in the event of a Corporate Transaction each Award which is at the time outstanding under the Plan shall automatically become fully vested and exercisable and be released from any restrictions on transfer (other than transfer restrictions applicable to Options) and repurchase or forfeiture rights, immediately prior to the specified effective date of such Corporate Transaction, for all of the Shares at the time represented by such Award if the Award is not assumed by the successor corporation or the Parent thereof in connection with the Corporate Transaction. For the purposes of accelerating the vesting and the release of restrictions applicable to Awards pursuant to this subsection (but not for purposes of termination of such Awards), the Award shall be considered assumed if, in connection with the Corporate Transaction, the Award is replaced with a comparable Award with respect to shares of capital stock of the successor corporation or Parent thereof or is replaced with a cash incentive program of the successor corporation or Parent thereof which preserves the compensation element of such Award existing at the time of the Corporate Transaction and provides for subsequent payout in accordance with the same vesting schedule applicable to such Award. The determination of Award comparability above shall be made by the Administrator and its determination shall be final, binding and conclusive.

Choice 4 - Double Trigger - Acceleration of vesting upon termination without cause or with good reason within 12 months of Corporate Transaction if the Award has been assumed; acceleration prior to the Corporate Transaction.

---

[1] In order to qualify as "performance based" under I.R.C. § 162(m), the Plan must set limits on the number of options awardable to an individual.

[2] The 85% figure is conservative. See note on Deep Discount NSOs.

[3] The importance of a carefully drafted adjustment provision was highlighted by the Delaware Court of Chancery's holding in Sanders v. Wang.

In Wang, the court held that the board of directors that administered a stock option plan exceeded its administrative authority by granting options for additional shares of stock in order to adjust the number of shares subject to previously granted options for stock splits. The plan considered in Wang permitted the board to adjust the number of shares under the options and the exercise price for stock splits, but did not authorize an adjustment of the maximum number of shares available under the plan to account for stock splits or other recapitalizations. The court stated that the board exceeded the limitation on the maximum number of shares subject to options available for grant under the plan when it granted the additional options.

[4] If possible, stockholder approval should predate installation of the Plan. Advance approval is highly desirable for several reasons. Thus, if upon subsequent ratification the value of the stock has increased, any ISOs granted subject to ratification cannot qualify as ISOs unless the exercise price is increased to the fair market value on the date of ratification. Moreover, under the applicable accounting conventions, a charge to earnings may be required because, in theory, the option was granted at a discount. The answer is, currently, not entirely clear, the issue apparently hinging on whether subsequent shareholder approval was a formality (because of insider control) or in doubt at the time the option was granted. See Bachelder "Treatment of Stock Options," N. YLJ 3 (May 31, 1996), discussing FASB No. 123, "Accounting for Stock-Based Compensation" (1995). Bachelder also raises the question whether an option granted on day one and rising in value prior to

stockholder approval within the next 12 months would be deemed granted at an exercise price equal to fair market value for purposes of Internal Revenue Code § 162(m), which calculates the awards to be included in compensation for purposes of the $1 million deduction cap.

24

Model Stock Option Award Agreement

Option Award Agreement

1. Grant of Option

_____, Inc., a _____ corporation (the "Company"), hereby grants to the Grantee (the "Grantee") named in the Notice of Stock Option Award (the "Notice"), an option (the "Option") to purchase the Total Number of Shares of Common Stock subject to the Option (the "Shares") set forth in the Notice, at the Exercise Price per Share set forth in the Notice (the "Exercise Price") subject to the terms and provisions of the Notice, this Stock Option Award Agreement (the "Option Agreement") and the Company's [Year] Stock Incentive Plan, as amended from time to time (the "Plan"), which are incorporated herein by reference. Unless otherwise defined herein, the terms defined in the Plan shall have the same defined meanings in this Option Agreement.

If designated in the Notice as an Incentive Stock Option, the Option is intended to qualify as an Incentive Stock Option as defined in Section 422 of the Code. However, notwithstanding such designation, to the extent that the aggregate Fair Market Value of Shares subject to Options designated as Incentive Stock Options which become exercisable for the first time by the Grantee during any calendar year (under all plans of the Company or any Parent or Subsidiary) exceeds $100,000, such excess Options, to the extent of the Shares covered thereby in excess of the foregoing limitation, shall be treated as Non-Qualified Stock Options. For this purpose, Incentive Stock Options shall be taken into account in the order in which they were granted, and the Fair Market Value of the Shares shall be determined as of the date the Option with respect to such Shares is awarded.

2. Exercise of Option

(a) *Right to Exercise.* The Option shall be exercisable during its term in accordance with the Vesting Schedule set out in the Notice and with the applicable provisions of the Plan and this Option Agreement. The Option shall be subject to the provisions of Section 10(b) of the Plan relating to the exercisability or termination of the Option in the event of a Corporate Transaction. The Grantee shall be subject to reasonable limitations on the number of requested exercises during any monthly or weekly period as determined by the Administrator. In no event shall the Company issue fractional Shares.

(b) *Method of Exercise.* The Option shall be exercisable only by delivery of an Exercise Notice (attached as Exhibit A) which shall state the election to exercise the Option, the whole number of Shares in respect of which the Option is being exercised, and such other provisions as may be required by the Administrator. The Exercise Notice shall be signed by the Grantee and shall be delivered in person, by certified mail, or by such other method as determined from time to time by the Administrator to the Company accompanied by payment of the Exercise Price. The Option shall be deemed to be exercised upon receipt by the Company of such written notice accompanied by the Exercise Price, which, to the extent selected, shall be deemed to be satisfied by use of the broker-dealer sale and remittance procedure to pay the Exercise Price provided in Section 4(d), below.

(c) *Taxes.* No Shares will be delivered to the Grantee or other person pursuant to the exercise of the Option until the Grantee or other person has made arrangements acceptable to the Administrator for the satisfaction of applicable income tax, employment tax, and social security tax withholding obligations, including, without limitation, obligations incident to the receipt of Shares or the disqualifying disposition of Shares received on exercise of an Incentive Stock Option. Upon exercise of the Option, the Company or the Grantee's employer may offset or withhold (from any amount owed by the Company or the Grantee's employer to the Grantee) or collect from the Grantee or other person an amount sufficient to satisfy such tax obligations and/or the employer's withholding obligations.

3. Grantee's Representations

The Grantee understands that neither the Option nor the Shares exercisable pursuant to the Option have been registered under the Securities Act of 1933, as amended, or any United States securities laws. In the event the Shares purchasable pursuant to the exercise of the Option have not been registered under the Securities Act of 1933, as amended, at the time the Option is exercised, the Grantee shall, if requested by the Company, concurrently with the exercise of all or any portion of the Option, deliver to the Company his or her Investment Representation Statement in the form attached hereto as Exhibit B.

4. Method of Payment

Payment of the Exercise Price shall be made by any of the following, or a combination thereof, at the election of the Grantee; provided, however, that such exercise method does not then violate any Applicable Law:

(a) cash;

(b) check;

(c) {if the exercise occurs on or after the Registration Date, surrender of Shares or delivery of a properly executed form of attestation of ownership of Shares as the Administrator may require (including withholding of Shares otherwise deliverable upon exercise of the Option) which have a Fair Market Value on the date of surrender or attestation equal to the aggregate Exercise Price of the Shares as to which the Option is being exercised (but only to the extent that such exercise of the Option would not result in an accounting compensation charge with respect to the Shares used to pay the exercise price)};

(d) {if the exercise occurs on or after the Registration Date, payment through a broker-dealer sale and remittance procedure pursuant to which the Grantee (i) shall provide written instructions to a Company-designated brokerage firm to effect the immediate sale of some or all of the purchased Shares and remit to the Company, out of the sale proceeds available on the settlement date, sufficient funds to cover the aggregate exercise price payable for the purchased Shares and (ii) shall provide written directives to the Company to deliver the certificates for the purchased Shares directly to such brokerage firm in order to complete the sale transaction}; or

(e) {provided that the aggregate Exercise Price for the number of Shares being purchased exceeds _____ thousand dollars ($___,000)}, payment pursuant to a promissory note as described below.

(i) The promissory note shall have a term of _____ (__) years with principal and interest payable in _____ (__) equal annual installments;

(ii) The promissory note shall bear interest at the minimum rate required by the federal tax laws to avoid the imputation of interest income to the Company and compensation income to the Grantee;

(iii) The Grantee shall be personally liable for payment of the promissory note and the promissory note shall be secured by the Shares purchased upon delivery of the promissory note, or such other collateral of equal or greater value, in a manner satisfactory to the Administrator with such documentation as the Administrator may request; and

(iv) The promissory note shall become due and payable upon the occurrence of any or all of the following events: (A) the sale or transfer of the Shares purchased with the promissory note; (B) termination of the Grantee's Continuous Service for any reason other than death or Disability; or (C) the first anniversary of the termination of the Grantee's Continuous Service due to death or Disability.

5. Restrictions on Exercise

The Option may not be exercised if the issuance of the Shares subject to the Option upon such exercise would constitute a violation of any Applicable Laws. [In addition, the Option may not be exercised until such time as the Plan has been approved by the stockholders of the Company.]

6. Termination or Change of Continuous Service

In the event the Grantee's Continuous Service terminates, (other than for Cause,) the Grantee may, to the extent otherwise so entitled at the date of such termination (the "Termination Date"), exercise the Option during the Post-Termination Exercise Period. {In the event of termination of the Grantee's Continuous Service for Cause, the Grantee's right to exercise the Option shall, except as otherwise determined by the Administrator, terminate concurrently with the termination of the Grantee's Continuous

Service.} In no event shall the Option be exercised later than the Expiration Date set forth in the Notice. In the event of the Grantee's change in status from Employee, Director or Consultant to any other status of Employee, Director or Consultant, the Option shall remain in effect and, except to the extent otherwise determined by the Administrator, continue to vest; provided, however, with respect to any Incentive Stock Option that shall remain in effect after a change in status from Employee to Director or Consultant, such Incentive Stock Option shall cease to be treated as an Incentive Stock Option and shall be treated as a Non-Qualified Stock Option on the day three (3) months and one (1) day following such change in status. Except as provided in Sections 7 and 8 below, to the extent that the Grantee is not entitled to exercise the Option on the Termination Date, or if the Grantee does not exercise the Option within the Post-Termination Exercise Period, the Option shall terminate.

7. Disability of Grantee

In the event the Grantee's Continuous Service terminates as a result of his or her Disability, the Grantee may, but only within {twelve (12) months} from the Termination Date (and in no event later than the Expiration Date), exercise the Option to the extent he or she was otherwise entitled to exercise it on the Termination Date; provided, however, that if such Disability is not a "disability" as such term is defined in Section 22(e)(3) of the Code and the Option is an Incentive Stock Option, such Incentive Stock Option shall cease to be treated as an Incentive Stock Option and shall be treated as a Non-Qualified Stock Option on the day three (3) months and one (1) day following the Termination Date. To the extent that the Grantee is not entitled to exercise the Option on the Termination Date, or if the Grantee does not exercise the Option to the extent so entitled within the time specified herein, the Option shall terminate.

8. Death of Grantee

In the event of the termination of the Grantee's Continuous Service as a result of his or her death, or in the event of the Grantee's death during the Post-Termination Exercise Period or during the twelve (12) month period following the Grantee's termination of Continuous Service as a result of his or her Disability, the Grantee's estate, or a person who acquired the right to exercise the Option by bequest or inheritance, may exercise the Option, but only to the extent the Grantee could exercise the Option at the date of termination, within twelve (12) months from the date of death (but in no event later than the Expiration Date). To the extent that the Grantee is not entitled to exercise the Option on the date of death, or if the Option is not exercised to the extent so entitled within the time specified herein, the Option shall terminate.

9. Transferability of Option

The Option, if an Incentive Stock Option, may not be transferred in any manner other than by will or by the laws of descent and distribution and may be exercised during the lifetime of the Grantee only by the Grantee; provided, however, that the Grantee may designate a beneficiary of the Grantee's Incentive Stock Option in the event of the Grantee's death on a beneficiary designation form provided by the Administrator. The Option, if a Non-Qualified Stock Option, may be transferred to any person by will and by the laws of descent and distribution. Non-Qualified Stock Options also may be transferred during the lifetime of the Grantee by gift and pursuant to a domestic relations order to members of the Grantee's Immediate Family to the extent and in the manner determined by the Administrator. The terms of the Option shall be binding upon the executors, administrators, heirs, successors and transferees of the Grantee.

The 2/99 amendments to Form S-8 and Rule 701 allow Non-Qualified Stock Options to be transferred by gift or through a domestic relations order to a

Family Member defined as follows: "<u>Family Member</u>" means any child, stepchild, grandchild, parent, stepparent, grandparent, spouse, former spouse, sibling, niece, nephew, mother-in-law, father-in-law, son-in law, daughter-in-law, brother-in-law, or sister-in-law, including adoptive relationships, any person sharing the Grantee's household (other than a tenant or employee), a trust in which these persons have more than fifty percent of the beneficial interest, a foundation in which these persons (or the Grantee) control the management of assets, and any other entity in which these persons (or the Grantee) own more than fifty percent of the voting interests.

10. Term of Option

The Option may be exercised no later than the Expiration Date set forth in the Notice or such earlier date as otherwise provided herein.

11. Company's Right of First Refusal

(a) *Transfer Notice.* Neither the Grantee nor a transferee (either being sometimes referred to herein as the "Holder") shall sell, hypothecate, encumber or otherwise transfer any Shares or any right or interest therein without first complying with the provisions of this Section 11 or obtaining the prior written consent of the Company. In the event the Holder desires to accept a bona fide third-party offer for any or all of the Shares, the Holder shall provide the Company with written notice (the "Transfer Notice") of:

(i) The Holder's intention to transfer;

(ii) The name of the proposed transferee;

(iii) The number of Shares to be transferred; and

(iv) The proposed transfer price or value and terms thereof.

(b) *First Refusal Exercise Notice.* The Company shall have the right to purchase (the "Right of First Refusal") all but not less than all, of the Shares which are described in the Transfer Notice (the "Offered Shares") at any time during the period commencing upon receipt of the Transfer Notice and ending forty-five (45) days after the first date on which the Company determines that the Right of First Refusal may be exercised without incurring an accounting expense with respect to such exercise (the "Option Period") at the per share price or value and in accordance with the terms stated in the Transfer Notice, which Right of First Refusal shall be exercised by written notice (the "First Refusal Exercise Notice") to the Holder. {During the Option Period and the 120-day period following the expiration of the Option Period, the Company also may exercise its Repurchase Right in lieu or in addition to its Right of First Refusal if the Repurchase Right is or becomes exercisable during the Option Period or such 120-day period.}

(c) *Payment Terms.* The Company shall consummate the purchase of the Offered Shares on the terms set forth in the Transfer Notice within 15 days after delivery of the First Refusal Exercise Notice; provided, however, that in the event the Transfer Notice provides for the payment for the Offered Shares other than in cash, the Company and/or its assigns shall have the right to pay for the Offered Shares by the discounted cash equivalent of the consideration described in the Transfer Notice as reasonably determined by the Administrator. Upon payment for the Offered Shares to the Holder or into escrow for the benefit of the Holder, the Company or its assigns shall become the legal and beneficial owner of the Offered Shares and all rights and interest therein or related thereto, and the Company shall have the right to transfer the Offered Shares to its own name or its assigns without the further action by the Holder.

(d) *Assignment.* Whenever the Company shall have the right to purchase Shares under this Right of First Refusal, the Company may designate and assign one or more employees, officers, directors or stockholders of the

Company or other persons or organizations, to exercise all or a part of the Company's Right of First Refusal.

(e) *Non-Exercise.* If the Company and/or its assigns do not collectively elect to exercise the Right of First Refusal within the Option Period or such earlier time if the Company and/or its assigns notifies the Holder that it will not exercise the Right of First Refusal, then the Holder may transfer the Shares upon the terms and conditions stated in the Transfer Notice, provided that:

(i) The transfer is made within 120 days of the expiration of the Option Period; and

(ii) The transferee agrees in writing that such Shares shall be held subject to the provisions of this Option Agreement.

(f) *Expiration of Transfer Period.* Following such 120-day period, no transfer of the Offered Shares and no change in the terms of the transfer as stated in the Transfer Notice (including the name of the proposed transferee) shall be permitted without a new written Transfer Notice prepared and submitted in accordance with the requirements of this Right of First Refusal.

(g) *Exception for Certain Family Transfers.* Anything to the contrary contained in this section notwithstanding, the transfer by gift or pursuant to a domestic relations order of any or all of the Shares during the Grantee's lifetime to members of the Grantee's Immediate Family or to any person on the Grantee's death by will or by the laws of descent and distribution shall be exempt from the provisions of this Right of First Refusal (a "Permitted Transfer"); provided, however, that (i) the transferee or other recipient shall receive and hold the Shares so transferred subject to the provisions of this Option Agreement, and there shall be no further transfer of such Shares except in accordance with the terms of this Option Agreement and (ii) prior to any such transfer, each transferee shall execute an agreement pursuant to which such transferee shall agree to receive and hold such Shares subject to the provisions of this Option Agreement.

(h) *Termination of Right of First Refusal.* The provisions of this Right of First Refusal shall terminate as to all Shares upon the Registration Date.

(i) *Additional Shares or Substituted Securities.* In the event of any transaction described in Section <10> of the Plan, any new, substituted or additional securities or other property which is by reason of any such transaction distributed with respect to the Shares shall be immediately subject to the Right of First Refusal, but only to the extent the Shares are at the time covered by such right.

(j) *Corporate Transaction.* Immediately prior to the consummation of a Corporate Transaction described in Sections 2(m)(i),(ii), and (iii) of the Plan, the Right of First Refusal shall automatically lapse in its entirety, except to the extent this Option Agreement is assumed by the successor corporation (or its Parent) in connection with such Corporate Transaction, in which case the Right of First Refusal shall apply to the new capital stock or other property received in exchange for the Shares in consummation of the Corporate Transaction, but only to the extent the Shares are at the time covered by such right. {*Note to drafter: delete above Section 11 if Right of First Refusal is in the Bylaws and instead substitute the following:*

The Grantee acknowledges and agrees that the Shares are subject to a right of first refusal ("Right of First Refusal") as set forth in the Bylaws of the Company and that, except in compliance with such right of first refusal, neither the Grantee nor a transferee (either being sometimes referred to herein as the "Holder") shall sell, hypothecate, encumber or otherwise transfer any Shares or any right or interest therein.}

12. Company's Repurchase Right

(a) *Grant of Repurchase Right.* The Company is hereby granted the right to repurchase all or any portion of the Shares (the "Repurchase Right") exercisable at any time (i) during the period commencing on the Termination Date and ending ninety (90) days after the first date on which the Repurchase Right may be exercised without incurring an accounting expense with respect to such exercise or (ii) during the period commencing upon any exercise of the Option that occurs after the Termination Date and ending ninety (90) days after the first date on which the Repurchase Right may be exercised without incurring an accounting expense with respect to such exercise (together, the "Share Repurchase Period").

(b) *Exercise of the Repurchase Right.* The Repurchase Right shall be exercisable by written notice delivered to each Holder of the Shares prior to the expiration of the Share Repurchase Period. The notice shall indicate the number of Shares to be repurchased and the date on which the repurchase is to be effected, such date to be not later than the last day of the Share Repurchase Period. On the date on which the repurchase is to be effected, the Company and/or its assigns shall pay to the Holder in cash or cash equivalents (including the cancellation of any purchase-money indebtedness) an amount equal to the Fair Market Value on the date immediately prior to the day on which the repurchase is to be effected, of the Shares which are to be repurchased from the Holder. Upon such payment to the Holder or deposit of such amount into escrow for the benefit of the Holder, the Company and/or its assigns shall become the legal and beneficial owner of the Shares being repurchased and all rights and interest therein or related thereto, and the Company shall have the right to transfer to its own name or its assigns the number of Shares being repurchased, without further action by the Holder.

(c) *Assignment.* Whenever the Company shall have the right to purchase Shares under this Repurchase Right, the Company may designate and assign one or more employees, officers, directors or stockholders of the Company or other persons or organizations, to exercise all or a part of the Company's Repurchase Right.

(d) *Termination of the Repurchase Right.* The Repurchase Right shall terminate with respect to any Shares for which it is not timely exercised. In addition, the Repurchase Right shall terminate and cease to be exercisable with respect to all Shares upon the Registration Date.

(e) *Additional Shares or Substituted Securities.* In the event of any transaction described in Section <10> of the Plan, any new, substituted or additional securities or other property which is by reason of any such transaction distributed with respect to the Shares shall be immediately subject to the Repurchase Right, but only to the extent the Shares are at the time covered by such right. Appropriate adjustments to reflect the distribution of such securities or property shall be made to the price per share to be paid upon the exercise of the Repurchase Right in order to reflect the effect of any such transaction upon the Company's capital structure.

(f) *Corporate Transaction.* Immediately prior to the consummation of a Corporate Transaction described in Sections 2(m)(i),(ii), and (iii) of the Plan, the Repurchase Right to the extent it has not been exercised shall automatically lapse in its entirety,except to the extent this Option Agreement is assumed by the successor corporation (or its Parent) in connection with such Corporate Transaction, in which case the Repurchase Right shall apply to the new capital stock or other property received in exchange for the Shares in consummation of the Corporate Transaction, but only to the extent the Shares are at the time covered by such right. Appropriate adjustments shall be made to the price per share payable upon exercise of the Repurchase Right to reflect the effect of the Corporate Transaction upon the Company's capital structure.

13. Stop-Transfer Notices

In order to ensure compliance with the restrictions on transfer set forth in this Option Agreement, the Notice or the Plan, the Company may issue appropriate "stop transfer" instructions to its transfer agent, if any, and, if the Company transfers its own securities, it may make appropriate notations to the same effect in its own records.

14. Refusal to Transfer

The Company shall not be required (i) to transfer on its books any Shares that have been sold or otherwise transferred in violation of any of the provisions of this Option Agreement or (ii) to treat as owner of such Shares or to accord the right to vote or pay dividends to any purchaser or other transferee to whom such Shares shall have been so transferred.

15. Lock-Up Agreement

(a) *Agreement.* The Grantee, if requested by the Company and the lead underwriter of any public offering of the Common Stock or other securities of the Company (the "Lead Underwriter"), hereby irrevocably agrees not to sell, contract to sell, grant any option to purchase, transfer the economic risk of ownership in, make any short sale of, pledge or otherwise transfer or dispose of any interest in any Common Stock or any securities convertible into or exchangeable or exercisable for or any other rights to purchase or acquire Common Stock (except Common Stock included in such public offering or acquired on the public market after such offering) during the 180-day period following the effective date of a registration statement of the Company filed under the Securities Act of 1933, as amended, or such shorter period of time as the Lead Underwriter shall specify. The Grantee further agrees to sign such documents as may be requested by the Lead Underwriter to effect the foregoing and agrees that the Company may impose stop-transfer instructions with respect to such Common Stock subject until the end of such period. The Company and the Grantee acknowledge that each Lead Underwriter of a public offering of the Company's stock, during the period of such offering and for the 180-day period thereafter, is an intended beneficiary of this Section 16.

(b) _No Amendment Without Consent of Underwriter._ During the period from identification as a Lead Underwriter in connection with any public offering of the Company's Common Stock until the earlier of (i) the expiration of the lock-up period specified in Section 16(a) in connection with such offering or (ii) the abandonment of such offering by the Company and the Lead Underwriter, the provisions of this Section 16 may not be amended or waived except with the consent of the Lead Underwriter.

16. Entire Agreement: Governing Law

The Notice, the Plan and this Option Agreement constitute the entire agreement of the parties with respect to the subject matter hereof and supersede in their entirety all prior undertakings and agreements of the Company and the Grantee with respect to the subject matter hereof, and may not be modified adversely to the Grantee's interest except by means of a writing signed by the Company and the Grantee. Nothing in the Notice, the Plan and this Option Agreement (except as expressly provided therein) is intended to confer any rights or remedies on any persons other than the parties. The Notice, the Plan and this Option Agreement are to be construed in accordance with and governed by the internal laws of the State of without giving effect to any choice of law rule that would cause the application of the laws of any jurisdiction other than the internal laws of the State of to the rights and duties of the parties. Should any provision of the Notice, the Plan or this Option Agreement be determined by a court of law to be illegal or unenforceable, such provision shall be enforced to the fullest extent allowed by law and the other provisions shall nevertheless remain effective and shall remain enforceable.

17. Headings

The captions used in the Notice and this Option Agreement are inserted for convenience and shall not be deemed a part of the Option for construction or interpretation.

18. Dispute Resolution

The provisions of this Section 18 shall be the exclusive means of resolving disputes arising out of or relating to the Notice, the Plan and this Option Agreement. The Company, the Grantee, and the Grantee's assignees (the "parties") shall attempt in good faith to resolve any disputes arising out of or relating to the Notice, the Plan and this Option Agreement by negotiation between individuals who have authority to settle the controversy. Negotiations shall be commenced by either party by notice of a written statement of the party's position and the name and title of the individual who will represent the party. Within thirty (30) days of the written notification, the parties shall meet at a mutually acceptable time and place, and thereafter as often as they reasonably deem necessary, to resolve the dispute. If the dispute has not been resolved by negotiation, the parties agree that any suit, action, or proceeding arising out of or relating to the Notice, the Plan or this Option Agreement shall be brought in the United States District Court for the Southern District of New York (or should such court lack jurisdiction to hear such action, suit or proceeding, in a New York state court in the County of New York) and that the parties shall submit to the jurisdiction of such court. The parties irrevocably waive, to the fullest extent permitted by law, any objection the party may have to the laying of venue for any such suit, action or proceeding brought in such court. THE PARTIES ALSO EXPRESSLY WAIVE ANY RIGHT THEY HAVE OR MAY HAVE TO A JURY TRIAL OF ANY SUCH SUIT, ACTION OR PROCEEDING. If any one or more provisions of this Section 18 shall for any reason be held invalid or unenforceable, it is the specific intent of the parties that such provisions shall be modified to the minimum extent necessary to make it or its application valid and enforceable. [Select alternate forum if New York is not appropriate]

19. Notices

Any notice required or permitted hereunder shall be given in writing and shall be deemed effectively given upon personal delivery or upon deposit in the United States mail by certified mail (if the parties are within the United States) or upon deposit for delivery by an internationally recognized express mail courier service (for international delivery of notice), with postage and fees prepaid, addressed to the other party at its address as shown beneath its signature in the Notice, or to such other address as such party may designate in writing from time to time to the other party.

Exhibit A - Exercise Notice

EXHIBIT A
NEWCO, INC.
[YEAR] STOCK INCENTIVE PLAN

EXERCISE NOTICE

[COMPANY ADDRESS]

Attention: Secretary

1. Effective as of today, _____, 2002 the undersigned (the "Grantee") hereby elects to exercise the Grantee's option to purchase _____ shares of the Common Stock (the "Shares") of Newco, Inc. (the "Company") under and pursuant to the Company's [YEAR] Stock Incentive Plan, as amended from time to time (the "Plan") and the [ ] Incentive [ ] Non-Qualified Stock Option Award Agreement (the "Option Agreement") and Notice of Stock Option Award (the "Notice") dated _____, _____. Unless otherwise defined herein, the terms

defined in the Plan shall have the same defined meanings in this Exercise Notice.

2. *Representations of the Grantee.* The Grantee acknowledges that the Grantee has received, read and understood the Notice, the Plan and the Option Agreement and agrees to abide by and be bound by their terms and conditions.

3. *Rights as Stockholder.* Until the stock certificate evidencing such Shares is issued (as evidenced by the appropriate entry on the books of the Company or of a duly authorized transfer agent of the Company), no right to vote or receive dividends or any other rights as a stockholder shall exist with respect to the Shares, notwithstanding the exercise of the Option. The Company shall issue (or cause to be issued) such stock certificate promptly after the Option is exercised. No adjustment will be made for a dividend or other right for which the record date is prior to the date the stock certificate is issued, except as provided in Section {10(a)} of the Plan.

The Grantee shall enjoy rights as a stockholder until such time as the Grantee disposes of the Shares or the Company and/or its assignee(s) exercises the {Right of First Refusal} or {the Repurchase Right}. Upon such exercise, the Grantee shall have no further rights as a holder of the Shares so purchased except the right to receive payment for the Shares so purchased in accordance with the provisions of the Option Agreement, and the Grantee shall forthwith cause the certificate(s) evidencing the Shares so purchased to be surrendered to the Company for transfer or cancellation.

4. *Delivery of Payment.* The Grantee herewith delivers to the Company the full Exercise Price for the Shares, which, to the extent selected, shall be deemed to be satisfied by use of the broker-dealer sale and remittance procedure to pay the Exercise Price provided in Section 4(d) of the Option Agreement.

5. *Tax Consultation.* The Grantee understands that the Grantee may suffer adverse tax consequences as a result of the Grantee's purchase or disposition of the Shares. The Grantee represents that the Grantee has consulted with any tax consultants the Grantee deems advisable in connection with the purchase or disposition of the Shares and that the Grantee is not relying on the Company for any tax advice.

6. *Taxes.* The Grantee agrees to satisfy all applicable foreign, federal, state and local income and employment tax withholding obligations and herewith delivers to the Company the full amount of such obligations or has made arrangements acceptable to the Company to satisfy such obligations. In the case of an Incentive Stock Option, the Grantee also agrees, as partial consideration for the designation of the Option as an Incentive Stock Option, to notify the Company in writing within thirty (30) days of any disposition of any shares acquired by exercise of the Option if such disposition occurs within two (2) years from the Award Date or within one (1) year from the date the Shares were transferred to the Grantee. If the Company is required to satisfy any foreign, federal, state or local income or employment tax withholding obligations as a result of such an early disposition, the Grantee agrees to satisfy the amount of such withholding in a manner that the Administrator prescribes.

7. *Restrictive Legends.* The Grantee understands and agrees that the Company shall cause the legends set forth below or legends substantially equivalent thereto, to be placed upon any certificate(s) evidencing ownership of the Shares together with any other legends that may be required by the Company or by state or federal securities laws:

THE SECURITIES REPRESENTED HEREBY HAVE NOT BEEN REGISTERED UNDER THE SECURITIES ACT OF 1933 (THE "ACT") OR ANY STATE SECURITIES LAWS AND MAY NOT BE OFFERED, SOLD OR OTHERWISE TRANSFERRED, PLEDGED OR HYPOTHECATED UNLESS AND UNTIL REGISTERED UNDER THE

ACT OR, IN THE OPINION OF COUNSEL SATISFACTORY TO THE ISSUER OF THESE SECURITIES, SUCH OFFER, SALE OR TRANSFER, PLEDGE OR HYPOTHECATION IS IN COMPLIANCE THEREWITH.

THE SHARES REPRESENTED BY THIS CERTIFICATE ARE SUBJECT TO CERTAIN RESTRICTIONS ON TRANSFER, A [RIGHT OF FIRST REFUSAL AND A REPURCHASE RIGHT] HELD BY THE ISSUER OR ITS ASSIGNEE(S) AS SET FORTH IN THE OPTION AGREEMENT BETWEEN THE ISSUER AND THE ORIGINAL HOLDER OF THESE SHARES, A COPY OF WHICH MAY BE OBTAINED AT THE PRINCIPAL OFFICE OF THE ISSUER. SUCH TRANSFER RESTRICTIONS, [RIGHT OF FIRST REFUSAL AND REPURCHASE RIGHT] ARE BINDING ON TRANSFEREES OF THESE SHARES.

8. *Successors and Assigns.* The Company may assign any of its rights under this Exercise Notice to single or multiple assignees, and this agreement shall inure to the benefit of the successors and assigns of the Company. Subject to the restrictions on transfer herein set forth, this Exercise Notice shall be binding upon the Grantee and his or her heirs, executors, administrators, successors and assigns.

9. *Headings.* The captions used in this Exercise Notice are inserted for convenience and shall not be deemed a part of this agreement for construction or interpretation.

10. *Dispute Resolution.* The provisions of Section 19 of the Option Agreement shall be the exclusive means of resolving disputes arising out of or relating to this Exercise Notice.

11. *Governing Law; Severability.* This Exercise Notice is to be construed in accordance with and governed by the internal laws of the State of without giving effect to any choice of law rule that would cause the application of the laws of any jurisdiction other than the internal laws of the State of to the

rights and duties of the parties. Should any provision of this Exercise Notice be determined by a court of law to be illegal or unenforceable, such provision shall be enforced to the fullest extent allowed by law and the other provisions shall nevertheless remain effective and shall remain enforceable.

12. *Notices.* Any notice required or permitted hereunder shall be given in writing and shall be deemed effectively given upon personal delivery or upon deposit in the United States mail by certified mail (if the parties are within the United States) or upon deposit for delivery by an internationally recognized express mail courier service (for international delivery of notice), with postage and fees prepaid, addressed to the other party at its address as shown below beneath its signature, or to such other address as such party may designate in writing from time to time to the other party.

13. *Further Instruments.* The parties agree to execute such further instruments and to take such further action as may be reasonably necessary to carry out the purposes and intent of this agreement.

14. *Entire Agreement.* The Notice, the Plan and the Option Agreement are incorporated herein by reference and together with this Exercise Notice constitute the entire agreement of the parties with respect to the subject matter hereof and supersede in their entirety all prior undertakings and agreements of the Company and the Grantee with respect to the subject matter hereof, and may not be modified adversely to the Grantee's interest except by means of a writing signed by the Company and the Grantee. Nothing in the Notice, the Plan, the Option Agreement and this Exercise Notice (except as expressly provided therein) is intended to confer any rights or remedies on any persons other than the parties.

Submitted by: Accepted by:
GRANTEE: [COMPANY]
_____   By:
                                           _____

(Signature)   Title:
Address: Address:
_____   _____ [COMPANY ADDRESS]
_____   _____

Exhibit B - Investment Representation Statement

EXHIBIT B
NEWCO, INC.
[YEAR] STOCK INCENTIVE PLAN

INVESTMENT REPRESENTATION STATEMENT

GRANTEE: _____

COMPANY: _____

SECURITY: COMMON STOCK

AMOUNT: _____

DATE: _____

In connection with the purchase of the above-listed Securities, the undersigned Grantee represents to the Company the following:

(a) Grantee is aware of the Company's business affairs and financial condition and has acquired sufficient information about the Company to reach an informed and knowledgeable decision to acquire the Securities. Grantee is acquiring these Securities for investment for Grantee's own account only and not with a view to, or for resale in connection with, any "distribution" thereof within the meaning of the Securities Act of 1933, as amended (the "Securities Act").

(b) Grantee acknowledges and understands that the Securities constitute "restricted securities" under the Securities Act and have not been registered under the Securities Act in reliance upon a specific exemption therefrom, which exemption depends upon among other things, the bona fide nature of Grantee's investment intent as expressed herein. Grantee further understands that the Securities must be held indefinitely unless they are subsequently registered under the Securities Act or an exemption from such registration is available. Grantee further acknowledges and understands that the Company is under no obligation to register the Securities. Grantee understands that the certificate evidencing the Securities will be imprinted with a legend which prohibits the transfer of the Securities unless they are registered or such registration is not required in the opinion of counsel satisfactory to the Company.

(c) Grantee is familiar with the provisions of Rule 701 and Rule 144, each promulgated under the Securities Act, which, in substance, permit limited public resale of "restricted securities" acquired, directly or indirectly from the issuer thereof, in a non-public offering subject to the satisfaction of certain conditions. Rule 701 provides that if the issuer qualifies under Rule 701 at the time of the grant of the Option to the Grantee, the exercise will be exempt from registration under the Securities Act. In the event the Company becomes subject to the reporting requirements of Section 13 or 15(d) of the Securities Exchange Act of 1934, ninety (90) days thereafter (or such longer period as any market stand-off agreement may require) the Securities exempt under Rule 701 may be resold, subject to the satisfaction of certain of the conditions specified by Rule 144, including: (1) the resale being made through a broker in an unsolicited "broker's transaction" or in transactions directly with a market maker (as said term is defined under the Securities Exchange Act of 1934); and, in the case of an affiliate, (2) the availability of certain public information about the Company, (3) the amount of Securities being sold during any three month period not exceeding the limitations specified in Rule 144(e), and (4) the timely filing of a Form 144, if applicable.

In the event that the Company does not qualify under Rule 701 at the time of grant of the Option, then the Securities may be resold in certain limited circumstances subject to the provisions of Rule 144, which requires the resale to occur not less than one year after the later of the date the Securities were sold by the Company or the date the Securities were sold by an affiliate of the Company, within the meaning of Rule 144; and, in the case of acquisition of the Securities by an affiliate, or by a non-affiliate who subsequently holds the Securities less than two years, the satisfaction of the conditions set forth in sections (1), (2), (3) and (4) of the paragraph immediately above.

(d) Grantee further understands that in the event all of the applicable requirements of Rule 701 or 144 are not satisfied, registration under the Securities Act, compliance with Regulation A, or some other registration exemption will be required; and that, notwithstanding the fact that Rules 144 and 701 are not exclusive, the Staff of the Securities and Exchange Commission has expressed its opinion that persons proposing to sell private placement securities other than in a registered offering and otherwise than pursuant to Rules 144 or 701 will have a substantial burden of proof in establishing that an exemption from registration is available for such offers or sales, and that such persons and their respective brokers who participate in such transactions do so at their own risk. Grantee understands that no assurances can be given that any such other registration exemption will be available in such event.

(e) Grantee represents that he or she is a resident of the state of
_____.

Signature of Grantee:

_____

Date: _____, _____

25

Model Stock Appreciation Rights Agreement

STOCK APPRECIATION RIGHTS AGREEMENT

(Measured by Book Value)

THIS AGREEMENT, made and entered into this _____ day of
_____, 200_, by and between [John Smith] (Employee) and
NEWCO, INC. (the Company),

PREAMBLE:

The Company wishes to award stock appreciation rights to Employee,
subject to the provisions of this Agreement, as an incentive for Employee to
remain in the service of the Company.

NOW, THEREFORE, in consideration of the agreements set forth herein,
IT IS HEREBY AGREED by and between Employee and the Company as
follows:

1. *Award of Stock Appreciation Rights.* The Company hereby awards to Employee ___ stock appreciation right units (the Units).

2. *Exercise of Units.* Employee may elect to exercise the Units in accordance with the following:

(i) Employee may not exercise more than ___ Units during any Fiscal Year.

(ii) The aggregate number of Units that Employee may exercise as of any date may not exceed the number of Units in which he is vested as of that date (determined in accordance with the provisions of paragraph 3), reduced by the number of Units previously exercised.

(iii) Employee may not elect to exercise any Units as of a date occurring after the earlier of:

a. the date he ceases to be employed by the Company for any reason, including but not limited to death, disability or discharge without cause; or

b. March 31, 200_ (the Expiration Date).

(iv) Any election by Employee to exercise any Units shall be made in writing, shall be signed by Employee, shall specify the date as of which the exercise is to occur, shall be filed with the Secretary of the Company (the Secretary) prior to the date as of which the exercise is to occur, and shall be in such form, and shall contain such other information as the Secretary may reasonably require.

The filing of Employees election to exercise a Unit shall be deemed to have occurred on the date it is received by the Secretary of the Company or, if it is sent to the Secretary of the Company by registered mail, postage prepaid, return receipt requested, the date on which it is sent. For purposes of this Agreement, the term Fiscal Year shall mean each 12-consecutive-month period ending each March 31.

3. *Vesting*. Employee shall be vested in the Units if he remains in the full-time employ of the Company in accordance with the following schedule:

As of Any Date Occurring Before the Following Date	Employee Shall Be Vested in the Folling Number of Unites `
_____, 200_	Zero Units
_____, 200_	_____ Units
_____, 200_	_____ Units
_____, 200_	_____ Units
_____, 200_	_____ Units
_____, 200_	_____ Units

Employee shall forfeit, and shall not become vested in, any Units in which he is not vested as of the date on which his employment with the Company terminates. If any stock appreciation rights are not vested, or if vested are not exercised within the periods specified in Section 2, then such stock appreciation rights will automatically terminate and expire and be forfeited.

4. *Payment on Exercise*. For each Unit exercised by Employee, he (or in the event of his death, his personal representative) shall be entitled to a cash payment equal to the Unit Value as of the date the Unit is exercised, without regard to changes in the Book Value of a share of stock of the Company occurring after the date of exercise of the applicable Unit. The cash amount payable with respect to the exercise of a Unit under this paragraph 4 shall be made, without interest, as soon as practicable after the later of the date the Unit is exercised or the date on which the Unit Value has been determined. The Company shall take all reasonable steps to pay amounts due under this paragraph with respect to the exercise of a Unit not later than 30 days after the date the Unit is exercised. All payments in respect of the exercise or purchase of stock appreciation rights hereunder will be subject to the withholding and payment of applicable payroll, withholding and other taxes.

5. *Unit Value.* The Unit Value of a Unit as of any date is an amount equal to the excess of:

(i) The Book Value of a share of stock of the Company (determined as set forth below) as of that date;

(ii) The Book Value of a share of stock of the Company as of March 31, 200_.

For purposes of the Agreement, the Book Value of a share of stock of the Company as of any date shall be determined in accordance with the provisions of Exhibit I, which is attached to and forms a part of this Agreement.

6. *Limits on Transferability.* Employee may not sell, assign, pledge or transfer, other than by the law of descent or distribution, any Units, or any rights under this Agreement; and any Units, and any rights under this Agreement, shall not be subject to the claims of creditors of Employee other than the Company.

7. *Changes in Capitalization.* In the event of any change in the Book Value of the shares of stock of the Company by reason of any stock dividend, split, recapitalization, merger, consolidation, combination or exchange of shares or other similar corporate change, the number of Units awarded to Employee, the number of Units in which Employee is vested, and the method of computing the Book Value under this Agreement may be equitably adjusted by the Committee in its sole discretion to preserve the benefits of the Agreement for Employee and the Company.

8. *Successors.* This Agreement shall be binding upon and inure to the benefit of any assignee or successor in the interest of the Company, and shall be binding upon and inure to the benefit of any estate, legal representative, beneficiary or heir of Employee.

9. *Committee.* The authority to manage and control the operation and administration of this Agreement shall be vested in a committee (the Committee) consisting of at least __ persons who shall be appointed by, and may be removed by, the Board of Directors of the Company. The Committee's interpretation and construction of this Agreement shall be final.

10. *Agreement Not Contract of Employment.* This Agreement does not constitute a contract of employment, and does not give Employee the right to be employed by the Company.

11. *No Rights as Shareholder.* This Agreement does not confer on Employee any rights as a shareholder of the Company.

The parties agree and acknowledge that this Agreement does not confer upon Employee as the holder of the stock appreciation rights any rights or interests as a stockholder of the Company, and that no fiduciary duties are owed by the Company or its directors, officers and stockholders in respect of such stock appreciation rights. Employee further agrees and acknowledges that the Company is not, and shall not be, restricted or limited in any manner from engaging in transactions that may have dilutive effects, entering into or modifying any financing agreements that restrict or limit payments of dividends, engaging in reorganizations or recapitalizations, liquidating or otherwise taking actions that may affect the stock appreciation rights granted hereunder.

12. *Stockholder Approval.* This Agreement has been approved by the Company's stockholders for purposes of § 280G(b)(5)(B) of the Internal Revenue Code.

13. *Counterparts.* This Agreement may be executed in two or more counterparts, any one of which shall be deemed an original without reference to the others.

14. *Employee's Representation.* Employee hereby warrants and represents to the Company that Employee is not subject to any covenants, agreements or restrictions, including without limitation any covenants, agreements or restrictions which would be breached or violated by Employee's execution of this Agreement.

15. *Applicable Law.* The provisions of this Agreement shall be construed in accordance with the law of [New York].

16. *Amendment.* This Agreement may be amended at any time by the mutual written agreement of the Company and Employee without the consent of any other person and, no person, other than the parties hereto, shall have any rights under or interest in this Agreement or the subject matter hereof.

IN WITNESS WHEREOF, Employee has hereunto set his hand, and the Company has caused these presents to be executed in its name and on its behalf, and its corporate seal to be hereunto affixed and attested by its Secretary, all as of the date first above written.

[John Smith]

Newco, Inc.

By:

Its:

Exhibit I

Determination of Book Value

Book Value of a share of stock, for purposes of this Agreement, shall mean:

- The amount representing net shareholder's equity (or comparable entry) as reported on the most recent financial statements of the Company made available to the Company's Board of Directors as a group, assuming such statements meet the following standards.

- Such statements shall be audited or unaudited but, if unaudited, accompanied by a statement indicating the same have been reviewed by the Company's regularly retained public accountants or its chief financial officer;

- Preferred stock convertible at the option of the holder shall be included in net shareholder's equity;

- The statements have been prepared in accordance with generally accepted accounting principles consistently applied;

divided by:

- The number of primary common equity shares of the Company outstanding as of the date of calculation. Common equity shares shall mean that class or classes of shares most closely fitting the following description, Shares which enjoy the right to receive on liquidation the residue of the Company's assets, after distribution to all superior classes of the Company's securities, and are entitled to vote on (absent special circumstances) all matters appropriate for shareholder action.

26

Model Form: Loaning Money to a C-Level Employee–Special Employment Terms

Loan

The Parent Corporation XYZ or another company in the Group (the "Lender") shall provide you with a loan in the aggregate principal amount of U.S. $500,000 (the "Loan"). The proceeds of the Loan shall be paid to you against your furnishing the Lender with security, for the Loan and interest thereon, in the form of a mortgage on your home in _____ (the market value of which you have declared you believe to be not less than approximately $1 million, after deducting therefrom the amount (approximately $1 million) of an existing mortgage thereon), at the later of (a) the commencement of your employment under this Agreement and (b) ten (10) days after the Parent Corporation receives in hand the first payment by the investor(s) in the Private Placement. The Loan will bear simple interest at the rate in effect (from time to time as provided below) on U.S. three-year Treasury Notes. The rate of interest on the Loan shall be adjusted at six-month intervals to match the rate then in effect on such Treasury Notes, and such adjusted rate shall apply to the Loan, together with all interest accrued thereon to such date (such amount of principal plus such interest as of any date being referred to herein as the 'Loan Balance"), will, in all events, be repaid by you to the Lender promptly after the Closing of the initial public offering of the Common Stock of the Parent Corporation (the "IPO"), provided, however, that, if the Underwriting Agreement (or another agreement) relating to the IPO prevents your sale of your shares in the Parent Corporation until the passage of a specified number of days following the IPO, such repayment shall take place promptly after the passage of such number of days.

If your employment with your employer or the Group is terminated by reason of an Event of Acceleration, the Loan Balance shall be reduced (and, to that extent deemed forgiven), by 25% for each year you will have been employed hereunder prior to such termination (with partial years to be pro-rated), and the Loan Balance so reduced shall be repaid in two equal installments, the first of which will be due 30 days after the date of termination and the second of which (including accrued interest on the unpaid installment) shall be due six (6) months after the date of termination. Notwithstanding the foregoing, under the circumstances described in the immediately preceding sentence, and for purposes thereof, you will be deemed to have been employed for one full year longer than you will have actually been so employed prior to such termination. If your said employment is terminated otherwise than by reason of an Event of Acceleration the entire Loan Balance shall be repaid in installment as aforesaid, provided, however, anything herein to the contrary notwithstanding, that, if the IPO has not taken place by December 31, 2004 (you being still employed hereunder), if and when you are subsequently required to replay the Loan Balance (as reduced, if reduced, pursuant to this clause (B), you will have the right, but not the obligation to effect such payment by transferring to the Parent Corporation, or its designee, to the extent, if any, that it may lawfully purchase "your option shares" (hereinafter defined), such number of shares in the Parent Corporation acquired by you pursuant to the exercise of stock options ("your option shares"), and, after so transferring all such shares, to cancel such amount of your vested unexercised stock options, so will cause the aggregate value of such shares and options determined as hereinafter provided so transferred and cancelled (the "Aggregate Value") to equal the Loan Balance. It is understood (i) that if the Aggregate Value exceeds the Loan Balance, after transferring such shares and canceling such options with an Aggregate Value equal to the Loan Balance, your remaining option shares and vested options will be retained by you. For purposes of this clause (B), the value of such shares and options shall mean the fair market value thereof as of the date they are transferred or cancelled as aforesaid, less, in the case of such options, the exercise price thereof. Such fair market value shall be determined by the Supervisory Board on the basis of objective third party expert advice.

Upon your repayment of the Loan or its forgiveness as provided above, the Lender shall deliver to you appropriate documents releasing and satisfying any mortgage provided by you to secure the Loan.

Resignation

Notice to your employer of your resignation from your employment hereunder will, at the request of your employer be effective six (6) months (or such shorter period as may be designated by your employer) after such notice. During the period between such notice of resignation and the effectiveness thereof, you may search for other employment provided such search does not affect the performance of your obligation (hereinafter set forth) with regard to orderly transfer, and your employer will sympathetically consider a request by you for the right, during such period, to provide consulting services to others, provided that your employer, in its sole discretion, believes (as expressed in its written consent thereto) that the performance of such services will not restrict you in the performance of your duties hereunder (including without limitation such orderly transfer) prior to the effectiveness of your resignation.

Irrespective of the circumstances of the termination of your employment, unless terminated by your employer for cause, at your employer's request, for a period (the "Transfer Period") of up to six (6) months as may be determined by your employer, you will conscientiously do all things reasonably required to effect an orderly transfer of your functions and responsibilities to the person(s) who will replace you. Your employer shall be entitled to request you to continue working full time during the Transfer Period, or to work on a part-time or occasional basis, or to initially work full time and, after a period of full-time work, to work on a part-time or occasional basis, all as may be determined by your employer. It is understood and agreed (i) that, during the Transfer Period, so long as you are working full time, your salary will be in accordance with the provisions of Section 5(b), (ii) that, after you cease working full time, the scheduling of your work will be determined in good faith discussions between you and your employer (taking into account the needs of both parties), and that your salary will be on a basis proportionate to the time which you work unless otherwise agreed and (iii) that, for all purposes hereunder, the termination or cessation of your employment shall be deemed to have occurred on the date when you cease working full time.

Takeover: Consulting

Whereas, the Board of Directors ("Board") and Compensation Committee recognize that the possibility of an unsolicited tender offer or other takeover bid for the Company is unsettling to senior executives of the Company. Therefore, these arrangements are being made to help assure a continuing dedication by such senior executives to their duties to the Company notwithstanding the occurrence of a tender offer or takeover bid. In particular, the Board and the Committee believe it important, should the Company receive proposals from third parties with respect to its future, to enable senior executives, without being influenced by the uncertainties of their own situation, to assess and advise the Board whether such proposals would be in the best interests of the Company and its shareholders and to take such other action regarding such proposals the Board might determine to be appropriate. The Board and the Committee also wish to demonstrate to executives of the Company that the Company is concerned with the welfare of it executives and intends to see that loyal executives are treated fairly.

Cost of Living

Cost of Living increase in Base Salary. As promptly as practicable at the end of each year during the term of this Executive Employment Agreement, the Company shall compute the increase, if any, in the cost of living, using as the basis of such computation the "Consumers Price Index" hereinafter called the Index, published by the Bureau of Labor Statistics of the United States Department of Labor.

(A) January, 2004 shall be the "Base Year" and the corresponding Index number for the month of January on each anniversary of this Agreement, or any extension thereof, shall be the current Index number.

(B) Appropriate adjustments shall be promptly made in case there is a published amendment of the Index figures upon which the computation is based.

(C) If publication of the Index is discontinued, the parties hereto shall except comparable statistics on the cost of living for [New York City] as computed and published by an agency of the United States or by a responsible financial periodical of recognized authority then to be selected by the parties.

Acceleration of Compensation and Registration of Securities. In the event of the happening of any of the following:

(A) A tender offer for shares of the Company's Common Stock is made, which tender is not approved by the Company's Board of Directors, and a majority of the Company's outstanding stock is tendered thereunder;

(B) There is a contested election of Directors, and Directors not recommended by management are empanelled, or there is a change of control of the Company (hereinafter defined);

(C) Because John Smith is not elected or reelected to or is removed from an office or position at least equal to that which he held immediately prior to the change of control; or

(D) Because of a material change in the nature or scope of the authorities, powers, function, duties or responsibilities attached to John Smith's position without his express written consent as a result of which change his position with the Company shall be or become of less dignity, responsibility, importance or scope, or a reduction in base salary, which is not remedied within 30 days after receipt by the Company of written notice from John Smith; or

(E) Because of liquidation, dissolution, consolidation or merger of the Company or the transfer of all or substantially all of its assets unless a successor or successors (by merger, consolidation or otherwise) to which all or substantially all of its assets have been transferred shall have agreed to continue the employment upon terms and conditions satisfactory to John Smith.

Then and in any of the above events, the entire compensation required to be paid pursuant to this Agreement through January 31, 2006, shall be immediately due and payable at the option of John Smith and any and all options, shares of common stock and shares underlying options owned by John Smith shall forthwith, but in no event later than twenty (20) days after the happening of any of the events set forth in subparagraphs "A" through "E" above, become the subject of an appropriate registration statement, for the sale of such securities, which will be filed by the Company with the Securities and Exchange Commission, at the Company's expense. The Company officers shall take all steps necessary to qualify such options and shares for sale.

For the purpose of this Agreement, a change in control of the Company shall mean a change in control of a nature that would be required to be reported in response to Item 5(f) of Schedule 14A of Regulation 14A promulgated under the Securities Exchange Act of 1934 as in effect on the date of this Agreement; provided that, without limitation, such a change in control shall be deemed to have occurred if and when any "person" (as that term is used in Section 13(d) and 14(d)(2) of the Securities Exchange Act of 1934) becomes a beneficial owner directly or indirectly of securities of the Company representing 15% or more of the combined voting power of the Company's then outstanding securities.

In the alternative, John Smith may elect the option of serving as a consultant to the Company in lieu of receiving (or in partial lieu thereof) all of the compensation remaining to be paid as set forth under this Agreement and John Smith shall then serve as a consultant to the Company under the terms set forth below for a period to be co-terminus with the term set forth in this Agreement (the "Consultation Period").

During the Consultation Period, John Smith will supply advice from time to time on a reasonable advance notice with respect to the affairs of the Company, but John Smith may at his sole discretion serve as a full-time regular employee of any other business during the Consultation Period, and his consulting services shall not require his presence at times and places not compatible with such other full-time employment.   For such consulting services John Smith shall be paid an amount per month equal to one-twelfth (1/12) of the highest annual compensation (including bonuses and incentive compensation) received by John Smith from the Company in any twelve consecutive months preceding the termination date. John Smith shall also be provided by the Company with such insurance benefits (including life and medical insurance) as the Company generally provides for any group or class of employee of which John Smith would have been a member had his employment continued.

The payments provided in this paragraph shall be made without regard to whether John Smith is able to perform services for the Company during the Consultation Period or whether other full-time employment is available to John Smith or whether the Company desires consulting services from John Smith after the termination date. In the event of the death or disability of John Smith, the payments required by this paragraph shall be made to his surviving spouse, and if he is deceased without leaving a surviving spouse, said payment shall be made to the estate of John Smith.

John Smith agrees that without the consent of the Company he will not at any time after the termination date (except as required by law) disclose to any person confidential information concerning the Company or any of the Company's trade secrets.

27

Model Form: Consulting Agreement (Pro-Consultant)

Often two parties will enter into a simple consulting relationship prior to formalizing a detailed employment contract. The below agreement is *pro-consultant*, giving more flexibility to the C-level executive and his or her business.

Professional Services Agreement

This Professional Services Agreement ("Agreement"), dated _____, 200_ (the "Effective Date"), is by and between _____, a _____ corporation ("Customer"), and _____, a _____ corporation ("Consultant").

Services and Statements of Work.

Performance of Services. Customer may from time to time issue statements of work ("Statements of Work") in the form attached to this Agreement as *Exhibit A.* Each Statement of Work shall, when executed by Customer and Consultant, form a part of this Agreement and be subject to the terms and conditions set forth herein. Consultant agrees to use commercially reasonable efforts to perform or cause to be performed for Customer the services described in the Statements of Work ("Services") [and to deliver to Customer the deliverables set forth in the Statements of Work ("Deliverables")] according to the specifications ("Specifications") and schedule set forth therein.

    Personnel.

Consultant shall assign employees and subcontractors with suitable qualifications to perform the Services [and shall designate a project manager who shall confer with Customer regarding the status of the Services at a mutually agreed-upon minimum frequency]. While on Customer's premises, Consultant's employees and subcontractors shall comply with all reasonable security practices and procedures generally prescribed by Customer. Consultant employees and subcontractors shall not be required to sign any waivers, releases or other documents to gain access to Customer's premises in connection with the performance of the Services and any such waivers, releases or other documents shall be invalid and shall have no effect. Consultant may replace or change employees and subcontractors as required. For the term of each Statement of Work and for twelve (12) months thereafter, Customer agrees not to solicit or retain the services of any person who is an employee of Consultant and who performed Services pursuant to such Statement of Work.

Acceptance.

Customer shall have fifteen (15) days from its receipt of any deliverable developed by Consultant pursuant to a Statement of Work and delivered for use by Customer in performance of the Services under this Agreement ("Deliverable") to review and evaluate such Deliverable to determine whether the Deliverable meets the requirements specific to the particular Deliverable as set forth in the applicable Statement of Work. If no written rejection is given to Consultant by Customer within fifteen (15) days following Customer's receipt of any Deliverable, such Deliverable shall be deemed accepted. If Customer does not accept such Deliverable, it shall provide Consultant with a detailed written description of the inaccuracies, inadequacies, inconsistencies, defects, deficiencies or other problems in the Deliverable that led to the rejection. Consultant shall have [fifteen (15)] days following Consultant's receipt of Customer's notice of rejection in which to correct any such problems in the Deliverable and to deliver a corrected Deliverable to Customer for its review and acceptance as set forth above. Consultant shall not be responsible for any delays in the delivery schedule that are caused by Customer. [This procedure shall be repeated until the Deliverable is accepted by Customer.]

Customer's Obligations.

Customer acknowledges that Customer's timely provision of (and Consultant's access to) Customer facilities, equipment, assistance, cooperation, and complete and accurate information and data from Customer's officers, agents and employees ("Cooperation") is essential to the performance of the Services, and that Consultant shall not be liable for any deficiency in performing the Services if such deficiency results from Customer's failure to provide full cooperation as required hereunder. Cooperation includes, but is not limited to, designating a project manager to interface with Consultant during the course of the Services, allocating and engaging additional resources as may be required to assist Consultant in performing the Services, and [providing all necessary review and approval of Deliverables as required hereunder].

Payments.

Fees.

Unless otherwise specified in the applicable Statement of Work, all Services shall be provided on a time-and-materials basis at Consultant's then-current fees and charges therefore. Consultant's standard hourly billing rates for professional services are set forth [in Consultant's published billing rate schedule] [OR in Exhibit __] and are subject to change without prior notice to Customer.

Expenses.

Customer shall reimburse Consultant for all reasonable travel, lodging, communications, shipping charges and out-of-pocket expenses incurred by Consultant in connection with providing the Services.

Payment Terms.

Consultant shall invoice Customer for all Services, expenses incurred by Consultant in connection with performing the Services and other payments due under this Agreement and any Statement of Work and, unless otherwise specified in the applicable Statement of Work, Customer shall pay such invoiced amounts within thirty (30) days of the date of the invoice. Customer agrees to pay interest at the rate of one and one-half percent (1.5%) per month (or the maximum rate permitted by applicable law, whichever is less) for all amounts not paid within thirty (30) days from the date of the invoice therefor. [If Customer disputes an invoice, it may withhold the disputed portion but shall pay the undisputed portion. No interest shall be incurred on any unpaid or adjusted invoice unless it is determined that Consultant is due all or a portion of the disputed amount. Interest shall be charged at a rate of one and one-half percent (1.5%) per month (or the maximum rate permitted by applicable law, whichever is less), on all amounts that were disputed and not paid but were due Consultant.]

Taxes.

In addition to all charges specified in this Agreement and the Statements of Work, Customer shall pay or reimburse Consultant for all federal, state, local or other taxes, including, without limitation, sales, use, excise and property taxes, or amounts levied in lieu thereof, based on charges set forth in this Agreement or the Statement of Work; provided, however, Customer shall have no responsibility for taxes imposed on Consultant's net income by any taxing authority.

Termination.

Customer may terminate this Agreement and/or any Statement of Work at any time upon [fifteen (15) days] advance written notice to Consultant. In the event that either party shall fail to perform its obligations pursuant to this Agreement and/or any Statement of Work and such failure shall continue for a period of thirty (30) days following written notice from the other party, this Agreement and/or any Statement of Work may be terminated by the non-breaching party by giving a notice of termination to the other party. Notice of termination of any Statement of Work shall not be considered notice of termination of this Agreement unless specifically stated in the notice; provided, however, any termination of this Agreement shall automatically terminate all Statements of Work. Customer shall pay Consultant for all Services performed and expenses incurred up through the termination date. The provisions of Sections 0 (last sentence only), 0, 0, 0, 0, 0, 0 and 0 shall survive any termination of this Agreement.

Proprietary Rights.

Ownership of Work Product.

As used herein, the term "Work Product" means all materials, software, tools, data, inventions, works of authorship and other innovations of any kind, including, without limitation, [any Deliverables and] any improvements or modifications to Consultant proprietary computer software programs and related materials, that Consultant, or personnel working for or through Consultant, may make, conceive, develop or reduce to practice, alone or jointly with others, in the course of performing the Services or as a result of such Services, whether or not eligible for patent, copyright, trademark, trade secret or other legal protection. Customer agrees that all Work Product shall be the property of Consultant and hereby assigns all its rights in the Work Product and in all related patents, patent applications, copyrights, mask work rights, trademarks, trade secrets, rights of priority and other proprietary rights to Consultant. Customer acknowledges that Consultant, in its sole discretion, shall have the right to license the Work Product or any portion thereof, and/or incorporate the Work Product or any portion thereof into products or services, for use by other licensees or customers of Consultant. At Consultant's request and expense, Customer shall assist and cooperate with Consultant in all reasonable respects and shall execute documents, give testimony and take further acts as reasonably requested by Consultant to acquire, transfer, maintain and enforce patent, copyright, trademark, mask work, trade secret and other legal protection for the Work Product.

License of Work Product.

Subject to Customer's performance of its obligations hereunder, Consultant shall grant to Customer a worldwide, non-exclusive, non-transferable license during the term of this Agreement to use, within Customer's enterprise only, the Work Product solely for Customer's internal business purposes.

Customer shall not, without the written consent of Consultant: (a) decompile, disassemble or otherwise reverse engineer the Work Product or any portion thereof; (b) rent, lease, sublicense, sell, transfer or otherwise grant rights in or to the Work Product (in whole or in part) to any third party in any form; or (c) use the Work Product for third-party training, commercial time-sharing or service bureau use.

Reservation of Rights.

Except as otherwise expressly provided herein, nothing in this Agreement shall be deemed to grant, directly or by implication, estoppel or otherwise, any right or license with respect to any technology or other intellectual property rights, and each party retains all right, title and interest in and to their respective technologies and other intellectual property rights.

Limited Warranty.

Limited Warranty.

Consultant hereby represents and warrants to Customer that (a) the Services will be performed in a professional and workmanlike manner, [and (b) the Deliverables will conform to the Specifications for a period of [thirty (30)] days commencing on the date of delivery thereof][and (c) the Deliverables will not infringe or misappropriate any copyright or trade secret of any person]. In the event of a breach of the warranty set forth in this Section 0, Consultant agrees, as Consultant's sole and exclusive obligation and Customer's sole and exclusive remedy, to use commercially reasonable efforts to modify or correct the Deliverable.

No Other Warranties.

EXCEPT AS SPECIFICALLY PROVIDED IN THIS SECTION 0, CONSULTANT MAKES NO OTHER WARRANTIES, EITHER

EXPRESS OR IMPLIED, AS TO ANY OTHER MATTER
WHATSOEVER, INCLUDING, WITHOUT LIMITATION, THE
CONDITION OF THE SERVICES OR ANY WORK PRODUCT
DEVELOPED HEREUNDER, AND CONSULTANT HEREBY
EXPRESSLY DISCLAIMS ANY IMPLIED WARRANTIES OF
MERCHANTABILITY, FITNESS FOR ANY PARTICULAR PURPOSE
OR NEED, ACCURACY, NON-INFRINGEMENT OF THIRD PARTY
RIGHTS AND TITLE, AND ANY WARRANTIES THAT MAY ARISE
FROM COURSE OF DEALING, COURSE OF PERFORMANCE OR
USAGE OF TRADE.

Limitation of Liability.

General Limitation.

Consultant's aggregate liability to Customer for damages in connection with
this Agreement and the Services or any Work Product provided pursuant to
this Agreement, regardless of the form of action giving rise to such liability
(under any theory, whether in contract, tort, statutory or otherwise) shall
not exceed the aggregate fees paid by Customer to Consultant pursuant to
the Statement of Work giving rise to such damages.

Limitation on Other Damages.

To the extent permitted by applicable law and notwithstanding anything in
this Agreement to the contrary or any failure of essential purpose of any
limited remedy or limitation of liability, Consultant shall not be liable for any
indirect, exemplary, special, consequential or incidental damages of any
kind, or for any damages resulting from loss or interruption of business, lost
data or lost profits, arising out of or relating to this Agreement or the subject
matter hereof, however caused, even if Consultant has been advised of or
should have known of the possibility of such damages.

[*Contractual Statute of Limitations.*

Except for actions for nonpayment or breach of Contractor's proprietary rights in the Work Product, no action, regardless of form, arising out of this Agreement may be brought by either party more than two (2) years after the cause of action has accrued.]

Acknowledgment.

Customer acknowledges that the limitations of liability contained in this Section 0 are a fundamental part of the basis of Consultant's bargain hereunder, and Consultant would not enter into this Agreement absent such limitations.

Confidentiality.

Confidential Information.

By virtue of this Agreement, the parties may have access to information that is confidential to one another ("Confidential Information"). For purposes of this Agreement, "Confidential Information" of a party means information, ideas, materials or other subject matter of such party, whether disclosed orally, in writing or otherwise, that is provided under circumstances reasonably indicating that it is confidential or proprietary. Confidential Information includes, without limitation, the terms and conditions of this Agreement; all business plans, technical information or data, product ideas, methodologies, calculation algorithms and analytical routines; and all personnel, customer, contracts and financial information or materials disclosed or otherwise provided by such party ("Disclosing Party") to the other party ("Receiving Party"). Confidential Information does not include that which (a) is already in the Receiving Party's possession at the time of disclosure to the Receiving Party, (b) is or becomes part of public knowledge other than as a result of any action or inaction of the Receiving Party, (c) is obtained by the Receiving Party from an unrelated third party without a duty of confidentiality, or (d) is independently developed by the Receiving Party. Without limiting the generality of, and notwithstanding the exclusions described in, the foregoing, (i) Confidential Information of Consultant includes the Work Product, including any portion thereof (in both object code and source code form), modifications and derivatives thereof, and information or materials derived therefrom, whether or not marked as such, and (ii) Confidential Information of both parties includes the terms and pricing under this Agreement.

Restrictions on Use.

The Receiving Party shall not use Confidential Information of the Disclosing Party for any purpose other than in furtherance of this Agreement and the activities described herein. The Receiving Party shall not disclose Confidential Information of the Disclosing Party to any third parties except as otherwise permitted hereunder. The Receiving Party may disclose Confidential Information of the Disclosing Party only to those employees or consultants who have a need to know such Confidential Information and who are bound to retain the confidentiality thereof under provisions (including, without limitation, provisions relating to nonuse and nondisclosure) no less restrictive than those required by the Receiving Party for its own Confidential Information. The Receiving Party shall maintain Confidential Information of the Disclosing Party with at least the same degree of care it uses to protect its own proprietary information of a similar nature or sensitivity, but no less than reasonable care under the circumstances. Each party shall advise the other party in writing of any misappropriation or misuse of Confidential Information of the other party of which the notifying party becomes aware.

Exclusions.

Notwithstanding the foregoing, this Agreement shall not prevent the Receiving Party from disclosing Confidential Information of the Disclosing Party to the extent required by a judicial order or other legal obligation, provided that, in such event, the Receiving Party shall promptly notify the Disclosing Party to allow intervention (and shall cooperate with the Disclosing Party) to contest or minimize the scope of the disclosure (including application for a protective order). Further, each party may disclose the terms and conditions of this Agreement: (a) as required by the applicable securities laws, including, without limitation, requirements to file a copy of this Agreement (redacted to the extent reasonably permitted by applicable law) or to disclose information regarding the provisions hereof or performance hereunder to applicable regulatory authorities; (b) in confidence, to legal counsel; (c) in confidence, to accountants, banks, and financing sources and their advisors; and (d) in connection with the enforcement of this Agreement or any rights hereunder.

[*Source Code.*

With respect to any source code provided by Consultant to Customer, such source code shall be subject to all of the obligations of this Section 0 and the following additional restrictions on use and disclosure: (a) Customer shall allow use of or access to the source code only by employees of Customer who have a need to use the source code for exercise of Customer's rights with respect to the source code as set forth in this Agreement and who are bound to retain the confidentiality thereof under written non-disclosure agreements that include provisions (including, without limitation, provisions relating to nonuse and nondisclosure) no less restrictive than those required under this Agreement; (b) Customer shall maintain and use the source code only in secure, locked facilities to which access is limited to the employees set forth in subsection (a), above; (c) for source code that is useable or stored on any computer equipment (whether a multi-user system, network, stand-alone computer or otherwise), the equipment must have password-based access control, with each user having a unique user identification and associated password; (d) Customer shall use, and shall allow use of and access to, the source code only at its _____ facilities; and (e) Customer shall maintain a record of all personnel who use or have access to the source code, the number of copies made, if any, of the source code, and the computer equipment and storage media on which the source code is used or stored.]

Equitable Relief.

Each party (as Receiving Party) acknowledges that the Disclosing Party considers its Confidential Information to contain trade secrets of the Disclosing Party and that any unauthorized use or disclosure of such information would cause the Disclosing Party irreparable harm for which remedies at law would be inadequate. Accordingly, each party (as Receiving Party) acknowledges and agrees that the Disclosing Party will be entitled, in addition to any other remedies available to it at law or in equity, to the issuance of injunctive relief, without bond, enjoining any breach or threatened breach of the Receiving Party's obligations hereunder with respect to the Confidential Information of the Disclosing Party, and such further relief as any court of competent jurisdiction may deem just and proper.

Return of Materials.

Upon termination of this Agreement, each party (as Receiving Party) will immediately return to the Disclosing Party all Confidential Information of the Disclosing Party embodied in tangible (including electronic) form or, at the Disclosing Party's discretion, destroy all such Confidential Information and certify in writing to the Disclosing Party that all such Confidential Information has been destroyed.

General.

Integration and Severability.

This Agreement, including all Statements of Work, is the final, complete and exclusive agreement between the parties relating to the subject matter hereof, and supersedes all prior or contemporaneous proposals, understandings, representations, warranties, promises and other communications, whether oral or written, relating to such subject matter. If any provision of this Agreement or any Statement of Work is held by a court of competent jurisdiction to be unenforceable for any reason, the remaining provisions hereof and thereof shall be unaffected and remain in full force and effect.

Governing Law.

This Agreement is to be construed in accordance with and governed by the internal laws of the State of [New York (as permitted by Section 5-1401 of the New York General Obligations Law or any similar successor provision) OR California (as permitted by Section 1646.5 of the California Civil Code or any similar successor provision)] without giving effect to any choice of law rule that would cause the application of the laws of any jurisdiction other than the internal laws of the State of [New York OR California] to the rights and duties of the parties. Any legal suit, action or proceeding arising out of or relating to this Agreement shall be commenced in a federal court in the _____ District of _____ [STATE] or in state court in the County of _____, _____ [COUNTY, STATE], and each party hereto irrevocably submits to the exclusive jurisdiction and venue of any such court in any such suit, action or proceeding.

Modification and Waiver.

No amendment or modification to this Agreement or any Statement of Work shall be valid or binding upon the parties unless in writing and signed by an officer of each party. No failure or delay on the part of either party in the exercise of any right or privilege hereunder shall operate as a waiver thereof or of the exercise of any other right or privilege hereunder, nor shall any single or partial exercise of any such right or privilege preclude other or further exercise thereof or of any other right or privilege.

Non-Assignable.

No right or obligation of Customer under this Agreement may be assigned, delegated or otherwise transferred, whether by agreement, operation of law or otherwise, without the express prior written consent of Consultant, and any attempt to assign, delegate or otherwise transfer any of Customer's rights or obligations hereunder without such consent shall be void. Subject to the preceding sentence, this Agreement shall bind each party and its permitted successors and assigns.

Remedies.

All rights and remedies hereunder shall be cumulative, may be exercised singularly or concurrently and, unless otherwise stated herein, shall not be deemed exclusive. If any legal action is brought to enforce any obligations hereunder, the prevailing party shall be entitled to receive its attorneys' fees, court costs and other collection expenses, in addition to any other relief it may receive.

Notices.

Any notice or communication permitted or required hereunder shall be in writing and shall be delivered in person or by courier, sent by electronic facsimile (fax), delivered by overnight delivery service, or mailed by certified or registered mail, postage prepaid, return receipt requested, and addressed as set forth after the signatures of this Agreement or to such other address as shall be given in accordance with this Section 0. If notice is given in person, by courier or by fax, it shall be effective upon receipt; if notice is given by overnight delivery service, it shall be effective two (2) business days after deposit with the delivery service; and if notice is given by mail, it shall be effective five (5) business days after deposit in the mail.

Export Control.

Customer hereby agrees to comply with all export laws and regulations of the U.S. Department of Commerce and all other U.S. agencies and authorities, including without limitation the Export Administration Regulations of the U.S. Department of Commerce Bureau of Export Administration (as contained in 15 C.F.R. Parts 730-772), and not to export, or allow the export or re-export of, any Confidential Information of Consultant in violation of such laws and or regulations, or without all required licenses and authorizations.

Force Majeure.

Both parties shall be excused from performance under this Agreement and any related Statement of Work for any period to the extent that a party is prevented from performing any obligation, in whole or in part, as a result of causes beyond its reasonable control and without its negligent or willful misconduct, including without limitation, acts of God, natural disasters, war or other hostilities, labor disputes, civil disturbances, governmental acts, orders or regulations, third party nonperformance, or failures or fluctuations in electrical power, heat, light, air conditioning or telecommunications equipment.

Construction.

The captions and section and paragraph headings used in this Agreement are inserted for convenience only and shall not affect the meaning or interpretation of this Agreement.

Counterparts.

This Agreement and any Statement of Work may be executed in several counterparts, all of which shall constitute one agreement.

Relationship of Parties.

This Agreement shall not be construed as creating an agency, partnership, joint venture or any other form of association, for tax purposes or otherwise, between the parties, and the parties shall at all times be and remain independent contractors. Except as expressly agreed by the parties in writing, neither party shall have any right or authority, express or implied, to assume or create any obligation of any kind, or to make any representation or warranty, on behalf of the other party or to bind the other party in any respect whatsoever.

IN WITNESS WHEREOF, the parties have caused this Agreement to be executed by their duly authorized representatives as of the Effective Date.

CUSTOMER   CONSULTANT

_____   _____

BY:_____   BY:_____

NAME:_____   NAME:_____

TITLE:_____   TITLE:_____

ADDRESS:_____   ADDRESS:_____

_____   _____

Exhibit A-___

FORM OF STATEMENT OF WORK

This Statement of Work is entered into as of this ___ day of _____,
200_, by and between _____, a _____ corporation
("Consultant"), and _____ , a _____ corporation
("Customer"), pursuant to that certain Professional Services Agreement
dated as of _____, 200_ by and between Consultant and
Customer (the "Agreement"). Any term not otherwise defined herein shall
have the meaning set forth in the Agreement.

Description of Services

Specifications

Deliverables

Schedule

Miscellaneous Terms

CONSULTANT_____CUSTOMER_____

BY:_____BY:_____

NAME:_____NAME:_____

TITLE:_____TITLE:_____

VC EXPERTS

Expertise and Opportunity in Venture Capital

Visit us online at www.vcexperts.com
Subscribe to The Encyclopedia of Private Equity and Venture Capital

The Glossary of Private Equity and Venture Capital

The Glossary of Private Equity and Venture Capital is the perfect resource for professionals in the private equity and venture capital industries. This glossary is provided to the industry and may be redistributed freely, provided that it is unaltered. Be sure to check VCExperts.com for updates to this glossary and for the latest news, events and information in private equity and venture capital. This copy of the Glossary was prepared on Tuesday, January 06, 2004. Don't forget to download an updated version as the glossary is updated on a regular basis at www.vcexperts.com.

"A" Round : A financing event whereby venture capitalists invest in a company that was previously financed by founders and/or angels. The "A" is from Series "A" Preferred stock. See "B" round.

"B" Round: A financing event whereby professional investors such as venture capitalists are sufficiently interested in a company to provide additional funds after the "A" round of financing. Subsequent rounds are called "C", "D", and so on.

- # -

401(K) Plan: A type of qualified retirement plan in which employees make salary reduced, pre-tax contributions to an employee trust. In many cases, the employer will match employee contributions up to a specified level.

A -

Accredited Investor: Defined by Rule 501 of Regulation D, an individual (i.e. non-corporate) "accredited investor" is a either a natural person who has individual net worth, or joint net worth with the person's spouse, that exceeds $1 million at the time of the purchase OR a natural person with income exceeding $200,000 in each of the two most recent years or joint income with a spouse exceeding $300,000 for those years and a reasonable expectation of the same income level in the current year. For the complete definition of accredited investor, see the SEC website.

Accrued Interest: The interest due on preferred stock or a bond since the last interest payment was made.

Acquisition: The process of gaining control, possession or ownership of a private portfolio company by an operating company or conglomerate.

ACRS: Accelerated Cost Recovery System. The IRS approved method of calculating depreciation expense for tax purposes. Also known as **Accelerated Depreciation.**

ADR: American Depositary Receipt (ADR's). A security issued by a U.S. bank in place of the foreign shares held in trust by that bank, thereby facilitating the trading of foreign shares in U.S. markets.

Advisory Board: A group of external advisors to a private equity group or portfolio company. Advice provided varies from overall strategy to portfolio valuation. Less formal than a Board of Directors.

Allocation: The amount of securities assigned to an investor, broker, or underwriter in an offering. An allocation can be equal to or less than the amount indicated by the investor during the subscription process depending on market demand for the securities.

Alternative Assets: This term describes non-traditional asset classes. They include private equity, venture capital, hedge funds and real estate. Alternative assets are generally more risky than traditional assets, but they should, in theory, generate higher returns for investors.

Amortization: An Accounting procedure that gradually reduces the book value of an intangible asset through periodic charges to income.

AMT: Alternative Minimum Tax. A tax designed to prevent wealthy investors from using tax shelters to avoid income tax. The calculation of the AMT takes into account tax preference items.

Angel Financing: Capital raised for a private company from independently wealthy investors. This capital is generally used as seed financing.

Angel Investor : A person who provides backing to very early-stage businesses or business concepts. Angel investors are typically entrepreneurs who have become wealthy, often in technology-related industries.

Antidilution provisions: Contractual measures that allow investors to keep a constant share of a firm's equity in light of subsequent equity issues. These may give investors preemptive rights to purchase new stock at the offering price. [See Full Ratchet and weighted Average]

Archangel : Usually an outsider hired by a syndicate of angel investors to perform due diligence on investment opportunities and coordinate allotment of investment duties among members. Archangels typically have no financial commitment to the syndicate.

Asset-backed loan: Loan, typically from a commercial bank, that is backed by asset collateral, often belonging to the entrepreneurial firm or the entrepreneur.

Automatic conversion: Immediate conversion of an investor's priority shares to ordinary shares at the time of a company's underwriting before an offering of its stock on an exchange.

Average IRR: The arithmetic mean of the internal rate of return.

B

Balance Sheet: A condensed financial statement showing the nature and amount of a company's assets, liabilities, and capital on a given date.

Bankruptcy: An inability to pay debts. Chapter 11 of the bankruptcy code deals with reorganization, which allows the debtor to remain in business and negotiate for a restructuring of debt.

BATNA (best alternative to a negotiated agreement): A no-agreement alternative reflecting the course of action a party to a negotiation will take if the proposed deal is not possible.

Bear Hug: An offer made directly to the Board of Directors of a target company. Usually made to increase the pressure on the target with the threat that a tender offer may follow.

Best Efforts: An offering in which he investment banker agrees to distribute as much of the offering as possible, and return and unsold shares to the issuer.

Blue Sky Laws: A common term that refers to laws passed by various states to protect the public against securities fraud. The term originated when a judge ruled that a stock had as much value as a *patch of blue sky.*

Board rights : Allowing an investor to take a seat on a firm's board of directors.

Book Value: Book value of a stock is determined from a company's balance sheet by adding all current and fixed assets and then deducting all debts, other liabilities and the liquidation price of any preferred issues. The sum arrived at is divided by the number of common shares outstanding and the result is book value per common share.

Bootstrapping: Means of financing a small firm by employing highly creative ways of using and acquiring recources without raising equity from traditional sources or borowing money from the bank.

Bridge Financing: A limited amount of equity or short-term debt financing typically raised within 6-18 months of an anticipated public offering or private placement meant to "bridge" a company to the next round of financing.

Broad-Based Weighted Average Ratchet: A type of anti-dilution mechanism. A weighted average ratchet adjusts downward the price per share of the preferred stock of investor A due to the issuance of new preferred shares to new investor B at a price lower than the price investor A originally received. Investor A's preferred stock is repriced to a weighed average of investor A's price and investor B's price. A broad-based ratchet uses all common stock outstanding on a fully diluted basis (including all convertible securities, warrants and options) in the denominator of the formula for determining the new weighed average price. Compare **Narrow-Based Weighted Average ratchet** and Chapter 2.9.4.d.ii of the Encyclopedia.

Burn Out / Cram Down: Extraordinary dilution, by reason of a round of financing, of a non-participating investor's percentage ownership in the issuer.

Burn Rate: The rate at which a company expends net cash over a certain period, usually a month.

Business Development Company (BDC): A vehicle established by Congress to allow smaller, retail investors to participate in and benefit from investing in small private businesses as well as the revitalization of larger private companies.

Business Judgment Rule: The legal principle that assumes the board of directors is acting in the best interests of the shareholders unless it can be **clearly established** that it is not. If the board was found to violate the business judgment rule, it would be in violation of its fiduciary duties to the shareholders.

Business Plan: A document that describes the entrepreneur's idea, the market problem, proposed solution, business and revenue models, marketing strategy, technology, company profile, competitive landscape, as well as financial data for coming years. The business plan opens with a brief executive summary, most probably the most important element of the document due to the time constraints of venture capital funds and angels.

C -

CAGR: Compound Annual Growth Rate. The year over year growth rate applied to an investment or other aspect of a firm using a base amount.

Call Option: The right to **buy** a security at a given price (or range) within a specific time period.

Capital (or Assets) Under Management: The amount of capital available to a fund management team for venture investments.

Capital Call: Also known as a draw down - When a venture capital firm has decided where it would like to invest, it will approach its investors in order to "draw down" the money. The money will already have been pledged to the fund but this is the actual act of transferring the money so that it reaches the investment target.

Capital Gains: The difference between an asset's purchase price and selling price, when the selling price is greater. Long-term capital gains (on assets held for a year or longer) are taxed at a lower rate than ordinary income.

Capitalization Table: Also called a "Cap Table", this is a table showing the total amount of the various securities issued by a firm. This typically includes the amount of investment obtained from each source and the securities distributed -- e.g. common and preferred shares, options, warrants, etc. -- and respective capitalization ratios.

Capitalize: To record an outlay as an asset (as opposed to an Expense), which is subject to depreciation or amortization.

Captive funds : A venture capital firm owned by a larger financial institution, such as a bank.

Carried Interest: The portion of any gains realized by the fund to which the fund managers are entitled, generally without having to contribute capital to the fund. Carried interest payments are customary in the venture capital industry, in order to create a significant economic incentive for venture capital fund managers to achieve capital gains.

Cash Position: The amount of cash available to a company at a given point in time. Claim Dilution A reduction in the likelihood that one or more of the firm's claimants will be fully repaid, including time value of money considerations.

Catch-up: This is a common term of the private equity partnership agreement. Once the general partner provides its limited partners with their preferred return, if any, it then typically enters a catch-up period in which it receives the majority or all of the profits until the agreed upon profit-split, as determined by the carried interest, is reached.

Chapter 11: The part of the Bankruptcy Code that provides for **reorganization** of a bankrupt company's assets.

Chapter 7: The part of the Bankruptcy Code that provides for **liquidation** of a company's assets.

Chinese wall: A barrier against information flows between different divisions or operating groups within banks and securities firms. Examples incliude a policy barrier between the trust department from making investment decisions based on any substantive inside information that may come into the possession of other bank departments. The term also refers to barriers againt information flows between corporate finance and equity research and trading operations.

Clawback: A clawback obligation represents the general partner's promise that, over the life of the fund, the managers will not receive a greater share of the fund's distributions than they bargained for. Generally, this means that the general partner may not keep distributions representing more than a specified percentage (e.g., 20%) of the fund's cumulative profits, if any. When triggered, the clawback will require that the general partner return to the fund's limited partners an amount equal to what is determined to be "excess" distributions.

Closed-end Fund: A type of fund that has a fixed number of shares outstanding, which are offered during an initial subscription period, similar to an initial public offering. After the subscription period is closed, the shares are traded on an exchange between investors, like a regular stock. The market price of a closed-end fund fluctuates in response to investor demand as well as changes in the values of its holdings or its Net Asset Value. Unlike open-end mutual funds, closed-end funds do not stand ready to issue and redeem shares on a continuous basis.

Closing: An investment event occurring after the required legal documents are implemented between the investor and a company and after the capital is transferred in exchange for company ownership or debt obligation.

Co-investment: The syndication of a private equity financing round or an investment by an individuals (usually general partners) alongside a private equity fund in a financing round.

Collar Agreement: Agreed upon adjustments in the number of shares offered in a stock-for-stock exchange to account for price fluctuations before the completion of the deal.

Committed Capital: The total dollar amount of capital pledged to a private equity fund.

Committed funds or raised funds : Capital committed by investors. Cash to the maximum of these commitments may be requested or drawn down by the private equity managers usually on a deal-by-deal basis. This amount is different from invested funds for three reasons. Firstly, most partnerships will initially invest only between 80% and 95% of committed funds (possibly even less). Second, it may be necessary in early years to deduct the annual management fee that is used to cover the cost of operation of a fund. Third, payback to investors usually begins before the final draw down of commitments has taken place. To the extent that capital invested does not equal capital committed, limited partners will have their private equity returns diluted by the much lower cash returns earned on the uninvested portion. Avoiding this situation is the main reason for the Partners Group over-commitment model, which aims to keep Partners Group products as close 100% invested as possible.

Common Stock: A unit of ownership of a corporation. In the case of a public company, the stock is traded between investors on various exchanges. Owners of common stock are typically entitled to vote on the selection of directors and other important events and in some cases receive dividends on their holdings. Investors who purchase common stock hope that the stock price will increase so the value of their investment will appreciate. Common stock offers no performance guarantees. Additionally, in the event that a corporation is liquidated, the claims of secured and unsecured creditors and owners of bonds and preferred stock take precedence over the claims of those who own common stock.

Company buy-back: The redemption of private of restricted holdings by the portfolio company itself. In essence the company is buying out the VC's interest.

Consolidation: Also called a leveraged rollup, this is an investment strategy in which a leveraged buyout (LBO) firm acquires a series of companies in the same or complementary fields, with the goal of becoming a dominant regional or nationwide player in that industry. In some cases, a holding company will be created to acquire the new companies. In other cases, an initial acquisition may serve as the platform through which the other acquisitions will be made.

Conversion Ratio: The number of shares of stock into which a convertible security may be converted. The conversion ration equals the par value of the convertible security divided by the conversion price.

Convertible Security: A bond, debenture or preferred stock that is exchangeable for another type of security (usually common stock) at a pre-stated price. Convertibles are appropriate for investors who want higher income, or liquidation preference protection, than is available from common stock, together with greater appreciation potential than regular bonds offer. **(See Common Stock, Dilution, and Preferred Stock)**.

Corporate Charter: The document prepared when a corporation is formed. The Charter sets forth the objectives and goals of the corporation, as well as a complete statement of what the corporation can and cannot do while pursuing these goals.

Corporate Resolution: A document stating that the corporation's board of directors has authorized a particular individual to act on behalf of the corporation.

Corporate Venturing: Venture capital provided by [in-house investment funds of] large corporations to further their own strategic interests.

Corporation: A legal, taxable entity chartered by a state or the federal government. Ownership of a corporation is held by the stockholders.

Covenant: A protective clause in an agreement.

Cumulative Dividends: Dividends that accrue at a fixed rate until paid are "Cumulative Dividends" which are payments to shareholders made with respect to an investor's Preferred Stock. Generally, holders of Preferred Shares are contractually entitled to receive dividends prior to holders of Common Stock. Dividends can accumulate at a fixed rate (for example 8%) or simply be payable as and when determined by a company's Board of Directors in such amount as determined by the board. Because venture backed companies typically need to conserve cash, the use of Cumulative Dividends is customary with the result that the Liquidation Preference increases by an amount equal to the Cumulative Dividends. Cumulative Dividends are often waived if the Preferred Stock converts to Common Stock prior to an IPO but may be included in the aggregate value of Preferred Stock applied to the Conversion Ratio for other purposes. Dividends that are not cumulative are generally called "when, as and if declared dividends."

Cumulative Preferred Stock: A stock having a provision that if one or more dividend payments are omitted, the omitted dividends (arrearage) must be paid **before** dividends may be paid on the company's common stock.

Cumulative Voting Rights: When shareholders have the right to pool their votes to concentrate them on an election of one or more directors rather than apply their votes to the election of all directors. For example, if the company has 12 openings to the Board of Directors, in statutory voting, a shareholder with 10 shares casts 10 votes for each opening (10x12 = 120 votes). Under the cumulative voting method however, the shareholder may opt to cast all 120 votes for **one** nominee (or any other distribution he might choose). **Compare Statutory Voting.**

D -

Deal Flow: The measure of the number of potential investments that a fund reviews in any given period.

Deficiency Letter: A letter sent by the SEC to the issuer of a new issue regarding omissions of material fact in the registration statement.

Demand Rights: Contemplate that the company must initiate and pursue the registration of a public offering including, although not necessarily limited to, the shares proffered by the requesting shareholder(s).

Depreciation: An expense recorded to reduce the value of a long-term tangible asset. Since it is a non-cash expense, it increases free cash flow while decreasing the amount of a company's reported earnings.

Dilution: A reduction in the percentage ownership of a given shareholder in a company caused by the issuance of new shares.

Dilution Protection: Mainly applies to convertible securities. Standard provision whereby the conversion ratio is changed accordingly in the case of a stock dividend or extraordinary distribution to avoid dilution of a convertible bondholder's potential equity position. Adjustment usually requires a split or stock dividend in excess of 5% or issuance of stock below book value. Share Purchase Agreements also typically contain anti-dilution provisions to protect investors in the event that a future round of financing occurs at a valuation that is below the valuation of the current round.

Director: Person elected by shareholders to serve on the board of directors. The directors appoint the president, vice president and all other operating officers, and decide when dividends should be paid (among other matters).

Disbursement: The investments by funds into their portfolio companies.

Disclosure Document: A booklet outlining the risk factors associated with an investment.

Distressed debt: Corporate bonds of companies that have either filed for bankruptcy or appear likely to do so in the near future. The strategy of distressed debt firms involves first becoming a major creditor of the target company by snapping up the company's bonds at pennies on the dollar. This gives them the leverage they need to call most of the shots during either the reorganization, or the liquidation, of the company. In the event of a liquidation, distressed debt firms, by standing ahead of the equity holders in the line to be repaid, often recover all of their money, if not a healthy return on their investment. Usually, however, the more desirable outcome a reorganization that allows the company to emerge from bankruptcy protection. As part of these reorganizations, distressed debt firms often forgive the debt obligations of the company, in return for enough equity in the company to compensate them. (This strategy explains why distressed debt firms are considered to be private equity firms.)

Distribution: Disbursement of realized cash or stock to a venture capital fund's limited partners upon termination of the fund.

Diversification: The process of spreading investments among various different types of securities and various companies in different fields.

Dividend: The payments designated by the Board of Directors to be distributed pro-rata among the shares outstanding. On preferred shares, it is generally a fixed amount. On common shares, the dividend varies with the fortune of the company and the amount of cash on hand and may be omitted if business is poor or if the Directors determine to withhold earnings to invest in capital expenditures or research and development.

Down Round: Issuance of shares at a later date and a lower price than previous investment rounds.

Drag-Along Rights: A majority shareholders' right, obligating shareholders whose shares are bound into the shareholders' agreement to sell their shares into an offer the majority wishes to execute.

Due Diligence: A process undertaken by potential investors -- individuals or institutions -- to analyze and assess the desirability, value, and potential of an investment opportunity.

E -

Early Stage: A state of a company that typically has completed its seed stage and has a founding or core senior management team, has proven its concept or completed its beta test, has minimal revenues, and no positive earnings or cash flows.

EBITDA: "Earnings Before Interest, Taxes, Depreciation and Amortization": A measure of cash flow calculated as: Revenue - Expenses (excluding tax, interest, depreciation and amortization). EBITDA looks at the cash flow of a company. By not including interest, taxes, depreciation and amortization, we can clearly see the amount of money a company brings in. This is especially useful when one company is considering a takeover of another because the EBITDA would cover any loan payments needed to finance the takeover.

Economies of Scale: Economic principle that as the volume of production increases, the cost of producing each unit decreases.

Elevator Pitch: An extremely concise presentation of an entrepreneur's idea, business model, company solution, marketing strategy, and competition delivered to potential investors. Should not last more than a few minutes, or the duration of an elevator ride.

Employee Stock Option Plan (ESOP): A plan established by a company whereby a certain number of shares is reserved for purchase and issuance to key employees. Such shares usually vest over a certain period of time to serve as an incentive for employees to build long term value for the company.

Employee Stock Ownership Plan: A trust fund established by a company to purchase stock on behalf of employees.

Equity Kicker: Option for private equity investors to purchase shares at a discount. Typically associated with mezzanine financings where a small number of shares or warrants are added to what is primarily a debt financing.

ERISA: ERISA shall mean the United States Employee Retirement Income Security Act of 1974, as amended, including the regulations promulgated thereunder.

ERISA Significant Participation Test: A test that is satisfied if the General Partner determines in its reasonable discretion that Persons that are "benefit plan investors" within the meaning of Section (f)(2) of the Final Regulation constitute or are expected to constitute at least 25 percent in interest of the Limited Partners. *Note that the test is 25% of the interests of all the limited* *partners, which means 20% (+/-) in the partnership as a whole, taking into account the general partner's interest.*

Evergreen Promise: This occurs when the company agrees to pay an employee's salary for a number of years, regardless of when termination occurs, the day after he or she is employed or 10 years after.

Exercise price: The price at which an option or warrant can be exercised.

Exit Strategy: A fund's intended method for liquidating its holdings while achieving the maximum possible return. These strategies depend on the exit climates including market conditions and industry trends. Exit strategies can include selling or distributing the portfolio company's shares after an initial public offering (IPO), a sale of the portfolio company or a recapitalization.

Exiting climates: The conditions that influence the viability and attractiveness of various exit strategies.

Exits (AKA divestments or realizations): The means by which a private equity firm realizes a return on its investment. Private equity investors generally receive their principal returns via a capital gain on the sale or flotation of investments. Exit methods include a trade sale (most common), flotation on a stock exchange (common), a share repurchase by the company or its management or a refinancing of the business (least common). A Secondary purchases of the company by another private equity firm are becoming an increasingly common phenomenon. Within Partners Goup, secondary purchases are often used to quickly reach a high investment level in a new product.

F.

Factoring: A procedure in which a firm can sell its accounts receivable invoices to a factoring firm, which pays a percentage of the invoices immediately, and the remainder (minus a service fee) when the accounts receivable are actually paid off by the firm's customers.

Final Regulation: An ERISA term, it is the United States Department of Labor's Final Regulation relating to the definition of "plan assets" in (29 C.F.R. §2510.3-101).

Finder: A person who helps to arrange a transaction.

Flipping: The act of buying shares in an IPO and selling them immediately for a profit. Brokerage firms underwriting new stock issues tend to discourage flipping, and will often try to allocate shares to investors who intend to hold on to the shares for some time. However, the temptation to flip a new issue once it has risen in price sharply is too irresistible for many investors who have been allocated shares in a hot issue.

Flotation: When a firm's shares start trading on a formal stock exchange, such as the NASDAQ or the NYSE. This is probably the most profitable exit route for entrepreneurs and their financial backers.

Follow-on funding : Companies often require several rounds of funding. If a private equity firm has invested in a particular company in the past, and then provides additional funding at a later stage, this is known as 'follow-on funding'.

Form 10-K: This is the annual report that most reporting companies file with the Commission. It provides a comprehensive overview of the registrant's business. The report must be filed within 90 days after the end of the company's fiscal year.

Form 10-KSB: This is the annual report filed by reporting "small business issuers." It provides a comprehensive overview of the company's business, although its requirements call for slightly less detailed information than required by Form 10-K. The report must be filed within 90 days after the end of the company's fiscal year.

Form S-1: The form can be used to register securities for which no other form is authorized or prescribed, except securities of foreign governments or political sub-divisions thereof.

Form S-2: This is a simplified optional registration form that may be used by companies that have been required to report under the '34 Act for a minimum of three years and have timely filed all required reports during the 12 calendar months and any portion of the month immediately preceding the filing of the registration statement. Unlike Form S-1, it permits incorporation by reference from the company's annual report to stockholders (or annual report on Form 10-K) and periodic reports. Delivery of these incorporated documents as well as the prospectus to investors may be required.

Form SB-2: This form may be used by "small business issuers" to register securities to be sold for cash. This form requires less detailed information about the issuer's business than Form S-1.

Founders' Shares: Shares owned by a company's founders upon its establishment.

Free cash flow: The cash flow of a company available to service the capital structure of the firm. Typically measured as *operating cash flow less capital expenditures and tax obligations.*

Full Ratchet Antidilution: The sale of a single share at a price less than the favored investors paid reduces the conversion price of the favored investors' convertible preferred stock "to the penny". For example, from $1.00 to 50 cents, regardless of the number of lower priced shares sold.

Fully Diluted Earnings Per Share: Earnings per share expressed as if all outstanding convertible securities and warrants have been exercised.

Fully Diluted Outstanding Shares: The number of shares representing total company ownership, including common shares and current conversion or exercised value of the preferred shares, options, warrants, and other convertible securities.

Fund age: The age of a fund (in years) from its first takedown to the time an IRR is calculated.

Fund Focus : The indicated area of specialization of a venture capital fund usually expressed as Balanced, Seed and Early Stage, Later Stage, Mezzanine or Leveraged Buyout (LBO).

Fund of funds: A fund set up to distribute investments among a selection of private equity fund managers, who in turn invest the capital directly. Fund of funds are specialist private equity investors and have existing relationships with firms. They may be able to provide investors with a route to investing in particular funds that would otherwise be closed to them. Investing in fund of funds can also help spread the risk of investing in private equity because they invest the capital in a variety of funds.

Fund Size: The total amount of capital committed by the investors of a venture capital fund.

- G -

GAAP: Generally Accepted Accounting Principles. The common set of accounting principles, standards and procedures. GAAP is a combination of authoritative standards set by standard-setting bodies as well as accepted ways of doing accounting.

Gatekeeper : Specialist advisers who assist institutional investors in their private equity allocation decisions. Institutional investors with little experience of the asset class or those with limited resources often use them to help manage their private equity allocation. Gatekeepers usually offer tailored services according to their clients' needs, including private equity fund sourcing and due diligence through to complete discretionary mandates.

GDR's: Global Depositary Receipt (GDR's). Receipts for shares in a foreign based corporation traded in capital markets around the world. While ADR's permit foreign corporations to offer shares to American citizens, GDR's allow companies in Europe, Asia and the US to offer shares in many markets around the world.

General Partner (GP): The partner in a limited partnership responsible for all management decisions of the partnership. The GP has a fiduciary responsibility to act for the benefit of the limited partners (LPs), and is fully liable for its actions.

General partner clawback: This is a common term of the private equity partnership agreement. To the extent that the general partner receives more than its fair share of profits, as determined by the carried interest, the general partner clawback holds the individual partners responsible for paying back the limited partners what they are owed.

General partner contribution: The amount of capital that the fund manager contributes to its own fund in the same way that a limited partner does. This is an important way in which limited partners can ensure that their interests are aligned with those of the general partner. The U.S. Department of Treasury recently removed the legal requirement of the general partner to contribute at least 1 percent of fund capital. However, a 1 percent general partner contribution remains common, particularly among venture capital funds.

Golden Handcuffs: This occurs when an employee is required to relinquish unvested stock when terminating his employment contract early.

Golden Parachute: Employment contract of upper management that provides a large payout upon the occurrence of certain control transactions, such as a certain percentage share purchase by an outside entity or when there is a tender offer for a certain percentage of a company's shares. Discussed in more detail at The Executive Employment Agreement

- H -

Hedge of hedging: The practice of reducing price fluctuation risk by taking a position in futures equal and opposite to an existing or anticipated cash position, or by shorting a security similar to one in which the long position is established. It is used by banks, corporations and individuals by buying (long) or selling (short) in the financial futures market, and it is also used in covering long or short positions in foreign currencies.

Hockey stick projections: The general shape and form of a chart showing revenue, customers, cash, or some other financial or operational measure that increases dramatically at some point in the future. Entrepreneurs often develop business plans with hockey stick charts to impress potential investors.

Holding Company: A corporation that owns the securities of another, in most cases with voting control.

Holding Period: The amount of time an investor has held an investment. The period begins on the date of purchase and ends on the date of sale, and determines whether a gain or loss is considered short-term or long-term, for capital gains tax purposes.

Hot Issue: A newly issued stock that is in great public demand. Technically, it is when the *secondary market price on the effective date is above the new* *issue offering price.* Hot issues usually experience a dramatic rise in price at their initial public offering because the market demand outweighs the supply.

Hurdle Rate: The internal rate of return that a fund must achieve before its general partners or managers may receive an increased interest in the proceeds of the fund. Often, if the expected rate of return on an investment is below the hurdle rate, the project is not undertaken.

I -

Incubator : An entity designed to nurture business concepts or new technologies to the point that they become attractive to venture capitalists. An incubator typically provides both physical space and some or all of the services-legal, managerial, and/or technical-needed for a business concept to be developed. Incubators often are backed by venture firms, which use them to generate early-stage investment opportunites.

Initial Public Offering (IPO): The sale or distribution of a stock of a portfolio company to the public for the first time. IPOs are often an opportunity for the existing investors (often venture capitalists) to receive significant returns on their original investment. During periods of market downturns or corrections the opposite is true.

Institutional Investors: Organizations that professionally invest, including insurance companies, depository institutions, pension funds, investment companies, mutual funds, and endowment funds.

Intellectual property : A venture's intangible assets, such as patents, copyrights, trademarks, and brand name.

Investment Company Act of 1940: Investment Company Act shall mean the Investment Company Act of 1940, as amended, including the rules and regulations promulgated thereunder.

Investment Letter: A letter signed by an investor purchasing unregistered long securities under Regulation D, in which the investor attests to the long-term investment nature of the purchase. These securities must be held for a minimum of 1 year before they can be sold.

IRA Rollover: The reinvestment of assets received as a lump-sum distribution from a qualified tax-deferred retirement plan. Reinvestment may be the entire lump sum or a portion thereof. If reinvestment is done within 60 days, there are no tax consequences.

IRR: Internal Rate of Return. A typical measure of how VC Funds measure performance. IRR is a technically a discount rate: the rate at which the present value of a series of investments is equal to the present value of the returns on those investments.

ISO: Incentive Stock Option. Plan which qualifying options are free of tax at the date of grant and the date of exercise. Profits on shares sold after being held at least 2 years from the date of grant or 1 year from the date of exercise are subject to favorable capital gains tax rate.

Issue Price : The price per share deemed to have been paid for a series of Preferred Stock. This number is important because Cumulative Dividends, the Liquidation Preference and Conversion Ratios are all based on Issue Price. In some cases, it is not the actual price paid. The most common example is where a company does a bridge financing (a common way for investors to provide capital without having to value the Company as a whole) and sells debt that is convertible into the next series of Preferred Stock sold by the Company at a discount to the Issue Price.

Issued Shares: The amount of common shares that a corporation has sold (issued).

Issuer: Refers to the organization issuing or proposing to issue a security.

J-Curve Effect: The curve realized by plotting the returns generated by a private equity fund against time (from inception to termination). The common practice of paying the management fee and start-up costs out of the first draw-down does not produce an equivalent book value. As a result, a private equity fund will initially show a negative return. When the first realizations are made, the fund returns start to rise quite steeply. After about three to five years, the interim IRR will give a reasonable indication of the definitive IRR. This period is generally shorter for buyout funds than for early-stage and expansion funds.

Key Employees: Professional management attracted by the founder to run the company. Key employees are typically retained with warrants and ownership of the company.

Later Stage: A fund investment strategy involving financing for the expansion of a company that is producing, shipping and increasing its sales volume. Later stage funds often provide the financing to help a company achieve critical mass in order to position itself.

Lead Investor: Also known as a bell cow investor. Member of a syndicate of private equity investors holding the largest stake, in charge of arranging the financing and most actively involved in the overall project .

Lemon : An investment that has a poor or negative rate of return. An old venture capital adage claims that "lemons ripen before plums."

Leveraged Buyout (LBO): A takeover of a company, using a combination of equity and borrowed funds. Generally, the target company's assets act as the collateral for the loans taken out by the acquiring group. The acquiring group then repays the loan from the cash flow of the acquired company. For example, a group of investors may borrow funds, using the assets of the company as collateral, in order to take over a company. Or the management of the company may use this vehicle as a means to regain control of the company by converting a company from public to private. In most LBOs, public shareholders receive a premium to the market price of the shares.

Lifestyle firms : Catagory comprising around 90 percent of all start-ups. These firms merely afford a reasonable living for their founders, rather than incurring the risks associated with high growth. These ventures typically have growth rates below 20 percent annually, have five-year revenue projections below $10 million, and are primarily funded internally-only very rarely with outside equity funds.

Limited Partner (LP): An investor in a limited partnership who has no voice in the management of the partnership. LP's have limited liability and usually have priority over GP's upon liquidation of the partnership.

Limited partner clawback: This is a common term of the private equity partnership agreement. It is intended to protect the general partner against future claims, should the general partner of the limited partnership become the subject of a lawsuit. Under this provision, a fund's limited partners commit to pay for any legal judgement imposed upon the limited partnership or the general partner. Typically, this clause includes limitations in the timing or amount of the judgement, such as that it cannot exceed the limited partners' committed capital to the fund.

Limited Partnerships: An organization comprised of a general partner, who manages a fund, and limited partners, who invest money but have limited liability and are not involved with the day-to-day management of the fund. In the typical venture capital fund, the general partner receives a management fee and a percentage of the profits (or carried interest). The limited partners receive income, capital gains, and tax benefits.

Liquidation: 1) The process of converting securities into cash. 2) The sale of the assets of a company to one or more acquirers in order to pay off debts. In the event that a corporation is liquidated, the claims of secured and unsecured creditors and owners of bonds and preferred stock take precedence over the claims of those who own common stock.

Liquidation Preference: The amount per share that a holder of a given series of Preferred Stock will receive prior to distribution of amounts to holders of other series of Preferred Stock of Common Stock. This is usually designated as a multiple of the the Issue Price, for example 2X or 3X, and there may be multiple layers of Liquidation Preferences as different groups of investors buy shares in different series. For example, holders of Series B Preferred Stock may be entitled to receive 3X their Issue Price, and then if any money is left, holders of Series A Preferred Stock may be entitled to receive 2X their Issue Price and then holders of Common Stock receive whatever is left. The trigger for the payment of the Liquidation Preference is a sale or liquidation of the company, such as a merger or other transaction where the company stockholders end up with less than half of the ownership of the new entity or a liquidation of the company.

Liquidity Event: An event that allows a VC to realize a gain or loss on an investment. The ending of a private equity provider's involvement in a business venture with a view to realizing an internal return on investment. Most common exit routes include Initial Public Offerings [IPOs], buy backs, trade sales and secondary buy outs. See also: Exit strategy

Lock-up Period: The period of time that certain stockholders have agreed to waive their right to sell their shares of a public company. Investment banks that underwrite initial public offerings generally insist upon lockups of at least 180 days from large shareholders (1% ownership or more) in order to allow an orderly market to develop in the shares. The shareholders that are subject to lockup usually include the management and directors of the company, strategic partners and such large investors. These shareholders have typically invested prior to the IPO at a significantly lower price to that offered to the public and therefore stand to gain considerable profits. If a shareholder attempts to sell shares that are subject to lockup during the lockup period, the transfer agent will not permit the sale to be completed.

Lower quartile: The point at which 75% of all returns in a group are greater and 25% are lower.

- M -

Management buy-out (MBO): A private equity firm will often provide financing to enable current operating management to acquire or to buy at least 50 per cent of the business they manage. In return, the private equity firm usually receives a stake in the business. This is one of the least risky types of private equity investment because the company is already established and the managers running it know the business - and the market it operates in - extremely well.

Management Fee: Compensation for the management of a venture fund's activities, paid from the fund to the general partner or investment advisor. This compensation generally includes an annual management fee.

Management Team: The persons who oversee the activities of a venture capital fund.

Mandatory Redemption: is a right of an investor to require the company to repurchase some or all of an investor's shares at a stated price at a given time in the future. The purchase price is usually the Issue Price, increased by Cumulative Dividends, if any. Mandatory Redemption may be automatic or may require a vote of the series of Preferred Stock having the redemption right.

Market Capitalization: The total dollar value of all outstanding shares. Computed as shares multiplied by current price per share. Prior to an IPO, market capitalization is arrived at by estimating a company's future growth and by comparing a company with similar public or private corporations. (See also Pre-Money Valuation)

Merchant banking: An activity that includes corporate finance activities, such as advice on complex financings, merger and acquisition advice (international or domestic), and at times direct equity investments in corporations by the banks.

Merger: Combination of two or more corporations in which greater efficiency is supposed to be achieved by the elimination of duplicate plant, equipment, and staff, and the reallocation of capital assets to increase sales and profits in the enlarged company.

Mezzanine Financing: Refers to the stage of venture financing for a company immediately prior to its IPO. Investors entering in this round have lower risk of loss than those investors who have invested in an earlier round. Mezzanine level financing can take the structure of preferred stock, convertible bonds or subordinated debt.

Middle-market firms: Firms with growth prospects of more than 20 percent annually and five-year revenue projections between $10 million and $50 million. Less than 10 percent of all start-ups annually, these entrepreneurial firms are the backbone of the U.S. economy and attractive to business angel investors.

Mutual Fund: A mutual fund, or an open-end fund, sells as many shares as investor demand requires. As money flows in, the fund grows. If money flows out of the fund the number of the fund's outstanding shares drops. Open-end funds are sometimes closed to new investors, but existing investors can still continue to invest money in the fund. In order to sell shares an investor usually sells the shares back to the fund. If an investor wishes to buy additional shares in a mutual fund, the investor must buy newly issued shares directly from the fund. (See Closed-end Funds)

~ N ~

Narrow-based weighted average ratchet: A type of anti-dilution mechanism. A weighted average ratchet adjusts downward the price per share of the preferred stock of investor A due to the issuance of new preferred shares to new investor B at a price lower than the price investor A originally received. Investor A's preferred stock is repriced to a weighed average of investor A's price and investor B's price. A narrow-based ratchet uses only common stock outstanding in the denominator of the formula for determining the new weighed average price. Compare **Broad-Based Weighted Average Ratchet** and Chapter 2.9.4.d.ii of the Encyclopedia for specific examples.

NASD: The **National Association of Securities Dealers**. An mandatory association of brokers and dealers in the over the counter securities business. Created by the *Maloney Act of 1938*, an amendment to the Securities Act of 1934.

NASDAQ: An automated information network which provides brokers and dealers with price quotations on securities traded over the counter.

NDA (Non-disclosure agreement): An agreement issued by entrepreneurs to potential investors to protect the privacy of their ideas when disclosing those ideas to third parties.

Net Asset Value (NAV): NAV is calculated by adding the value of all of the investments in the fund and dividing by the number of shares of the fund that are outstanding. NAV calculations are required for all mutual funds (or open-end funds) and closed-end funds. The price per share of a closed-end fund will trade at either a premium or a discount to the NAV of that fund, based on market demand. Closed-end funds generally trade at a discount to NAV.

Net Financing Cost: Also called the cost of carry or, simply, carry, the difference between the cost of financing the purchase of an asset and the asset's cash yield. Positive carry means that the yield earned is greater than the financing cost; negative carry means that the financing cost exceeds the yield earned.

Net income: The net earnings of a corporation after deducting all costs of selling, depreciation, interest expense and taxes.

Net Present Value: An approach used in capital budgeting where the present value of cash inflow is subtracted from the present value of cash outflows. NPV compares the value of a dollar today versus the value of that same dollar in the future after taking inflation and return into account.

Net present value (NPV): A firm or project's net contribution to wealth. This is the present value of current and future income streams, minus initial investment.

New Issue: A stock or bond offered to the public for the first time. New issues may be initial public offerings by previously private companies or additional stock or bond issues by companies already public. New public offerings are registered with the Securities and Exchange Commission. (See Securities and Exchange Commission and Registration).

Newco: The typical label for any newly organized company, particularly in the context of a leveraged buyout.

No Shop, No Solicitation Clauses: A no shop, no solicitation, or exclusivity, clause requires the company to negotiate exclusively with the investor, and not solicit an investment proposal from anyone else for a set period of time after the term sheet is signed. The key provision is the length of time set for the exclusivity period.

Non-Compete Clause: An agreement often signed by employees and management whereby they agree not to work for competitor companies or form a new competitor company within a certain time period after termination of employment. Governed by state law.

Nonaccredited: An investor not considered accredited for a Regulation D offering. (Accredited Investor)

NYSE: The **New York Stock Exchange.** Founded in 1792, the largest organized securities market in the United States. The Exchange itself does not buy, sell, own or set prices of stocks traded there. The prices are determined by public supply and demand. Also known as the Big Board.

- O -

Open-end Fund: An open-end fund, or a mutual fund, generally sells as many shares as investor demand requires. As money flows in, the fund grows. If money flows out of the fund the number of the fund's outstanding shares drops. Open-end funds are sometimes closed to new investors, but existing investors can still continue to invest money in the fund. In order to sell shares an investor generally sells the shares back to the fund. If an investor wishes to buy additional shares in a mutual fund, the investor generally buys newly issued shares directly from the fund.

Option Pool: The number of shares set aside for future issuance to employees of a private company.

Original Issue Discount: OID. A discount from par value of a bond or debt-like instrument. In structuring a private equity transaction, the use of a preferred stock with liquidation preference or other clauses that guarantee a fixed payment in the future can potentially create adverse tax consequences. The IRS views this cash flow stream as, in essence, a zero coupon bond upon which tax payments are due yearly based on "phantom income" imputed from the difference between the original investment and "guaranteed" eventual payout. Although complex, the solution is to include enough clauses in the investment agreements to create the possibility of a material change in the cash flows of owners of the preferred stock under different scenarios of events such as a buyout, dissolution or IPO.

OTC: Over-the-Counter. A market for securities made up of dealers who may or may not be members of a formal securities exchange. The over-the-counter market is conducted over the telephone and is a negotiated market rather than an auction market such as the NYSE.

Outstanding Stock: The amount of common shares of a corporation which are in the hands of investors. It is *equal to the amount of issued shares less treasury stock.*

Oversubscription: Occurs when demand for shares exceeds the supply or number of shares offered for sale. As a result, the underwriters or investment bankers must allocate the shares among investors. In private placements, this occurs when a deal is in great demand because of the company's growth prospects.

Oversubscription Privilege: In a rights issue, arrangement by which shareholders are given the right to apply for any shares that are not purchased.

P -

Paid-in Capital: The amount of committed capital a limited partner has actually tranferred to a venture fund. Also known as the cumulative takedown amount.

Pari Passu: At an equal rate or pace, without preference.

Participating Preferred: A preferred stock in which the holder is entitled to the stated dividend, and also to additional dividends on a specified basis upon payment of dividends to the common stockholders. The preferred stock entitles the owner to receive a predetermined sum of cash (usually the original investment plus accrued dividends) if the company is sold or has an IPO. The common stock represents additional continued ownership in the company.

Participation: Describes a right of a holder of Preferred Stock to enjoy both the rights associated with the Preferred Stock and also participate in any benefit available to Common Stock, without converting to Common Stock. This may occur with Liquidation Preferences, for example, a series of Preferred Stock may have the right to receive its Liquidation Preference and then also share in whatever money is left to be distributed to the holders of Common Stock. Dividends may also be "Participating" where after a holder of Preferred Stock receives its Cumulative Dividend it also receives any dividend paid on the Common Stock.

Partnership: A nontaxable entity in which each partner shares in the profits, loses and liabilities of the partnership. Each partner is responsible for the taxes on its share of profits and loses.

Partnership agreement: The contract that specifies the compensation and conditions governing the relationship between investors (LP's) and the venture capitalists (GP's) for the duration of a private equity fund's life.

Pay to Play: A "Pay to Play" provision is a requirement for an existing investor to participate in a subsequent investment round, especially a Down Round. Where Pay to Play provisions exist, an investor's failure to purchase its rata portion of a subsequent investment round will result in conversion of that investor's Preferred Stock into Common Stock or another less valuable series of Preferred Stock.

Penny Stocks: Low priced issues, often highly speculative, selling at less than $5/share.

Piggyback Registration: A situation when a securities underwriter allows existing holdings of shares in a corporation to be sold in combination with an offering of new public shares.

PIK Debt Securities: (Payment in Kind) PIK Debt are bonds that may pay bondholders compensation in a form other than cash.

PIV: Pooled Investment Vehicle. A legal entity that pools various investor's capital and deploys it according to a specific investment strategy.

Placement Agent: A company that specializes in finding institutional investors that are willing and able to invest in a private equity fund or company issuing securities. Sometimes the "issuer" will hire a placement agent so the fund partners can focus on management issues rather than on raising capital. In the U.S., these companies are regulated by the NASD and SEC.

Plain English Handbook: The Securities and Exchange Commission online version of Plain English Handbook: How to Create Clear SEC Disclosure Documents

Plum: An investment that has a very healthy rate of return. The inverse of an old venture capital adage (see Lemons) claims that "plums ripen later than lemons."

Poison Pill: A right issued by a corporation as a preventative antitakeover measure. It allows rightholders to purchase shares in either their company or in the combined target and bidder entity at a **substantial discount,** usually 50%. This discount may make the takeover prohibitively expensive.

Pooled IRR: A method of calculating an aggregate IRR by summing cash flows together to create a portfolio cash flow. The IRR is subsequently calculated on this portfolio cash flow.

Portfolio Companies: Companies in which a given fund has invested.

Post-Money Valuation: The valuation of a company immediately after the most recent round of financing. For example, a venture capitalist may invest $3.5 million in a company valued at $2 million "pre-money" (before the investment was made). As a result, the startup will have a post-money valuation of $5.5 million.

Pre-Money Valuation: The valuation of a company prior to a round of investment. This amount is determined by using various calculation models, such as discounted P/E ratios multiplied by periodic earnings or a multiple times a future cash flow discounted to a present cash value and a comparative analysis to comparable public and private companies.

Preemptive Right: A shareholder's right to acquire an amount of shares in a future offering at current prices per share paid by new investors, whereby his/her percentage ownership remains the same as before the offering.

Preference shares: Shares of a firm that encompass preferential rights over ordinary common shares, such as the first right to dividends and any capital payments.

Preferred Dividend: A dividend ordinarily accruing on preferred shares payable where declared and superior in right of payment to common dividends.

Preferred return (AKA Hurdle Rate): The minimum return to investors to be achieved before a carry is permitted. A hurdle rate of 10% means that the private equity fund needs to achieve a return of at least 10% per annum before the profits are shared according to the carried interest arrangement.

Preferred Stock: A class of capital stock that may pay dividends at a specified rate and that has priority over common stock in the payment of dividends and the liquidation of assets. Many venture capital investments use preferred stock as their investment vehicle. This preferred stock is convertible into common stock at the time of an IPO.

Private Equity: Equity securities of companies that have not "gone public" (are not listed on a public exchange). Private equities are generally illiquid and thought of as a long-term investment. As they are not listed on an exchange, any investor wishing to sell securities in private companies must find a buyer in the absence of a marketplace. In addition, there are many transfer restrictions on private securities. Investors in private securities generally receive their return through one of three ways: an initial public offering, a sale or merger, or a recapitalization.

Private investment in public equities (PIPES): Investments by a private equity fund in a publicly traded company, usually at a discount.

Private Placement : Also known as a **Reg. D offering.** The sale of a security (or in some cases, a bond) directly to a limited number of investors. Avoids the need for S.E.C. registration if the securities are purchased for investment as opposed to being resold. The size of the issue is not limited, but its sale is limited to a maximum of thirty-five nonaccredited investors.

Private Placement Memorandum : Also known as an **Offering Memorandum.** A document that outlines the terms of securities to be offered in a private placement. Resembles a business plan in content and structure.

Private Securities: Private securities are securities that are not registered and do not trade on an exchange. The price per share is set through negotiation between the buyer and the seller or issuer.

Prospectus: A formal written offer to sell securities that provides an investor with the necessary information to make an informed decision. A prospectus explains a proposed or existing business enterprise and must disclose any material risks and information according to the securities laws. A prospectus must be filed with the SEC and be given to all potential investors. Companies offering securities, mutual funds, and offerings of other investment companies including Business Development Companies are required to issue prospectuses describing their history, investment philosophy or objectives, risk factors and financial statements. Investors should carefully read them prior to investing.

Put option: The right to **sell** a security at a given price (or range) within a given time period.

- Q -

QPAM: Qualified professional asset manager as defined by ERISA.

- R -

Recapitalization: The reorganization of a company's capital structure. A company may seek to save on taxes by replacing preferred stock with bonds in order to gain interest deductibility. Recapitalization can be an alternative exit strategy for venture capitalists and leveraged buyout sponsors. (See Exit Strategy and Leveraged Buyout)

Reconfirmation: The act a broker/dealer makes with an investor to confirm a transaction.

Red Herring: The common name for a preliminary prospectus, due to the red SEC required legend on the cover. (See Prospectus)

Redeemable Preferred Stock: Redeemable preferred stock, also known as exploding preferred, at the holder's option after (typically) five years, which in turn gives the holders (potentially converting to creditors) leverage to induce the company to arrange a liquidity event. The threat of creditor status can move the founders off the dime if a liquidity event is not occurring with sufficient rapidity.

Redemption: The right or obligation of a company to repurchase its own shares.

Registration: The SEC's review process of all securities intended to be sold to the public. The SEC requires that a registration statement be filed in conjunction with any public securities offering. This document includes operational and financial information about the company, the management and the purpose of the offering. The registration statement and the prospectus are often referred to interchangeably. Technically, the SEC does not "approve" the disclosures in prospectuses.

Registration Rights: The right to require that a company register restricted shares. Demand Registered Rights enable the shareholder to request registration at any time, while Piggy Back Registration Rights enable the shareholder to request that the company register his or her shares when the company files a registration statement (for a public offering with the SEC).

Regulation A: SEC provision for simplified registration for small issues of securities. A Reg. A issue may require a shorter prospectus and carries lesser liability for directors and officers for misleading statements. The conditional small issues securities exemption of the Securities Act of 1933 is allowed if the offering is a maximum of $5,000,000 U.S. Dollars.

Regulation C: The regulation that outlines registration requirements for Securities Act of 1933.

Regulation D: Regulation D, is the rule (Reg. D is a "regulation" comprising a series of "rules") that allow for the issuance and sale of securities to purchasers if they qualify as accredited investors.

Regulation D Offering: (See Private Placement)

Regulation S: The rules relating to Offers and Sales made outside the US without SEC Registration.

Regulation S-B : Reg. S-B of the Securities Act of 1933 governs the Integrated Disclosure System for Small Business Issuers.

Regulation S-K : The Standard Instructions for Filing Forms Under Securities Act of 1933, Securities Exchange Act of 1934 and Energy Policy and Conservation Act of 1975.

Regulation S-X: The regulation that governs the requirements for financial statements under the Securities Act of 1933, and the Securities Exchange Act of 1934.

Reorganization or Corporate Reorganization: Reorganizations are significant changes in the equity base of a company such as converting all outstanding shares to Common Stock, or combining outstanding shares into a smaller number of shares (a reverse split). A Reorganization is frequently done when a company has already had a few rounds of venture financing but has not been able to successfully increase the value of the company and therefore is doing a Down Round that is essentially a restart of the company.

Restricted Securities: Public securities that are not freely tradable due to SEC regulations. (See Securities and Exchange Commission)

Restricted Shares: Shares acquired in a private placement are considered restricted shares and may not be sold in a public offering absent registration, or after an appropriate holding period has expired. Non-affiliates must wait one year after purchasing the shares, after which time they may sell less than 1% of their outstanding shares each quarter. For affiliates, there is a two-year holding period.

Revlon Duties: The legal principle that actions, such as anti-takeover measures, that **promote** the value of an auction process are allowable, whereas those that thwart the value of an auction process are not allowed. The duty is triggered when a company is in play as a target acquisition.

Right of First Refusal: The right of first refusal gives the holder the right to meet any other offer before the proposed contract is accepted.

Rights Offering: Issuance of "rights" to current shareholders allowing them to purchase additional shares, usually at a discount to market price. Shareholders who do not exercise these rights are usually diluted by the offering. Rights are often transferable, allowing the holder to sell them on the open market to others who may wish to exercise them. Rights offerings are particularly common to closed-end funds, which cannot otherwise issue additional ordinary shares.

Risk: The chance of loss on an investment due to many factors including inflation, interest rates, default, politics, foreign exchange, call provisions, etc. In Private Equity, risks are outlined in the Risk Factors section of the Placement Memorandum.

Rule 144: Rule 144 provides for the sale of restricted stock and control stock. Filing with the SEC is required prior to selling restricted and control stock, and the number of shares that may be sold is limited.

Rule 144A: A safe harbor exemption from the registration requirements of

Section 5 of the 1933 Act for resales of certain restricted securities to qualified institutional buyers, which are commonly referred to as "QIBs." In particular, Rule 144A affords safe harbor treatment for reoffers or resales to QIBs - by persons other than issuers - of securities of domestic and foreign issuers that are not listed on a U.S. securities exchange or quoted on a U.S. automated inter-dealer quotation system. Rule 144A provides that reoffers and resales in compliance with the rule are not "distributions" and that the reseller is therefore not an "underwriter" within the meaning of Section 2(a)(11) of the 1933 Act. If the reseller is not the issuer or a dealer, it can rely on the exemption provided by Section 4(1) of the 1933 Act. If the reseller is a dealer, it can rely on the exemption provided by Section 4(3) of the 1933 Act.

Rule 147: Provides an exemption from the registration requirements of the Securities Act of 1933 for intrastate offerings, if certain requirements are met. One requirement is that 100% of the purchasers must be from within one state.

Rule 501: Rule 501 of Regulation D defines Accredited Investor.

Rule 505: Rule 505 of Regulation D is an exemption for limited offers and sales of securities not exceeding $5,000,000.

Rule 506: Rule 506 of Regulation D is considered a "safe harbor" for the private offering exemption of Section 4(2) of the Securities Act of 1933. Companies using the Rule 506 exemption can raise an unlimited amount of money if they meet certain exemptions.

- S -

S Corporation: A corporation that limits its ownership structure to 100. An S corporation does not pay taxes, rather, similar to a partnership, its owners pay taxes on their proportion of the corporation's profits at their individual tax rates.

SBIC : Small Business Investment Company. A company licensed by the Small Business Administration to receive government leverage in order to raise capital to use in venture investing.

SBIR: Small Business Innovation Research Program. See Small Business Innovation Development Act of 1982.

Secondary funds : Partnerships that specialize in purchasing the portfolios of investee company invesments of an existing venture firm. This type of partnership provides some liquidity for the original investors. These secondary partnerships, expecting a large return, invest in what they consider to be undervalued companies. The big difference is that they are buying their interests in a fund after the fund has been at least partially deployed in underlying portfolio companies. Unlike fund of fund managers, which generally invest in blind pools, secondary buyers can evaluate the underlying companies that they are indirectly investing in.

Secondary Market: The market for the sale of partnership interests in private equity funds. Sometimes limited partners chose to sell their interest in a partnership, typically to raise cash or because they cannot meet their obligation to invest more capital according to the takedown schedule. Certain investment companies specialize in buying these partnership interests at a discount.

Secondary Sale: The sale of private or restricted holdings in a portfolio company to other investors. See secondary market definition.

Securities Act of 1933: The federal law covering new issues of securities. It provides for full disclosure of pertinent information relating to the new issue and also contains antifraud provisions.

Securities Act of 1934: The federal law that established the Securities and Exchange Commission. The act outlaws misrepresentation, manipulation and other abusive practices in the issuance of securities.

Securities and Exchange Commission : The SEC is an independent, nonpartisan, quasi-judicial regulatory agency that is responsible for administering the federal securities laws. These laws protect investors in securities markets and ensure that investors have access to all material information concerning publicly traded securities. Additionally, the SEC regulates firms that trade securities, people who provide investment advice, and investment companies.

Seed Money: The first round of capital for a start-up business. Seed money usually takes the structure of a loan or an investment in preferred stock or convertible bonds, although sometimes it is common stock. Seed money provides startup companies with the capital required for their initial development and growth. Angel investors and early-stage venture capital funds often provide seed money.

Seed Stage Financing: An initial state of a company's growth characterized by a founding management team, business plan development, prototype development, and beta testing.

Senior Securities: Securities that have a preferential claim over common stock on a company's earnings and in the case of liquidation. Generally, preferred stock and bonds are considered senior securities.

Series A Preferred Stock: The first round of stock offered during the seed or early stage round by a portfolio company to the venture investor or fund. This stock is convertible into common stock in certain cases such as an IPO or the sale of the company. Later rounds of preferred stock in a private company are called Series B, Series C and so on.

Shell Corporation: A corporation with no assets and no business. Typically, shell corporations are designed for the purpose of going public and later acquiring existing businesses. Also known as Specified Purpose Acquisition Companies (SPACs).

Small Business Administration (SBA): Provides loans to small business investment companies (SBICs) that supply venture capital and financing to small businesses.

Small Business Innovation Development Act of 1982: The Small Business Innovation Research (SBIR) program is a set-aside program (2.5% of an agency's extramural budget) for domestic small business concerns to engage in Research/Research and Development (R/R&D) that has the potential for commercialization. The SBIR program was established under the Small Business Innovation Development Act of 1982 (P.L. 97-219), reauthorized until September 30, 2000 by the Small Business Research and Development Enhancement Act (P.L. 102-564), and reauthorized again until September 30, 2008 by the Small Business Reauthorization Act of 2000 (P.L. 106-554).

Special purpose vehicle : A special company, usually outside the United States, established by a company to meet a specific financial problem, often to pay lower taxes (e.g., a reinvoicing subsidiary or offshore insurance company).

Spin out: A division or subsidiary of a company that becones an independant business. Typically, private equity investors will provide the necessary capital to allow the division to "spin out" on its own; the parent company may retain a minority stake.

Staggered Board: This is an antitakeover measure in which the election of the directors is split in separate periods so that only a percentage (e.g. one-third) of the total number of directors come up for election in a given year. It is designed to make taking control of the board of directors more difficult.

Statutory Voting: A method of voting for members of the Board of Directors of a corporation. Under this method, a shareholder receives one vote for each share and may cast those votes for each of the directorships. For example: An individual owning 100 shares of stock of a corporation that is electing six directors could cast 100 votes for each of the six candidates. This method tends to favor the larger shareholders. *Compare* **Cumulative Voting.**

Stock Options: 1) The right to purchase or sell a stock at a specified price within a stated period. Options are a popular investment medium, offering an opportunity to hedge positions in other securities, to speculate on stocks with relatively little investment, and to capitalize on changes in the market value of options contracts themselves through a variety of options strategies. 2) A widely used form of employee incentive and compensation. The employee is given an option to purchase its shares at a certain price (at or below the market price at the time the option is granted) for a specified period of years.

Strategic Investors: Corporate or individual investors that add value to investments they make through industry and personal ties that can assist companies in raising additional capital as well as provide assistance in the marketing and sales process.

Subscription Agreement: The application submitted by an investor wishing to join a limited partnership. All prospective investors must be approved by the General Partner prior to admission as a partner.

Sweat Equity: Ownership of shares in a company resulting from work rather than investment of capital--usually founders receive "sweat equity".

Syndicate: Underwriters or broker/dealers who sell a security as a group. (See Allocation)

Syndication : A number of investors offering funds together as a group on a particular deal. A lead investor often coordinates such deals and represents the group's members. Within the last few years, syndication among angel investors (an angel alliance) has become more common, enabling them to fund larger deals closer to those typifying a small venture capital fund.

T -

Tag-Along Rights / Rights of Co-Sale: A minority shareholder protection affording the right to include their shares in any sale of control and at the offered price.

Takedown Schedule: A takedown schedule means the timing and size of the capital contributions from the limited partners of a venture fund.

Tax-free reorganizations: Types of business combinations in which shareholders do not incur tax liabilities. There are four types-A, B, C, and D reorganizations. They differ in various ways in the amount of stock/cash that can be offered. *See Internal Revenue Code Section 368.*

Tender offer: An offer to purchase stock made directly to the shareholders. One of the more common ways hostile takeovers are implemented.

Term Sheet: A summary of the terms the investor is prepared to accept. A non-binding outline of the principal points which the Stock Purchase Agreement and related agreements will cover in detail.

Time Value of Money: The basic principle that money can earn interest, therefore something that is worth $1 today will be worth more in the future if invested. This is also referred to as future value.

Trade sale: The sale of the equity share of a portfolio company to another company.

Treasury Stock: Stock issued by a company but later reacquired. It may be held in the company's treasury indefinitely, reissued to the public, or retired. Treasury stock receives no dividends and does not carry voting power while held by the company.

- U -

UBTI: UBTI, Unrelated Business Taxable Income, is a concern to tax exempt investors in a hedge fund because the receipt of UBTI requires the tax exempt entity to file a tax return that it would not otherwise have to file and pay taxes on income that would otherwise be exempt, at the corporate rate. UBTI includes most business operations income and does not include interest, dividends and gains from the sale or exchange of capital assets. Hedge Funds trade their own securities and therefor the tax exempt investor's share of such income of the hedge fund is not UBTI and not subject to federal income tax. However, hedge funds may subject tax exempt entities to UBTI under certain circumstances where the hedge fund is borrowing or purchasing securities on margin. Such transactions may subject the tax exempt to UBTI tax.

ULPA: Uniform Limited Partnership Act, see also the RULPA, Revised Uniform Limited Partnership Act U.L.P.A. § 101 et seq. (1976), as amended in 1985 (R.U.L.P.A.).

Upper quartile: The point at which 25% of all returns in a group are greater and 75% are lower.

- V -

Venture Capital Financing: An investment in a startup business that is perceived to have excellent growth prospects but does not have access to capital markets. Type of financing sought by early-stage companies seeking to grow rapidly.

Vesting schedules: Timetables for stock grants and options mandating that entrepreneurs earn (vest) their equity stakes over a number of years, rather than upon conversion of the stock options. This guarantees to investors and the market that the entrepreneurs will stick around, rather than converting and cashing in their shares.

Vintage Year: The year in which the venture firm began making investments. Often, those funds with "vintage years" at the top of the market will have lower than average returns because portfolio company valuations were high, e.g an Internet Fund started in vintage year 1998.

Voluntary Redemption: is the right of a company to repurchase some or all of an investors' outstanding shares at a stated price at a given time in the future. The purchase price is usually the Issue Price, increased by Cumulative Dividends.

Voting Right: The common stockholders' right to vote their stock in the affairs of the company. Preferred stock usually has the right to vote when preferred dividends are in default for a specified amount of time. The right to vote may be delegated by the stockholder to another person.

W -

Warrant: A type of security that entitles the holder to buy a proportionate amount of common stock or preferred stock at a specified price for a period of years. Warrants are usually issued together with a loan, a bond or preferred stock --and act as sweeteners, to enhance the marketability of the accompanying securities. They are also known as stock-purchase warrants and subscription warrants.

Wash-Out Round: A financing round whereby previous investors, the founders, and management suffer significant dilution. Usually as a result of a washout round, the new investor gains majority ownership and control of the company. Also known as burn-out or cram-down rounds.

Weighted Average Antidilution: The investor's conversion price is reduced, and thus the number of common shares received on conversion increased, in the case of a down round; it takes into account both: (a) the reduced price and, (b) how many shares (or rights) are issued in the dilutive financing. See Broad-Based Ratchet and Narrow-Based Ratchet definitions.

Williams Act of 1968: An amendment of the Securities and Exchange Act of 1934 that regulates tender offers and other takeover related actions such as larger share purchases.

Workout: A negotiated agreement between the debtors and its creditors outside the bankruptcy process.

Write-off: The act of changing the value of an asset to an expense or a loss. A write-off is used to reduce or eliminate the value an asset and reduce profits.

Write-up/Write-down: An upward or downward adjustment of the value of an asset for accounting and reporting purposes. These adjustments are estimates and tend to be subjective; although they are usually based on events affecting the investee company or its securities beneficially or detrimentally.

ABOUT THE AUTHORS

Joseph Bartlett

Mr. Bartlett, Founder and Chairman of the Board at VC Experts, is of counsel at the law firm of Fish & Richardson LP, one of the largest intellectual property law firms in the world. He is also an adjunct professor at New York University School of Law and the Johnson School of Business at Cornell.

A former Undersecretary of Commerce, law clerk to Chief Justice Earl Warren and President of the Boston Bar Association, Mr. Bartlett graduated from Stanford Law School where he was president of the Law Review. Mr. Bartlett has acted as counsel to, a director of, and shareholder in, a number of development stage companies during his 38 year career in the venture capital business. He was a founding stockholder and a director of GMIS, Inc.; chairman of a publicly traded REIT. Mr. Bartlett has been a director of Advanced Telecommunications Corp.; Shawmut Bank N.A.; the Shawmut Corporation; the Harbor National Bank; and the Northeast Federal Savings and Loan Association. He has served as a trustee of a series of public mutual funds and as counsel to asset managers throughout his career, including the managers of public and privately invested assets. He has been a limited partner in a number of pooled investment vehicles, including Bain Capital and Needham Emerging Growth Partners.

Mr. Bartlett literally wrote the book on venture capital financing, having published numerous articles and books including: Equity Finance: Venture Capital, Buyouts, Restructurings and Reorganizations, Corporate Restructurings: Reorganizations and Buyouts, and Venture Capital: Law, Business Strategies and Investment Planning. He has been an acting professor of law at Stanford and an instructor in law at Boston University Law School. He currently teaches Fundamentals of Venture Capital at NYU School of Law. Mr. Bartlett has been profiled in trade publications as one of the leading practitioners in venture capital nationwide.

Ross P. Barrett

Mr. Barrett is a General Partner with Louisiana Ventures, LP and a Partner at VCE Capital. He was a Co-founder of VC Experts, Inc. Previously, he worked on Capitol Hill as a legislative aide to senior U.S. Senator, J. Bennett Johnston, where he specialized in risk assessment and regulatory reform.

Mr. Barrett received a Masters degree in taxation from New York University School of Law. Prior to NYU Law, he earned a J.D. from Louisiana State University School of Law. In law school, he was selected to participate in the National Tugel Moot Court Competition. Prior to that, he earned a B.A. in Political Science from Southern Methodist University, graduating with honors.

He is the author of several articles, including: *The New Markets Tax Credit: Good Opportunity But Needs Tweaking* (Venture Capital Journal Oct. 2003); *The Private Equity Secondary Market: Direct Sales* (Benefits & Risks) (Start-Up and Emerging Companies Newsletter 2003); *Investment Banks, Placement Agents and Full Ratchet Dilution* (Start-Up and Emerging Companies Newsletter 2003);*Venture Capital Investing: Quick Facts* (Louisiana Bar Journal 2001); *Project Financing of the Channel Tunnel; Private Company Valuation: Minority Discounts and the Estate & Gift Tax Regime.* In addition, Mr. Barrett is the co-author and co-editor of the soon to be published *Advanced Private Equity: Series A Documents and Term Sheets* (American Lawyer 2004).

Mr. Barrett is active with his church, Redeemer Presbyterian Church, and sits on the Board of Hope for New York, an umbrella organization of thirty charities associated with Redeemer that promotes volunteerism in New York. He is head of its due diligence committee. He also sits on the Board of Mark Ventures, LLC., a New York based venture capital fund that focuses on early stage companies. He is registered with the Series 7, 24 and 63.